Money and the Economic Process

to Anna

Money and the Economic Process

Sheila C Dow
Reader in Economics
University of Stirling

Edward Elgar

Published by

Edward Elgar Publishing Limited
Gower House
Croft Road
Aldershot Hants GU11 3HR
England

Edward Elgar Publishing Company
Old Post Road
Brookfield
Vermont 05036
USA

A CIP catalogue record for this book is
available from the British Library.

ISBN 1 85278 566 7

're

Contents

List of Figures and Tables

Acknowledgements

Many people have influenced the development of ideas represented by this volume. Those who had a pivotal influence at particular junctures are noted in the introductory chapter; additional acknowledgements are noted at the start of each chapter. To these people I would like to express my warm gratitude. Some I would like to single out as having had a pervasive influence on my views on monetary theory: Victoria Chick, Paul Davidson, Hyman Minsky and Peter Earl. These four are owed a special debt of gratitude. The most pervasive and constant influence on my thinking is my husband Alistair; I would like to express my gratitude for this, and for other forms of support he has provided over the years.

In addition, I would like to thank Geoff Harcourt not only for the intellectual guidance and leadership he has provided, but also for the initial suggestion that I put together a selection of papers for publication in a volume. I am grateful too to Edward Elgar for agreeing to the theme I have chosen, and for encouraging its execution. Special thanks are due to Lorraine Annand and Lynne McNaughton for preparing the manuscript for publication.

The volume is dedicated to my younger daughter Anna.

I acknowledge the cooperation of the following in agreeing to the reprinting of material they had originally published:

Presses Universitaires de Grenoble: 'Methodology and the Analysis of a Monetary Economy', *Economies et Sociétés*, 18, *Monnaie et Production*, 1, pp. 7-35, 1984. 'Speculation and the Monetary Circuit', *Economies et Sociétés*, 20, *Monnaie et Production*, 3, pp. 95-109, 1986. 'Money Supply Endogeneity', *Economie Appliquée*, 41(1), pp. 19-39, 1988.

M E Sharpe: 'Post Keynesian Monetary Theory for an Open Economy', *Journal of Post Keynesian Economics*, 9(2), pp. 237-59, 1986-87.

Scottish Journal of Political Economy: 'The Regional Composition of the Money Multiplier Process', *Scottish Journal of Political Economy*, 29(1), pp. 22-44, 1982.

Journal of Regional Science: 'The Treatment of Money in Regional Economics', *Journal of Regional Science*, 27(1), pp. 13-24, 1987.

Pion Limited: 'Incorporating Money in Regional Economic Models', *London Papers in Regional Science*, 19, pp. 208-18, 1988.

Urban Studies: 'The Capital Account and Regional Balance of Payments Problems', *Urban Studies*, 23(2), pp. 173-84, 1986.

Studies in Political Economy: 'Money and Regional Development', *Studies in Political Economy*, 23(2), pp. 73-94, 1987.

1. Introduction

This book is motivated by the conviction that money is integral to the capitalist process and that there is much in common between its role at the regional, national and international levels. The material offered here therefore is juxtaposed to the conventional separation of money and the real economy in much of economics, and to the conventional separation of regional economics, macroeconomics and international finance into distinct fields.

A theory of money and the economic process in the regional, national and international contexts has theoretical significance. But it has increasing policy significance in a world where the distinctions between regional and national boundaries are being broken down and reformulated, and where new institutional arrangements are being designed for financial systems.

This volume brings together a selection of papers published over the period 1984-88 in a range of outlets, some less accessible than others, and some directed at particular audiences. The purpose in reprinting them here, in slightly amended form, is to stress the integrated nature of the arguments represented in the papers, ranging from methodological foundations to regional economic modelling. There is a common theme that a distinctive methodology is required to capture the integral role of money in the economic process, with the different contexts being used to illustrate that methodology. The final two chapters are new: they develop the theory in connection with developing countries and then analyse institutional arrangements within the international financial system, respectively.

Although it is not chronologically the first, the paper reprinted as Chapter 2 sets the scene for the rest of the volume by discussing the significance of methodological framework for incorporating money in economic analysis; it is argued that orthodox methodology does not allow for money to play an integral role, or indeed for theory to analyse economic process. The methodological requirements of a theory to incorporate money in the economic process are explored.

Two of the subsequent chapters illustrate the dangers in starting from an orthodox framework. Chapters 5 and 6 are the earliest papers; they run into limitations by starting from a global monetarist and a bank multiplier framework, respectively. There are accordingly some inconsistencies between particular chapters and these two. They have been included nevertheless in that they may act as a bridge for readers who themselves approach this book from an orthodox perspective. What is being presented here is a way of thinking about money. The methodology employed involves a range of methods deliberately chosen to try to contribute to knowledge about a complex process. Accordingly for those who do not share this way of thinking, a range of approaches will be necessary in order to communicate what it involves; a simple closed model cannot suffice. Making explicit the route by which I arrived at this way of thinking may be of some assistance to others with an interest in the same destination.

My first interest in money was sparked off by my husband Alistair's interest in it as a graduate student at Simon Fraser University. I was employed there briefly as research assistant to his instructor, Michael Porter. My earlier training at St Andrews University had been Keynesian. It therefore came as a shock to find Keynesian ideas being questioned, from a monetarist perspective. From this experience stemmed an awareness of schools of thought in economics, and a need to think through one's own preferred arguments.

When I was employed later by the Bank of England, I was involved in work on international monetary reform at the time of the suspension of dollar convertibility. I developed a particular interest in the distributional aspects of the system, a subject which I then developed in my Master's thesis at the University of Manitoba under the supervision of Clarence Barber. From there I worked for the Government of Manitoba, where I was thrown into a lively debate over the regional consequences of bank behaviour and consideration of possible policy responses. When I went next to MacMaster University I developed the idea of regional bank multipliers under the guidance of Syed Ahmed. When I transferred to Glasgow University to work on my PhD thesis under Tom Wilson, he persuaded me of the commonality between arguments about finance and distribution in the regional and international contexts; my thesis accordingly dealt with both.

The framework within which I was working was still quite orthodox. But under the influence and encouragement of Brian Loasby and Peter Earl at Stirling University and Vicky Chick whom I had met while at Glasgow, the 'struggle to escape' was given a methodological foundation. The final push came during a seminar presentation at the University of Ottawa, when the audience (notably Alain Parguez of ISMEA, Mario Seccareccia, Marc Lavoie and Jacques Henry) voiced their impatience with the standard (at that time) statement of where one's theory differed from orthodox theory; for the first time it seemed that I did not have to justify my rejection of the orthodox approach. In the meantime, the *Journal of Post Keynesian*

Economics had been established. Through this forum many people like myself discovered that we were not alone in using what we now realised was Post Keynesian theory. The subsequent development of my ideas benefited tremendously from the encouragement from and work of an increasing body of Post Keynesian economists.

The Ottawa/ISMEA connection is responsible for Chapters 2 to 4. Chapter 2, on methodological foundations, was written for the new *Monnaie et Production* series of *Economies et Sociétés* at the invitation of Alain Parguez. Chapter 3 explores further the concept of the endogeneity of the money supply which was touched on in Chapter 2 and was prepared for a conference at the University of Ottawa. Out of this paper arose further work on endogeneity (Dow and Dow, 1988) which combined endogeneity theory with liquidity preference theory. Chapter 4 was written for an ISMEA seminar on the monetary circuit approach; it develops the idea of endogenous money within the circuit and at the same time develops further the notion of outside money; the focus is on the possibility of credit being created to finance speculation.

Chapter 5 sets the scene for the subsequent chapters on regional and international money, by combining endogenous money theory with liquidity preference theory in an open economy context. This chapter started off with a diagrammatic comparison between global monetarism and a Post Keynesian theory of money in an open economy. But the logical impossibility of doing this satisfactorily eventually was overwhelming. Nevertheless the compulsion to try to present such a comparison in simple form persisted for many years, and was only finally laid to rest (to my satisfaction at least) in the paper reprinted here as Chapter 8.

Chapters 6 to 10 develop ideas on money in a regional context. Chapter 6 analyses money flows between regions by means of bank multipliers; credit creation is endogenous to the region but the presumption still is of aggregate credit creation being tied by the volume of reserves. Regional differences are demonstrated in the multiplier process, and differences in regional confidence are investigated. A series of papers was published around that time in the US, incorporating money in regional models. Chapter 7 reviews that literature and attempts to take it forward in a Post Keynesian vein, adapting a four-quadrant diagram framework. This allowed a formal treatment of regional confidence and regional financial market segmentation. But my uneasiness with this framework led to the paper reprinted as Chapter 8 which explains why money (as understood in Post Keynesian theory) cannot be incorporated in general equilibrium models. This chapter draws on the methodological ideas developed in Chapter 2. Chapter 9 develops more explicitly the role of the capital account of the regional balance of payments in regional development;

Chapter 10 develops these ideas further in relation to theories of regional economic development, illustrated by the Canadian case. A framework is developed which combines liquidity preference theory (and endogenous money theory) with dependency theory and cumulative causation theory facilitating a further development of the idea that money plays an active role in regional disparities. This work was subsequently taken forward by combining it with Chick's (1986) stages of banking framework in Chick and Dow (1988). Fuller development of the Canadian case study was published in Dow (1990), and of a Scottish case study in Dow (1991a, 1991b and 1992).

The final two chapters bring the analysis to the international level, at which distributional concerns are more urgent. In particular, the theory developed so far can be adapted in order to understand the causes and nature of the debt crisis. Because it is suggested that the process of which money is a part can promote economic divergence, questions naturally arise as to the possible policy actions which might be taken to limit this divergence. An argument is presented for a world central bank, and some concerns are expressed about the distributional consequences of current plans for European Monetary Union.

2. Methodology and the Analysis of a Monetary Economy

This chapter is a slightly amended version of an article of the same title which was published in Economies et Sociétés, *18,* Monnaie et Production *1, pp. 7-35, 1984. It benefited from helpful discussions with Alexander Dow and Peter Earl.*

INTRODUCTION

> ... it is my belief that the far-reaching and in some respects fundamental differences between the conclusions of a monetary economy and those of the more simplified real-exchange economy have been greatly underestimated by the exponents of the traditional economics ... The idea that it is comparatively easy to adapt the hypothetical conclusions of a real wage economics to the world of monetary economics is a mistake ... Accordingly I believe that the next task is to work out in some detail a monetary theory of production.
>
> (Keynes, *C.W. XIII*, pp. 410-11)

Keynes, in this passage, indicates clearly his belief that a theory of production in a monetary economy requires a different framework from a theory of production in a real exchange model. Accordingly, the *General Theory* was put forward as a theory of production with money incorporated from the outset. The methodological framework itself was designed to portray a monetary economy rather than a real exchange economy.[1]

But Keynes' theory was interpreted by the orthodoxy as if he had simply incorporated some new variables, or restrictions on coefficients, into the old real exchange framework. It was thus straightforward to isolate these factors and then attempt to belittle their importance. As a result, Post Keynesian critiques of the orthodoxy have tended to respond by reasserting the importance of the factors which Keynes had emphasised: not only money as a store of wealth, but also expectations formation under uncertainty, and historical rather than logical time. Any one of these factors can be shown to throw a monkey wrench in the general equilibrium machine.

Such critiques in fact employ the orthodox framework. The term 'orthodox' is being used here to refer to mainstream economics in its neo-classical synthesis, pure general equilibrium theory, or rational expectations form; the common methodological foundations are set out in Dow (1985). The conventional mode of analysis within the orthodoxy is to ask what difference is made to the final equilibrium position, or the stability properties of the model, when a new variable is incorporated, an exogenous variable shifts, or a restriction is placed on the value of a parameter or endogenous variable. Such questions are suited to closed, simultaneous equation systems. They lead to the urge to identify key variables or factors: what is a necessary and sufficient condition for an unemployment equilibrium position to emerge within a general equilibrium model?

Such a question is a product of the orthodox method itself. Yet, because the Post Keynesian *critique* (or at least that part which draws the attention of the orthodox oligarchy) is conducted largely in terms of orthodox method, there is a danger that Post Keynesian *analysis* also may be influenced by that method. Its influence can indeed be seen in discussions within Post Keynesian analysis about which variables or concepts are key.

In the same paper as that quoted above, Keynes insists that money is not a key variable, although he has just demonstrated its non-neutrality:

> This is not the same thing as to say that the problem of booms and depressions is a purely monetary problem. For this statement is generally meant to imply that a complete solution is to be found in banking policy. I am saying that booms and depressions are phenomena peculiar to an economy in which ... money is not neutral.
>
> (Keynes, *C.W. XIII*, p. 411)

The purpose of this chapter is to underline Keynes' original position that it is the difference in *method* or framework which allows analysis of a monetary economy. This method is built on the unique properties of money, on expectations formation under uncertainty, and on historical rather than logical time, each of which *necessarily* implies the other two; any analysis which involves only one or two of the factors is both logically incomplete and irrelevant to a monetary economy.

Davidson (1978) particularly has already strongly emphasised the interdependence of these factors. The need to reiterate and elaborate on this position arises from two sources of concern. First, if a monetary theory of production requires its own method, criticising the orthodoxy by means of the orthodox method is inadequate and misleading.[2] Temporary equilibrium theorists, for example, claim to take account of money, expectations and time,[3] but remain at odds with the conclusions of Post Keynesian theory. To be more effective, the Post Keynesian critique should thus be conducted at a more fundamental level in order to ferret out the real differences in approach.

Second, there are worrying signs that within Post Keynesian analysis there is a willingness to focus on some key variables to the exclusion of others. In particular, many expositions of (Post) Keynesian analysis are conducted with scant reference to money. While this may be a somewhat justifiable reaction to what may have seemed like a dominance of concern with money, rather than uncertainty and/or time, there is a danger that the pendulum will swing the other way.

A particular question to be addressed here is whether the role of money and the rate of interest is significantly diminished by the endogeneity of the money supply; that is, whether money may be excluded because of its endogeneity, even if not on logical grounds.

We start by considering the significance of method for the content of theories, as well as for the way in which they are understood (and misunderstood). Section three is devoted to comparing (Post) Keynesian methodology with general equilibrium methodology. Then the particular case is made that, within the Post Keynesian method, money, expectations formation under uncertainty and historical time are logically interdependent (as well as reflections of reality); the argument throws doubt on the validity of models set in historical time which ignore money.

THE SIGNIFICANCE OF THE METHODOLOGICAL FRAMEWORK

Traditionally, methodology in economics has dealt with how theories are formulated and tested, frequently referring to the methodology of the physical sciences. It has also traditionally been developed along normative lines, that is, advocating particular practices as being appropriate to the discipline.

Given the complexity of reality, theories by their very nature must abstract in some way from reality. Physical scientists can abstract from reality by conducting laboratory experiments (although interpreting laboratory results in a real-world situation is subject to serious problems). The abstractions used by physical scientists are suggested to a considerable extent by the nature of laboratory experiments; certain variables are more easily controlled than others. Social scientists cannot (in general) conduct laboratory experiments; in a social science such as economics, then, the choice of abstractions is unconstrained.

Any abstraction prevents a theory from being definitively tested against reality. Indeed, even if that were not the case, reference to reality involves induction, and thus cannot allow definite conclusions; because facts have confirmed (or refuted) a theory in the past, there is no guarantee that they will confirm (or refute) the theory in the future.[4]

It is in the nature of a social science, therefore, that an extremely wide range of methods of theory formulation and testing can in principle be justified. At one end of the spectrum, formal empirical testing may be eschewed, and theory consists of logical deductions from basic axioms; but then the range of possible axioms is enormous. At the other end of the spectrum, only those theories may be considered which could be subjected to some sort of empirical test; but again this leaves scope for a wide range of views as to what constitutes a test. In between these two extremes lies an array of possible combinations of induction and deduction.

Now, if this were all there was to the methodology of economics, one would expect economics to be a discipline in which 'a hundred flowers blossomed'.[5] Preferences have oscillated over the years between induction and deduction, but no categoric *methodological* basis has been established for choosing between any one combination of induction and deduction, far less any one set of axioms and testing procedures.

In practice, however, to continue the metaphor, economics has always been dominated by one strain of flower (although the dominant strain has changed under changing environmental conditions) while a few other varieties have struggled to survive alongside. At risk of stretching the metaphor unduly, one might say that the struggle of these other varieties was made harder by accusations that they were encroaching weeds, not flowers at all.

Nor is economics (or social science) alone in this actual outcome of a dominant orthodoxy, which changes from time to time. Indeed more recent approaches to scientific methodology have attempted to grapple with this reality. Inspired by Kuhn (1970), Lakatos (1978) and Feyerabend (1975), they have attempted to explain why one method should dominate for some time, and what leads to its supplanting by another.

It is worthwhile to consider this new methodology here not only in order to explain why Keynes' method was not adopted (while his liquidity trap, for example, was) but also so that we can proceed in the next section to discuss the significance of the particular method Keynes advocated.

The new methodology analyses the choice of approach to a discipline in terms of the behaviour of the practitioners as a group. It specifies those features of a discipline necessary to allow the group to function as such, for the term 'discipline' to have any meaning. First, an essential feature of group behaviour is the capacity to communicate; this in itself has a profound influence on limiting the admissible range of approaches.[6] Language itself plays a powerful role; an economist, for example, uses the term rational in a very particular, technical way which conveys meaning to other economists, but would be misunderstood by non-economists.

Of course behavioural micro-theorists, for example, would take exception to that use of the term. Its technical meaning is derived from a set of axioms about behaviour (defined to be rational) which would be unacceptable. This is the second aspect of communication: the model to which the language refers. For effective communication, not only must language be used in a similar way, but there must be a full understanding of the underlying models being used. Popper (1970) advocates that scientists be familiar enough with a range of theories (research programmes) to allow choice between them. In practice it is extremely difficult *fully* to understand more than one approach to economics. From a practical point of view it requires a large commitment of energy to keep abreast even of one approach. But, more important, theories are ideologically based,[7] and it is difficult to sustain more than one ideology at a time.

Third, aside from the internal logic and aesthetic appeal of a theory it can be assessed with reference to its ability to explain or predict events. But all perception is subjective, is described using language, and is coloured by the observer's theoretical approach both at the technical level and at the ideological level.[8] For a group to share theories which refer to the real world, there must be some commonality in perception, some common view as to what would constitute an empirical refutation of a theory.

The orthodoxy in economics is thus a matter of convention, what happens to be the language and analytical structure of the dominant group. The conventions feed upon themselves, as practitioners within the profession perform what Kuhn (1970) calls normal science, using the language models, exemplars and testing procedures of the orthodoxy. Keynes did not conceal the fact that he was attempting to overthrow what was then the orthodoxy. He was also aware of how difficult it was for someone brought up in the orthodoxy to develop a new framework, with its new language, models and empirical reference points:

> The composition of this book has been for the author a long struggle of escape, and so must the reading of it be for most readers if the author's assault upon them is to be successful, - a struggle of escape from habitual modes of thought and expression ... The difficulty lies, not in the new ideas, but in escaping from the old ones, which ramify, for those brought up as most of us have been, into every corner of our minds.
>
> (Keynes, *C.W. VII*, p. xxiii)

Unless Keynes' readers also struggled to escape, then they approached his theory with the language and modes of thought of the orthodoxy; there was a *failure of communication*. From the point of view of the orthodoxy (which in Keynes' day had much in common with the current orthodoxy), if Keynes was claiming to be saying something new, then he must have done one of three things: introduced a new exogenous variable (animal spirits), or placed a constraint on a parameter (the liquidity trap) or a variable (money wages).[9] To a Post Keynesian, the notion that this constitutes Keynes' contribution is ludicrous, but it remains the dominant view of the orthodoxy.[10] Further, because the first and third are, on the basis of orthodox micro-theory, irrational (although observed to occur) and the second (although rational) has never been observed, even this meagre representation of Keynes' contribution has been belittled significantly. This outcome is the result of a (deliberate, or unwitting) *failure to understand* Keynes' method.

Post Keynesians have through continued efforts[11] emphasised the point that Keynes had also dealt with money as a store of wealth, expectations formation under uncertainty, and historical time. Some within the orthodoxy at times have understood this,[12] but have explicitly stayed with their choice of the general equilibrium approach, which precludes these elements of Keynes' method. Tobin (1958) attempts to incorporate uncertainty into his model of portfolio selection. But he is using the term in a completely different way from the way Post Keynesians use it.[13] Similarly, when money is given a role in general equilibrium models it is, in Keynes' terms (when defining money in a real exchange economy):

> ... as a neutral link between transactions in real things and real assets and does not ... enter into motives or decisions.
>
> (Keynes, *C.W. XIII*, p. 408)

The word money thus conveys something quite different within a general equilibrium model from money in a Post Keynesian model. By and large, there is a widespread misunderstanding within the orthodoxy that more than one meaning exists; the same can be said for the word time. It is because of these failures of communication that Post Keynesians should beware of conducting critiques of the orthodoxy in the orthodoxy's own terms; there is a danger that the orthodoxy will persist in presuming that language and concepts are being used in the same way by all concerned.

Nor does it seem that critiques of the internal logic of the orthodoxy or the realism of its assumptions will be sufficient to persuade its practitioners to change paradigms: the orthodoxy has proved to be very resilient to such critiques. Any theory must abstract, Post Keynesian or orthodox; it is not a valid critique that a theory is unrealistic (or at least not without a careful specification of what would be entailed by a realistic theory). What is valid is an assertion along the lines that economics should abstract in a particular way, for example to incorporate the features of a monetary economy rather than of a real exchange economy. Many general equilibrium theorists (with notable exceptions, such as Hahn) appear to be under the impression that their theory *does* deal with a monetary economy. It seems therefore that, as an extension of the argument in favour of analysing monetary economies, the case must be made explicitly that the general equilibrium method precludes such analysis.

THE DIFFERENT METHODOLOGICAL BASES OF POST KEYNESIAN AND ORTHODOX ECONOMICS

The difference in methodological approach between Post Keynesian economics and the orthodoxy is deep-rooted. It means, for example, that an orthodox economist would not accept the new methodology outlined above; rather economics is seen as a science in traditional terms, an objective analytical structure on which all can (in theory) be expected to agree. By implication, there is a scientific method, all other methods being unscientific, or at least less scientific. The presumption that methods can be ranked according to objective criteria (mirroring the objective ranking of goods and services by utility-maximising consumers) provides justification for the practice of ignoring the alternative methodology within which a new theory is presented, and reinterpreting the theory in terms of the orthodox methodology. In this way the orthodoxy is perpetuated, giving the illusion of dealing with alternative theories.

The orthodoxy's mode of thought derives support from the long-standing Cartesian-Euclidean tradition in Western thought. According to this tradition, the ideal of scientific thought is a linear system of logic whereby theorems are derived from basic axioms. The tradition is so ingrained that this may seem at first sight to be innocuous. First, however, the specification of an ideal raises problems. If it is unattainable, a Second Best Theorem of methodology might suggest that approximating as closely as possible to the ideal is not necessarily the best approach. Wimsatt (1981) demonstrates that derivation of theorems from a set of axioms compounds in the theorems the shortcomings of the axioms:

> In the attempt to secure high reliability, the focus is on total elimination

> of error, not on recognising that it will occur and on controlling its effects.
>
> (Wimsatt, 1981, p. 131)

And, second, the ideal may be irrelevant as well as unattainable if there is no way of categorically establishing the basic axioms. General equilibrium theory can present an aesthetically appealing, flawless logical structure, but if its basic axioms are unacceptable, then the structure loses its value. The Duhem-Quine thesis shows that the axioms or assumptions incorporated in any economic proposition are so complex, applying at a number of levels, that even the strictest falsification procedure cannot isolate which axioms have been falsified by the evidence (see Cross, 1982).

A corollary of the position that a set of axioms *can* be categorically established is 'a metaphysical stance which, in effect, assumes that the scientist is an omniscient and computationally omnipotent LaPlacean demon'.[14] In other words, if the axioms are to bear any relation to reality, then the problems of perception and induction are presumed to have been solved. For economics, the presumption is much stronger than for a physical science: not only must the economist have objective knowledge of the past and the future, but so must the economic agents under study. Only if it is presumed that agents act rationally on the basis of 'the' model of the economy, where variables conform to a known probability distribution can the economist establish definitive axioms as to the behaviour of economic agents.[15]

Of course, in practice, economists have had to face up to their inability to perform scientific tests of their theories. The history of economic methodology has followed a cyclical path, swinging from aspiring to pure deduction to aspiring to pure induction, as each approach in turn has proved impractical. The practical reality of economic analysis has enforced some compromise position. But this is viewed with some dissatisfaction, one or other extreme being the ideal. Indeed dualism pervades the Cartesian-Euclidean tradition and is apparent in the introduction to many an economics textbook: note the dualism of induction-deduction, normative-positive, endogenous-exogenous, fixed-variable. In the theory of expectations, dualism emerges in the contrast between known and not-known; there is no room for 'expected to be likely, with a low degree of confidence'.

Post Keynesian methodology starts from the position that it is impossible to establish any one set of axioms which is broad enough to support an adequate theoretical structure. Axioms such as 'households maximise utility' and 'firms maximise profits' are not adequate without further axioms specifying how they deal with limited knowledge of the past and absence of knowledge about the future. Even if accounts of such behaviour could be formalised, they would be unlikely to have universal application, but rather be specific to a particular institutional setting. An economist must deal with this in a manner analogous to the way in which economic agents deal with uncertainty: a combination of approaches, none of which in itself is sufficient.

Stohs describes this as a Babylonian approach:

> According to it, there is no single chain from axioms to theorems; but there are several parallel, intertwined, and mutually reinforcing sets of chains, such that no particular axiom is logically basic.
>
> (Stohs, 1983, p. 87)

An alternative pedigree can be traced from the Stoics, through Roman thought to the Scottish tradition of Political Economy.[16] Macfie (1955) argues that Adam Smith was an important contributor to that tradition, with the formal comparative statics of Book I of the *Wealth of Nations* complemented by the combination of philosophical, historical and sociological approaches developed in the rest of his work. Modern logical positivism can thus claim only an incomplete portion of Smith's method for precedent.

According to Macfie:

> In fact Smith was a philosophic writer ... His aim was to present all the relevant facts critically. Modern writers start from a totally different angle. They found on the law of non-contradiction. They aim at isolating one aspect of experience and breaking it down by analysis into its logical components.
>
> (Macfie, 1955, p. 84)

and again

> The central assumptions of Benthamite Utilitarianism are themselves antithetic to the whole spirit of the Scottish social school. The main philosophic contrast is between a mechanistic psychology, which inevitably eliminates any truly moral theory, and the forward-looking assumptions of the Scottish school; or again it is seen in the fact that the Scots saw the central fact as a growing society, a creature quite different from any mere individual, whereas to Bentham any society was merely an aggregate of individuals ... The static equilibrium theory of 'normal' value is therefore itself inevitably mechanistic ... it is not equipped to

deal with changes away from equilibrium. Yet these changes seem to dominate our economic fates.

(Macfie, 1955, p. 96)

In line with these two traditions, then, the Post Keynesian approach requires that a problem be addressed from a variety of angles. Bringing to bear historical, political, sociological and psychological considerations allows conjectures to be made as to the behaviour of economic agents within a particular historical context. Only then can pure logic be brought to bear, and even then it cannot be guaranteed to provide knowledge of the future.

A business manager studies a potential project from a variety of angles, more or less formal; a large proportion of the final decision rests on an immersion in the facts. Priorities must be established among the characteristics of different approaches in order for a final assessment to be made, priorities which will vary with the individual and project concerned. Similarly an economist can derive an understanding of the economy which transcends the formality of either mathematical or econometric modelling. The somewhat maligned concept of intuition may in fact be the brain's efficient way of getting round the problems of cognition. Intuition suggests outcomes on the basis of a distilling of a broader range of evidence than is normally brought to a formal agreement. While, to be useful, economics must always be able to provide reasons for its conclusions, the 'ordinary logic' approach, enhanced by intuition, guides the reasoning process.[17]

This type of approach precludes the type of reasoning possible in a purely analytic approach. No one variable can be described as the key if no one component of the theory (analytic, historical, political, etc.) can stand on its own as a complete account of the theory. A variable may be key in the analytic component, but if the essence of the method is to overcome the limits to formal logic applied to a social science, then the variable cannot be concluded to be key to the entire theory. The key variables in general equilibrium theory are the exogenous variables; their key role derives from the fact that they are exogenous. But if a variable which is endogenous in another (the money supply, for example, viewed in a particular institutional setting), then the endogeneity-exogeneity distinction is no longer crucial. Rather, if anything is key, it is the way in which the variables and the components of the analysis are combined.

Second, this approach precludes the identification of general necessary and sufficient conditions for particular events (although Keynes himself indulged in this practice[18]). Within a closed model, such conditions are a matter of logic. But they are strongly predicated on the assumptions of the model. It is useful as a critique to show, for example, that a restriction on the value or flexibility of one variable is sufficient to generate an unemployment equilibrium within the general equilibrium framework, but that result relies on all the other features of that model. It is illegitimate to conclude that that one variable is *actually* solely responsible (or even partly responsible) for an observed level of unemployment.

MONEY, UNCERTAINTY AND HISTORICAL TIME

The methodological framework, in the sense of mode of thought as outlined above, determines broadly the scope of the theoretical structure to be employed. A general equilibrium framework, which is the logical outcome of a Cartesian-Euclidean approach to economics, cannot incorporate money, uncertainty and historical time in the sense of the terms employed by Post Keynesians. Similarly, the Post Keynesian framework, which is the logical outcome of a Roman-Stoic approach, cannot generate universal theorems from basic axioms.

The marginalist revolution provided the axiomatic basis for general equilibrium theory. It allowed a complete logical system to be built up, linking microeconomics and macroeconomics, and the short run and the long run. The realism to which appeal was made by the marginalists was the realism of individual behaviour; since market forces are the aggregation of individual action, the basic axioms had to refer to individual behaviour.[19] Hence arose the axioms of utility maximising behaviour, with application to all sectors and activities.

The solution of the system required axioms relating to the functioning of markets. The Walrasian system, which dominates general equilibrium analysis, is timeless, does not require money, and involves no uncertainty. The time-consuming process of establishing prices, during which there is uncertainty as to the outcome, which could be mitigated by holding money rather than entering the market for producible goods, is eliminated by the assumption that the auctioneer established the price by *tâtonnement*, with recontracting wiping out false trades. The longrun is only distinguished from the shortrun by the *ad hoc* introduction of restrictions on price flexibility, which in turn induce market responses to ensure the realisation of the full market-clearing general equilibrium position in the long-run. (Firms not maximising profits for any reason go bankrupt or are taken over by profit maximisers; full employment real wages are restored by price movements even if money wages are fixed; and so on). The shortrun and longrun do not have a time dimension in the historical sense; it is a logical distinction between consecutive events.

The introduction of such restrictions into the pure Walrasian system represents an injection of realism; it is an attempt to deal with sources of conflict between the Walrasian system and the real world. Similarly, general equilibrium theorists have been receptive to suggestions that greater realism would be achieved by incorporating expectations formation under uncertainty, and money. But true uncertainty by definition cannot be modelled deterministically; herein lies its significance for decision-making. It refers to an absence of knowledge, a lack of confidence in one's predictions. Uncertainty has instead been equated with knowledge expressed in terms of quantitative probability distributions, in order to allow it to be systematised. The actual future value of a variable is not known (there is uncertainty as to its value), but its mean value and variance are assumed to be known. This misrepresentation of true uncertainty, the lack of confidence in predictions, generates an axiomatic treatment of decision-making with respect to the future. The axiomatic form of the model has put limits on the extent to which expectations can be modelled.[20]

Although expectations are necessitated by time (either historical or logical) expectations with risk but no uncertainty can refer only to logical time. Similarly they limit the functions of money, since it need not act as a receptacle for uncertainty. The only rationale within the general equilibrium framework for holding money as a store of value is provided by Tobin's (1958) theory of portfolio selection. In the frozen instant of logical time, the probability distributions of the expected returns (including capital gains and losses) on all financial assets are known.

Holding money, which earns no interest, as an asset is justified only as a means of spreading risk. In fact, Chick (1983, pp. 213-17) demonstrates that, given the logic of a static portfolio choice model such as this, there is no reason to hold money at all. Since there is no scope for switching assets during the period in question (which is unspecified anyway, being in logical time only), there is no scope for speculation in the normal sense of the word, only for insurance. Since actual returns are randomly distributed about an estimated mean, which is positive for non-money financial assets, there is no reason to hold money whose expected return is known to be zero.

These probability distributions are based on objective evidence as to the distribution of returns in the past. There is nothing within the financial sector of the model to generate changes in past distributions, and thus estimates of risk. The demand for money is stable; it can only change if some exogenous shock (a change in expected returns to capital expenditure, for example) alters the relative returns to all assets. Money does not play an active role, any more than any other asset.

Indeed it is inherent in the general equilibrium method that change is not generated endogenously, only exogenously, beyond the scope of the model. This contrasts with Shackle's (1974) analysis of the originative process by which both business and financial investors use their imagination to attempt to steal a march on their competitors. Far from being exogenous, this concept in Shackle's hands is the central motive force of capitalism. It does however require uncertainty, and differences of opinion as to the future, to make sense.

Money enters into disequilibrium models or temporary equilibrium models as a unique kind of asset, one which acts as an intermediary element in exchange in a non-barter economy. Clower (1969) inspired much of this development, which stresses the information problems which emerge when the sale of one good or service (particularly labour) is not the direct counterpart of demand for another good or service. There is no mechanism by which the unemployed can convey to potential employers what their demand for goods would be if only they were employed.

It is certainly true that payment of incomes in money (where that term is broad enough to include any non-reproducible good) prevents adjustment in the labour market. If payment were in reproducible goods, the value of the wage would automatically adjust with the market value of output, and unemployment need not emerge.[21] But the implications are not drawn in this type of analysis of the possibility of *holding* a non-reproducible asset. It is assumed that workers automatically spend whatever income they receive; there is no question of holding money for other than transactions purposes. In effect, money is simply introduced as an impediment to full information in the market process, since the consequences of giving money its full role as a receptacle for uncertainty cannot be accommodated by analysis within a closed deterministic system. It is perhaps the restrictiveness of the general equilibrium method which accounts for the 'split-personalities' aspect of the writing of Clower and Leijonhufvud. In much of their writing, they mirror the (Post) Keynesian method, but the mode of formal expression of their ideas, designed often as critiques of the orthodoxy, forces them to accept the limitations of general equilibrium theory.

We have thus shown that the general equilibrium method precludes the consideration of money, time and uncertainty in the senses in which they are incorporated into the Post Keynesian model. The task before us now is to show that, as soon as any one of these three factors is employed within a compatible framework, the others necessarily follow. In particular, we consider the arguments for incorporating money and uncertainty in any model involving historical time.

As soon as time is introduced in either the logical or historical sense, it must be admitted that both the past and the future play a role in the economy. Not only are the market structures within which values are established the product of institutions formed and decisions taken in the past but also any new decision refers to the future and is thus influenced by expectations. Most explicitly, the investment decision is based on expectations of future returns, but so also is the decision to hold particular financial assets. Even decisions as to current (far less durable) consumption expenditure involve expectations about future earning streams, price trends, etc. It is crucial, then, how these expectations are viewed as being formed. As we have seen, within logical time, a deterministic model requires that expectations also be deterministically formed. Historical time, in contrast, does not come in discrete lumps; there is no universal day on which all accounts are settled, and all take stock. Historical time is also irreversible. False trades cannot be recontracted. Rather windfall losses and gains are made which, being unforeseen, have unforeseen consequences for the composition and level of expenditure. Some experiments are crucial in Shackle's terms; in other words, acting on a particular expectation itself changes the environment for the next set of observations, so that no sample can be compiled on which to base quantitative probability estimates.

Modelling historical time thus precludes the use of simultaneous systems. A simultaneous formation of expectations, and action upon them in effect presumes that decision-makers know the outcome of their collective actions and that any mistakes can be reversed and corrected with no consequences. In fact, at no point can a decision-maker know what will happen in the future. Past experience provides information and some understanding of how the relevant market works as well as the particular institutions within which values are formed and decisions are effected. A particular cause for uncertainty within historical time is in fact the *timing* of actions; experiments may be crucial for other participants in a market than the conductor of the experiment. The introduction of a new product or production process changes the entire market environment for competitors as well as for consumers, in a way which cannot be foreseen.

A dualistic mode of thought interprets an absence of perfect knowledge as no knowledge. Rather, within the framework of ordinary logic, there is a collection of information, subjectively gathered from a variety of sources and means of enquiry, which allows some kind of conjectures about the future. (It is this type of conjecture which allows us to function in our daily lives.) Some conjectures are held with more confidence than others; there are varying degrees of uncertainty. But the method does allow conjectures as to future values of economic variables, or, at another level, as to the behaviour of individuals forming their conjectures as to the future. The method is thus capable of dealing with uncertainty as well as historical time without being rendered nihilistic. Each is less than fully captured, but then, according to this approach, no theoretical structure can *fully* capture anything.

It is rare to come across a society without money, in the sense of a non-reproducible asset which can act as a store of wealth as well as a means of payment and unit of account. The palpable existence of a variable does not necessarily mean that it must be included in an economic theoretical framework; any such framework must abstract from some variables. One important argument in favour of incorporating money is that it is the outlet for expression of uncertainty in a monetary economy.

In a pure barter system, uncertainty is expressed by holding on to one type of producible good as a store of value, before deciding when and how to exchange it for other goods. But the only adjustment required is a change in the relative values of goods, and thus of incomes-in-kind. Unemployment would not result. In contrast, in a monetary economy, money is a non-reproducible good. A relative increase in the demand for money constitutes a reduction in aggregate demand for producible goods or less liquid financial assets. Further, the relative price shift in favour of non-reproducible goods dampens expectations as to the profitability of possible investment projects, further reducing expenditure plans and increasing liquidity preference.

The fact that almost every society employs some form of money is in itself a response to uncertainty. Denominating contracts in an intermediate commodity, money, allows a sharing of uncertainty between the buyer and the seller. In the same way, international transactions are frequently denominated in terms of a third currency (the US dollar, or Special Drawing Rights - SDR - for example) since each of two currencies is likely to fluctuate less against the third (if it is a stable world currency) than against each other. It is this need to reduce the uncertainty endemic to most decisions which accounts for the relative stickiness of money wages and of some prices. Thus current levels of wages and prices cannot be abstracted from the past formation of conventions as to wage-bargaining and price-setting. These conventions arise because of the impracticality of operating markets on Walrasian lines, with fully flexible wages and prices.

The institutionalisation of money allows the development of a system of money contracts. It also allows financial intermediation and credit creation; the development of a complex financial system increases the range of assets which are available as a store of wealth, as well as the range of liabilities which can finance investment spending. Not only money can be held as a means of postponing expenditure on investment or consumer goods; there is also a wide array of financial assets of varying degrees of liquidity.

In its simplified form, Keynes' theory of liquidity preference was expressed in terms of a choice between money and bonds. But the theory has broader generality, referring to the choice between assets of long and short-term, real and financial.[22] The important point is that an increase in uncertainty, a collapse of confidence, in the capital goods sector, translates into a preference for more liquid assets (or a reduction in illiquid liabilities, that is, debt) among entrepreneurs and into more liquid assets among financial investors. This in turn raises the cost of raising equity capital, raises the long-term rate of interest relative to the short-term rate, and raises further the liquidity premium on money and other liquid financial assets.

It is important from a methodological point of view to note that all the features of a Post Keynesian model have followed naturally, one from the other. The uncertainties associated with taking action with respect to an unknown future (actions which cannot be reversed) have historically encouraged the widespread use of money contracts which promote relative stickiness of wages and prices. Money performs the additional function of separating transactions in time (and place) allowing postponement until the uncertainty surrounding a particular purchase is reduced. The more sophisticated the financial system, the more choice is available of stores of value, but the greater the range of uncertainty as to the prices of a greater range of assets. Expectations as to the value of new capital goods relative to existing assets are unlikely to be independent of expectations as to the relative (objective and subjective) returns on financial assets, some of which are titles to the return on capital goods. Both sets of expectations determine preferences as to the liquidity structure of assets and liabilities, and thus the willingness to invest and the return on alternative assets. All these features are part of a package: it makes little sense either to isolate any one factor as being most important, or to eliminate one as unnecessary.

By extending the theory of liquidity preference to all assets, the significance of money may appear to have been downgraded. But, first, all the transactions involved in a shift in liquidity preference in favour of more liquid assets (or less liquid assets) involve money; one participant in each transaction must be willing to part with money. That willingness is a function not only of objective rates of return, but also of the subjective liquidity premium attached to money. It is for this reason that the rate of return on money 'rules the roost'.

Second, the fact remains that a financial system cannot function without money. The system of inside money (assets matched by liabilities within the financial system) relies on the existence of outside money. This can take the form of the liabilities of the central monetary authority, gold, or a foreign currency (such as the US dollar). Something has to provide the confidence which is necessary to the functioning of the financial system, the building of an inverted pyramid of credit on a narrow base of outside money. Backing with outside money confers money-like qualities on inside money.

The dramatic rate of growth of the inside money system in the post-war years has encouraged the notion that the supply of money is endogenous. Certainly, the lender-of-last-resort function of central monetary authorities has provided outside money on demand for banks' reserves, while innovation within the financial system has allowed inside money to grow as an increasing multiple of outside money. Particularly in the longrun, financial development is strongly correlated with economic development. This elasticity of the money supply seems to suggest that finance is not an effective constraint on expenditure, especially in the longrun; although money exists, it has therefore been presumed reasonable by many to exclude it from analysis.

The counter-argument can be expressed in three stages: a financial system cannot persist with a fully endogenous money supply; money supply growth is at its most accommodating in boom times, when a financial crisis can have long-lasting consequences for output; the endogenous contraction of monetary growth in recessions similarly can have damaging effects on output extending into the long run.

First, then, if a financial system relies on outside money, its supply cannot be fully endogenous. Outside money can be defined as a money whose supply is sufficiently constrained that its value is stable relative to other assets; holders are confident that its value will be maintained. Elastic supply of such an asset, relative to other assets, would reduce its value and shake confidence in it as a store of value. If the asset were no longer acceptable as money, some other asset must perform that function, an asset which does satisfy the condition of relative inelasticity of supply; the system would continue to be based on outside money, although the asset serving that function had changed. In practice, there is resistance to giving up one form of money for another even in inflationary conditions, simply because its liquidity premium derives from its general acceptability as a means of payment. Only a hyper-inflation has in practice been sufficient to persuade people to change transactions habits.

In fact the consequences of money supply endogeneity vary significantly depending on the economic conditions prevailing at the time. An economy in the boom phase of the cycle will have a demand for money which is expanding rapidly to finance transactions, although expanding less rapidly than the value of transaction themselves, given ever-falling rates of liquidity preference. The returns on all assets in relatively fixed supply rise relative to returns on producible assets. Progressively more activity is channelled into speculative markets, where euphoric attitudes encourage a high degree of layering. Output and employment are stunted by the relative unattractiveness of producible assets.

Speculative activity depends on expanding bank credit and credit from non-bank financial intermediaries. Increasing interest rates are unlikely to deter financial speculation as long as capital gains are anticipated with confidence. But direct controls on credit and on the capacity for non-bank financial intermediaries to expand, combined with institutional controls on asset purchases on margin can limit the amount of finance made available. Without such controls, euphoric markets always carry the potential for crisis and collapse, as Minsky (1982) has so fully demonstrated. In a boom situation, a perfectly elastic money supply would endanger the entire financial system. Some other form of money would take the place of the old eventually; the new money might be the liabilities of a new monetary administration renewing confidence in the old currency by implementing controls. But the crisis and ensuing transition would have long-run consequences as investment plans are held in abeyance and capital losses absorbed.

Less dramatic, although potentially more significant in the long run, is the third consideration: the *inelasticity* of the money supply in the downturn phase. Irrespective of the behaviour of the monetary authorities, the general rush for liquidity on the part of business and financial investors is shared by financial institutions. Demand for credit during a recession is more likely to be to finance working capital than the installation of new capital equipment. The greater sensitivity of financial institutions to default risk reduces the availability of credit for 'distress borrowing', thereby increasing the incidence of bankruptcy, and discouraging growth of output and employment. Just as the prospect of capital gains outweigh interest rate considerations in the upturn, the prospect of capital losses limits the extent to which the monetary authorities can induce banks to lend more in the downturn by reducing interest rates.

Keynes (*C.W. VII*, Chapter 22) argued that employment and output can be kept perpetually below their long-run potential by the diversion of borrowed money into non-productive markets promising capital gains, during upswings, and into holdings of idle balances to avoid capital losses, during downswings. This perpetuation of unemployment is an inevitable feature of a monetary capitalist economy without active government intervention. It is the outcome of the accumulation motive which drives the system.[23] The urge to accumulate thrives on uncertainty; it is the prospect of higher profits or capital gains at the expense of those with different expectations which determines investment decisions in real and financial markets. An economy with a sophisticated financial system provides far more scope for increased profitability as well as capital gains than one where accumulation consists purely of amassed savings in the form of stocks of commodities, or money. As the linchpin of the financial system - the means of payment and the last refuge of uncertainty - money plays a crucial role in the shortrun and in the longrun. This role cannot however be dissociated from the setting of historical time and the formation of expectations under the uncertainty that entails.

CONCLUSION

It has been the purpose of this chapter to examine the Post Keynesian method of analysing a monetary economy. In so doing, it was necessary to examine the way in which the orthodox methodology has influenced critiques of its content and thereby alternative approaches themselves. Some critiques have taken the form of accusations that one or other of time, uncertainty and money have been excluded from the real exchange model of the orthodoxy. The response has been to include time, uncertainty or money with little impact on the conclusions of the orthodox model. In fact these concepts mean something totally different, depending on whether they are employed in the Post Keynesian or orthodox frameworks.

We then explored the fundamental difference in mode of thought between the two frameworks, the orthodox methodology employing what has been the dominant (Cartesian-Euclidean) strand in Western scientific thought. The orthodox interpretation of alternative theoretical approaches has been conditioned by the fact that the Cartesian-Euclidean scientific method claims exclusivity. The methodology underlying the Post Keynesian approach stresses the difference between methods used, rather than their ranking, and the sociological basis for theory appraisal. It was demonstrated that Post Keynesian methodology is not without historical precedent.

The aim then was to show the interdependence between historical time, expectations formation under uncertainty and an active role for money within the Post Keynesian framework. Once historical time was introduced, uncertainty and money logically followed. The level of investment, and thus output and employment, are the outcome of choices between assets based on expectations as to future asset values, and the avoidance of choice represented by the holding of money, all within the context of experience and institutions arising from the past. As a corollary, any long-run model based on historical time is incomplete without consideration also of uncertainty and money.

NOTES

1. Chick (1983) puts great emphasis on the significance of Keynes' method, which fundamentally affects the nature of his analysis. And indeed her exposition is itself an excellent example of Keynes' method in practice.
2. This argument is made with respect to the Cambridge capital controversies in Dow (1980).
3. See, for example, E.R. Weintraub's (1979, pp. 102-6) review.
4. See Boland (1982).
5. The full reference is as follows: 'Letting a hundred flowers blossom and a hundred schools of thought contend is the policy for promoting the progress of the arts and the sciences and a flourishing socialist culture in our land' (Mao Tse-Tung, 1967, pp. 302-3).
6. See McCloskey (1983) for a discussion of the exchange of economic ideas in terms of rhetoric or 'disciplined conversation'. See also Bausor (1983) for a discussion of the role of language and conceptual evolution in promoting the wide acceptance of the rational expectations hypothesis. See also Kuhn (1970, pp. 201-4) for the original statement.
7. Katouzian (1980, p. 135) makes this case. It can also be expressed in Kuhnian language; Kuhn (1974) defined paradigms (or bodies of theory) as consisting partly of the models by which they are expressed, but partly also by the world-view of the scientist. The way in which any individual goes about organising observations of phenomena into a coherent framework which allows life to be conducted determines a world-view (part ideology) which then influences any scientific enquiry.
8. An example would be the term 'unemployment'. The way in which data are collected reflects a particular theoretical framework (it does not capture 'discouraged workers', for example). For some 'unemployment' is presumed to be largely involuntary, while to others it is entirely voluntary.
9. Leijonhufvud (1968) was the first to distinguish explicitly the *General Theory* from the neo-classical synthesis interpretation.
10. See Meltzer (1981) for a reassessment of Keynes' contribution from an orthodox perspective.
11. Most notably, Davidson (1978), Leijonhufvud (1968), Minsky (1976), Robinson (1965, section 2; 1979, sections 1 and 3), Shackle (1974) and S. Weintraub (1978).
12. Most notably, Hahn (1973), Tobin (1958) and E. R. Weintraub (1979).
13. See Chick (1983, pp. 213-17) for a thorough critique of Tobin's model and use of language.
14. Stohs (1983, p. 87).
15. This presumption is the basis of the Rational Expectations Hypothesis. It has been the achievement of this hypothesis to put its behavioural axioms on an epistemologically consistent basis, albeit vulnerable in their lack of realism.
16. See Macfie (1955). It has been argued that the Stoics in fact were influenced by the Babylonians; see Russell (1961, p. 260).
17. The term 'ordinary logic' is a reference to Keynes' epistemology. To those imbued with dualistic modes of thought, the notion of employing intuition will appear unscientific. It is certainly classified in a similar category to 'humanistic', 'sloppy', and 'vague' according to McCloskey's (1983, p. 510) representation of modernism. Introspection should however reveal that intuition plays a large part in providing the initial direction for research, or the insight into where to look for the weak point in an

argument, just as it plays a large part in innovation in the industrial or marketing setting, and indeed in the development of mathematics.

18. Chick (1983) shows how Keynes started with a pared-down static model to show how little it would take to violate Say's Law. Subsequent analysis in the *General Theory* built up the model gradually in such a way as to constitute an alternative to the orthodoxy.
19. There is some difference of opinion as to whether the axioms describe actual behaviour (see, for example, Hahn, 1973) or the behaviour of representative individuals (see, for example, Machlup, 1967).
20. See Davidson (1978, Chapter 2).
21. See Dow and Earl (1982, Chapter 8).
22. See Townshend (1937) for the earliest statement, and Dow and Earl (1982, Chapter 8) and Wells (1983) for restatements.
23. See Shapiro (1978).

3. Money Supply Endogeneity

This chapter is a slightly amended version of an article which appeared in Economie Appliqués, *41(1), pp. 19-39, 1988. The original paper was presented at the University of Ottawa-ISMEA Conference on The Cyclical Behaviour and Long-term Structural Movements of Contemporary Economies, Ottawa, 3-6 October 1984. It has benefited from comments made at the time by Victoria Chick, James Deane, John Foster and Mario Seccareccia.*

INTRODUCTION

The endogeneity or otherwise of the money supply process is an issue of central importance to macroeconomic theory and policy. For orthodox theorists, any exogenous variable is automatically significant as a cause of disturbance from equilibrium; the money supply has been the exogenous variable to receive most attention. Such a stance invites the critique that the money supply in reality is not exogenous, so that any model giving money such a powerful role is not helpful for policy purposes. But then, some have concluded that, if the money supply process is indeed endogenous in reality, then money loses all importance in macroeconomic analysis. Thus much Keynesian analysis has been conducted in real terms, allowing Johnson (1971) to associate the monetarist counter-revolution with a revival of concern with money, compared with the then Keynesian orthodoxy.

The endogeneity issue is a complex one, confused by the range of senses in which the terms endogeneity and exogeneity may be used. As in so many macroeconomic debates, a major factor has been the tendency to talk at cross-purposes; terms are used with different meanings by different participants, on the basis of their different theoretical frameworks. It is the primary purpose of this chapter to specify the range of uses of the relevant terms, and the significance of these uses.

These important semantic issues, symptoms of substantive differences in theoretical approach, were explicitly raised by Chick (1977, Chapter 5). It is again Chick (1983, Chapter 17) who has gone beyond these difficulties to pose the particular question as to the compatibility of money supply endogeneity with Keynes' treatment of the money supply as a 'given' in the *General Theory*. Chick concludes as follows:

> the elasticity of the postwar monetary system is probably the single most important area of departure from Keynes' assumptions and, with its corollaries for price expectations and the locus of the liquidity premium, represents the area of the theory most in need of thorough revamping.
>
> (Chick, 1983, p. 358)

By following upon Chick's discussion of endogeneity, this paper attempts a first step in the direction of that revamping. The context of the business cycle provides an ideal framework for this purpose, raising as it does questions of causality within a dynamic process.

The discussion will start with the general meaning of endogeneity and exogeneity within a theoretical framework. Much less straightforward is their meaning in reality. Any discussion in this second context must itself be theory-laden, in that our perceptions of reality are ordered implicitly by a general theoretical framework, or world-view. What are selected for discussion as separable variables, sectors and time-periods will reflect a particular theoretical stance. With this *caveat*, the third section discusses the various meanings of endogeneity and exogeneity in terms of perceptions of how the money supply process works in reality, and the implications these meanings hold for theory formulation with a view to policy prescription. It is concluded that, aside from acts of God, only the irreversible past can account for any exogeneity in a reality understood in terms of historical time. Theory formulation involves judgement as to what should and what should not in addition be represented as exogenous in abstracting from reality. In the fourth section we use the business cycle context in order to illustrate how such judgements may be made. In the process, it is demonstrated that money supply endogeneity as such is not incompatible with the necessary attributes of money, and that it by no means diminishes the role of money in economic fluctuations and the longterm.

THE MEANING OF ENDOGENEITY WITHIN A THEORETICAL FRAMEWORK

The notion of endogeneity is at its most straightforward in the context of a formal theoretical framework. That framework must make explicit the variables under consideration, and distinguish between those which are to be explained by the theory and those which are not. The former are the endogenous variables and the latter the exogenous variables. It would then appear at first sight to be a matter simply of testing the theory's predictions to assess whether the line between endogenous and exogenous has been drawn in the best place.

But we must consider further the significance of choosing particular variables as exogenous. Their primary significance lies in the implication of causality, that changes in exogenous variables cause changes in endogenous variables. Such an implication is only logically valid within the confines of the model itself; it is almost a matter of definition, a direct consequence of the choice of exogenous variables. By choosing to specify the money supply as exogenous, orthodox economists are thus begging the question of its causal role. The most direct attack on the orthodoxy's conclusions has been on their own ground, choosing alternative variables as exogenous and demonstrating their capacity to explain the money supply in much the same way as monetarists have sought to use the money supply to explain the general price level. (See for example Tobin, 1970 and Moore, 1979b). The further possibility can never be excluded of a common cause of changes in variables chosen as endogenous *and* exogenous. But, since the relevant variables follow similar time-trends, empirical testing has failed to settle the issue to the satisfaction of all concerned. The rationale for choosing one as exogenous must ultimately rest on other than empirical grounds. (The empirical basis for the endogeneity-exogeneity distinction is explored further in section 3. See Desai, 1981, Chapter 3, for a full methodological critique of monetarism.)

The theoretical meaning of exogeneity and endogeneity, and thus of causality-within-the-model, depends however on the type of theoretical framework employed. Orthodox theory is built on the presumption of private sector stability. The theoretical framework is one of general equilibrium, although different branches of the orthodoxy vary in the degree to which their theory is derived from the axioms of individual rationality. Even the disequilibrium and temporary equilibrium approaches take general equilibrium as their reference point. Private sector stability is represented by a closed system of equations whose solution is an equilibrium one, which, in the absence of market imperfections, is in some sense optimal, or at least efficient. That equilibrium solution can only be disturbed by an exogenous shock, a change in the value of an exogenous variable. Changes in technology or tastes are candidates for exogenous shocks, as Hahn (1983) pointed out in his critique of monetarism. But there is a sense of unease within the orthodoxy in relying on variables which ultimately should be explicable in terms of the rationality axioms: hence the strenuous attempts made to endogenise technical progress.

The public sector may provide a solution, in that its behaviour can be viewed as exempt from the axioms of individual rationality. Rational expectations theorists are moving in the direction of endogenising public sector behaviour too, further restricting the capacity of their theory to contribute to policy questions. (See Barro, 1984.) But for those in the neo-classical tradition, a separation between private sector and public sector behaviour is retained. Their judgement in this regard is reinforced by the capacity of the monetary authorities (subject to institutional constraints) to be a major influence on financial markets, as the issuer of a large proportion of financial assets. Exogeneity then arises from the degree of independence of the public sector from the private sector. Since the money supply in particular comes under the *aegis* of the public sector, it is a prime candidate for an exogenous variable, capable of periodically shocking the system away from equilibrium. As a corollary, only variables governed other than by individual rationality expressed through markets can have a causal role to play in the economy. (Temporary equilibrium theory can explain a continual state of flux in terms of the perpetual absence of complete futures markets. But additional factors are required to explain the relatively systematic flux of business cycles.)

Second, as Gale (1982, 1983) points out in his surveys of orthodox monetary theory, neither the full general equilibrium nor the disequilibrium framework is capable of incorporating the behaviour of financial institutions (or indeed the firm in general). The connection, then, between the public sector's involvement in money supply creation (the monetary base) and the more general monetary aggregates (made up mainly of bank deposits) can only be expressed in a mechanical way, by means of the bank multiplier, leaving the monetary base as the crucial variable. This limitation reinforces the focus on the money supply as an exogenous variable, under the control of the public sector.

The sharp distinction between endogenous and exogenous variables, which has such important consequences for perceptions of causality, is peculiar to theoretical frameworks which are closed systems of formal relations derived from a unique set of axioms. Since this system represents the theory in its entirety, either a variable is endogenous or it is not. But there are alternative ways of constructing theoretical frameworks whereby any formal equation system may form only part of the structure. (See Dow, 1985.) In the absence of a unifying set of axioms, such an approach allows several parallel chains of reasoning, each with different starting points. A variable may thus be exogenous to one chain of reasoning, but endogenous to another. Thus, for example, if the behaviour of financial institutions cannot be analysed in a formal, deterministic fashion, then a historical-institutional method could be used instead to generate conclusions about their influence on the money supply, and their reactions to action by the monetary authorities. (This historical-institutional method corresponds to Keynes', 1973b, broad notion of probability estimation: where a determinate basis for decision-making is lacking, predictions are based on informed judgement applied to both quantitative and non-quantitative information, of varying degrees of completeness.) Although the money supply might formally be exogenous within a macroeconomic equation system, its endogeneity within the analysis of the financial system would severely limit any tendency to infer causality on the part of the money supply.

The importance of identifying causal relations stems from the policy conclusions derived from theory. Once the money supply is identified as exogenous to the orthodox theoretical framework, it is an easy step to identify it as a cause of disturbance of the economy from its Pareto-efficient equilibrium. The inevitable policy conclusion is that the money supply should be controlled in such a way that these disturbances are avoided. The alternative theoretical approach *might* reach a similar conclusion from its formal analysis, but then the next step would be to turn to the analysis of financial institutions' behaviour for indications of the consequences of such action by the monetary authorities. This additional chain of reasoning might then lead to the conclusion that the monetary authorities would fail in their attempt to control the volume of bank deposits, and that other repercussions of the attempt (on investment plans or on price expectations, for example) should be fed back into the formal model.

Thus, within a theoretical framework, endogeneity and exogeneity and thus causality are matters of definition. The significance of the definition depends on the type of theoretical framework employed. A closed, axiomatic framework defines as exogenous those variables whose values cannot be derived ultimately from the axioms. Since the goal within this framework is to endogenise as much as possible, the range of exogenous variables which can account for systematic disturbance from equilibrium becomes narrow, and the importance of each enhanced. Within a theoretical framework made up of a collection of partial analyses, employing a variety of methods, endogeneity and exogeneity are matters of definition only within each partial analysis. Inference of causality is thus much more limited, since the cause within one chain of reasoning may be explained within another chain. Since different chains may require different methods of analysis - formal, or historical, for example - there is no scope for combining the parts into a complete, systematic whole. Nevertheless, the defusion of the notion of exogeneity allows a much more complex analysis of causal relations.

This discussion of endogeneity has been conducted at the abstract level of modes of theory construction. Theories are constructed as abstractions from reality, rather than mirrors of reality. But if conclusions are to be used for policy purposes, the connections between abstraction and reality are important. If the money supply is potentially to be regarded as a policy variable, then it is important whether its abstract representation as an exogenous variable is mirrored in reality. Thus, while many elements of abstract reasoning must necessarily be of an 'as if' character, the strong assumption of exogeneity necessary to justify policy conclusions must have a much stronger basis in perceptions of reality. We turn now in the next section to consider the possible meanings of endogeneity or exogeneity in perceptions of reality.

THE MEANING OF ENDOGENEITY 'IN REALITY'

The most immediate connection between theory and reality which provides its own meaning of endogeneity is econometric testing. Any theoretical framework can generate a conclusion of the form 'changes in variable A are explained by changes in variable B', where B has been defined as exogenous within the theoretical framework. Whether the conclusion refers to a particular, singular event (such as inflation in the 1970s) or a general kind of event (such as, simply, inflation), it is possible in general to test the conclusion with reference to measures of A and B. (See Addison *et al.*, 1984, for a discussion of the distinction between singular and general events.) Exogeneity within the model is confirmed by the statistical evidence if B is independent of A, that is, in a stochastic regression equation where A is the dependent variable, B in any one period is uncorrelated with the disturbance term in all periods.

In many instances such a clear-cut distinction between statistical endogeneity and exogeneity is not possible. If lagged values of dependent variables are used as explanatory variables, then the relevant distinction is rather between the jointly dependent variables (current values of endogenous variables) and predetermined variables (exogenous variables and lagged values of endogenous variables). But, for the moment let us consider the simpler case of a strictly exogenous variable which is statistically confirmed.

The first problem to face in drawing any policy conclusions is the problem of induction. If the theory is concerned with inflation in general, then observation of instances where inflation has been statistically explained in the past by money supply growth are not sufficient to infer that this will always be the case. An observation of a period in which money supply growth did not statistically explain the rate of change in the price level is sufficient to deny a *necessary* connection between one and the other. Thus Hendry and Eriksson (1983), for example, have demonstrated the significance of Friedman and Schwartz's (1982) insertion of shift factors in the demand for money equation for the UK to ensure its stability. (They also challenge Friedman and Schwartz's unexplained presumption that the money supply is exogenous.) As long as changes in one variable *can* be shown to be a necessary condition for changes in another, then control of the first variable is a sufficient condition for control of the other. (See Addison *et al.*, 1980). But the problem of induction prevents a categoric conclusion being reached as to whether or not a particular event *is* a necessary condition in reality.

If the theory refers to a particular, singular event, then it seeks to explain after the event rather than to predict. The problem of induction need not arise. But if the purpose of understanding particular events is to improve policy measures in the future, an element of prediction is necessary. Predictions however must extend to the conjunctural and institutional conditions expected to obtain in the future, and thus to how far past experience can provide clues as to the causal relations to obtain in the future. A necessary feature of such analysis is an understanding of the money supply process itself.

Once the money stock is viewed as the outcome of a process, the question arises as to the sense in which it might realistically be treated as exogenous, that is, independently determined. Indeed, there is a broader question as to what if anything is, in reality, exogenous to economic events. Ultimately everything is interconnected, so that the search for fundamental causes ends up on a path of infinite regress. For practical purposes, however, theories (and, indeed, disciplines) segment interconnected reality into manageable portions. The important question of judgement relates to where demarcation lines are drawn. Friedman (1970b), like many orthodox economists, in fact insists that he regards growth of the money supply as only a proximate cause of inflation. In other words, he admits that there may be more fundamental causes of the money supply increasing in the first place. But he stops at the money supply, treating it as an exogenous variable, on the grounds that its determinants are independent of the demand for money, supply being nominal, but demand being a demand for real balances. (See Friedman and Schwartz, 1982, pp. 32-6.)

Friedman's argument is subject to serious circularity. The theoretical conclusion that demand for money is a demand for real balances itself limits the scope for statistical correspondence between demand and supply. In any case, the technique for identifying demand and supply schedules from monetary data is by no means cut and dried (see Cooley and LeRoy, 1981). But, having concluded that demand and supply are independent, and having chosen the money supply as the exogenous variable, causality has thereby been imposed, on theoretical grounds, on the data. Friedman and Schwartz (1963a, p. 695) had no other basis for concluding that, while there is 'mutual interaction' between money supply changes and changes in money income and prices, money is 'rather clearly the senior partner in longer-run movements and in major cyclical movements'.

An argument can nevertheless be made in favour of choosing the money supply as an exogenous variable, on the grounds that it can be influenced (if not completely controlled) by the monetary authorities. As long as supply is subject to some influence which does not affect demand, the two can be regarded as independent. By defining the money supply as the monetary base times the bank multiplier, monetarists infer a very direct influence (indeed, control) on the part of the monetary authorities, as supplier of the monetary base. On the other hand, if the bank multiplier is variable, or if the monetary base is changed passively in response to demand, the authorities are at best influencing the stock of money, certainly not controlling it.

It has been the major Keynesian argument against the monetarist position that, while monetary growth *may* be a proximate cause of inflation, the fundamental cause of monetary growth is expenditure plans which bring forth an increased supply of credit. (See Kaldor, 1970a; Tobin, 1970; Davidson and Weintraub, 1973; and Godley and Cripps, 1983.) Inflation *may* ensue from this increased credit when the expenditure increase reflects increased unit costs, or for that matter increased profits. The expansion of credit is facilitated by two factors (see Kaldor, 1983a). First, the lender-of-last-resort facility ensures that banks can increase reserves at will, albeit at a cost. If, further, the monetary authorities are following the Keynesian monetary policy prescription of maintaining interest rate stability, additional reserves will not carry a penal interest rate. (Endogeneity of the money supply refers, then, to a particular policy stance chosen by the monetary authorities; it *could* be called an exogenously-determined endogeneity if public sector behaviour is defined as exogenous.) Second, if the monetary authorities were to try to discourage lender-of-last-resort borrowing of reserves, financial institutions are now sufficiently adaptable to be able to expand without increased reserves. The expansion of non-bank financial intermediaries during periods of attempted monetary control, and the need progressively to extend the coverage of money supply definitions attests to this capability. (The extent of the adaptability of financial institutions was one of the major subjects of the Radcliffe Report, 1959.)

This responsiveness of money supply to demand is reinforced in open economies by the capacity of firms to attract credit from foreign financial institutions as well as domestic ones. Indeed, a growing proportion of activity is conducted by firms which are themselves multinational and thus more free than domestic firms to borrow and lend internationally. At the international level, too, the development of credit markets in foreign currencies (of which the most important is the Euro-currency market) has increased the capacity to extend credit outside national regulatory frameworks. Even with floating exchange rates, particularly when the float is not pure, international financial intermediation allows increased credit capacity for each constituent economy.

The evidence thus suggests that the money supply process is endogenous, in the sense that it is responsive to demand, particularly if the money supply definition is allowed to change as new financial instruments emerge. Active monetary policy may nevertheless still have a role to play *if*, as Kahn (1976) suggests, monetary growth is still a necessary feature of inflation, even if not the fundamental cause, and *if* the monetary authorities can influence the money supply, even with private sector responses to such influence taken into account. The first condition is met only if the velocity of circulation is stable and/or there is no persistent stagnation of output accompanying inflation. Over the short period, velocity can speed up so that a given money supply finances rising nominal incomes. Also, rising costs due to a changing industrial structure or a change in the relative power of unions can coincide with stagnation of output, so that nominal expenditure does not increase, requiring additional finance. The conditions for monetary growth to accompany inflation are, however, more closely met the longer the period. But observed correlation between monetary growth and inflation in the long run, suggesting that the former is a proximate cause of the latter, is one thing. Drawing conclusions about the consequences of active intervention to present monetary growth is another. The problem of induction prevents us from concluding from past data that monetary growth will always be a necessary condition for inflation even in the longrun. And if the money supply is one element within a causal chain, breaking that link does not preclude the development of an alternative chain. The causal process requires further investigation.

The process of monetary control itself must thus be considered to assess whether any observed correlation between monetary growth and inflation is reversible, that is whether monetary contraction would lead to deflation, and indeed whether monetary control is possible at all. The monetary authorities can, if they choose, influence financial markets in the same way as any other major participant. By altering demand or supply in the money and bond markets, the monetary authority can influence the interest rate.

This is the element of exogeneity, the factor behind the money supply process which may be independent of demand. But if expected returns from alternative assets are rising faster in an inflationary boom period, higher interest rates will not discourage expenditure on those assets. They add to costs and they may be sufficiently high to discourage productive expenditure, in favour of speculative expenditure. Monetary control in such a situation would fail in its attempt to reduce inflation; rather it would increase inflation and reduce productive activity. This counter-example to the orthodox scenario demonstrates the importance of considering fundamental causes rather than proximate causes. Even if the money supply were exogenous, its control may produce effects opposite to those predicted by monetarist theory which starts analysis only at the moment of government's influence on the money supply.

The capacity to control the money supply in any case has been shown to be limited by the difficulties experienced by the US and UK authorities in reaching their monetary targets since 1979. As long as interest rates do not discourage borrowing, the lender-of-last-resort facility allows bank reserves to increase in response to demand. Further, rising interest rates attract capital inflows which allow credit demand to be satisfied by foreign capital if domestic credit is not forthcoming.

The question remains whether there exists an interest rate sufficiently high to discourage demand for credit, that is whether *in principle* governments could control the money supply if they had the political will to do so. This brings us to the essential element of exogeneity that underlies any financial system: its basis in outside money. If interest rates became so high that borrowing even for working capital could not be sustained, and if monetary targets were so rigidly adhered to that banks could not rely on the lender-of-last-resort facility, and thus could not satisfy demand for distress borrowing, bankruptcies and defaults would ensue. There would be multiple effects on the financial system which could not be averted by the authorities if they were committed to their monetary targets. In such a fragile situation, even high interest rates would not attract capital inflows if there was a danger of financial failure. (See Minsky, 1976, 1982, for a full analysis of the fragility of financial systems.)

What is the ingredient of a financial system which inspires confidence in it, which normally prevents such financial crises from arising? Confidence rests ultimately in the capacity of governments to regulate financial institutions to ensure prudent behaviour, and to provide lender-of-last-resort facilities for those encountering temporary liquidity shortages. It even rests in the willingness of the government to ensure an endogenous money supply, allowing financial institutions to expand in line with the growth of the economy. Any financial system must thus have an element of outside money in the sense of backing by government with its attendant regulatory and taxing power. If the domestic government does not inspire such confidence, a foreign currency performs the function of outside money. A paradox thus emerges that the outsideness of the monetary authorities' role in the provision of credit, that is, its exogeneity, relies on their willingness to allow the provision of credit to be endogenous, responding to demand.

The exogenous aspect of credit provision in reality is thus past experience of the behaviour of financial institutions, and whatever institution backs the financial system. It is a combination of actual behaviour in the past and current perceptions of it. If it were possible to control the money supply without disrupting the confidence derived from these perceptions then it would be legitimate to treat the money supply as itself exogenous. But it has not proved possible to do so. In the UK, for example, active policy influence has been applied further back along the chain of causation, so that inflation has been reduced by fiscal demand deflation. (This eventually has a side-effect of reducing the demand for credit, thus allowing the monetary targets to be approached.)

Within an orthodox framework, the econometric distinction between exogenous and other predetermined variables would be relevant here: 'the past' includes predetermined variables which are not exogenous (in a stochastic framework, their values are not independent of the disturbance terms in the equations explaining past values of dependent variables.) But in a historical time framework, the distinction loses significance since history is irreversible. A collapse of confidence due to (endogenous) inadequate supervision of banks in the past plays the same causal role in the future as a collapse of confidence due to an (exogenous) theft of the central bank's gold stocks if the collapse is irreversible. A causal role may thus be extended from strictly exogenous variables (in the econometric sense) to other predetermined variables which are subject to irreversible shifts. (See Termini, 1984, for a discussion of the significance of historical time, rather than mechanical time, for the concept of temporal causality.)

The problem remains as to whether this review of the money supply process precludes an active role for money in the economy. The problem is posed by the conclusion that the money supply process is endogenous. But, if anything but elements of the past is endogenous in reality, then endogeneity as such cannot be equated with economic insignificance. Clearly further investigation is required of the type of endogeneity involved. For example, when it was concluded above that the providers of outside money inspire confidence by making its provision endogenous, it is a particular type of endogeneity we have in mind: money supply growth in line with needs for productive purposes, in such a way that use of money for destabilising speculative purposes is discouraged. Limitless supplies of money regardless of economic conditions, as an alternative notion of endogeneity, would clearly not inspire confidence; the money asset would no longer be an acceptable store of value. It is partly for this reason that Keynes assumed inelasticity of supply with respect to demand. (It was inelasticity of production with respect to demand which he explicitly specified as a necessary attribute of money. See Keynes, *C.W. VII*, Chapter 17. But he proceeded to use the two notions interchangeably.)

To make sense of this attribute of inelasticity, within a world of increasing financial sophistication, it must be regarded as a relative concept - relative to other assets. At the same time, this allows us to analyse the growing moneyness of other assets in limited supply under conditions when their liquidity increases. Indeed, as Chick (1983, p. 308) points out, the form of endogeneity which the money supply takes, particularly as influenced by the private sector, is not always such as to generate the socially optimal elasticity.

We turn in the next section to an analysis of money's role in the business cycle to demonstrate the changing nature of its endogeneity under different economic conditions, and the prevailing importance of a given confidence in the financial system. The business cycle issue is significant, not only because it is the context of an important use of money supply exogeneity by the orthodoxy, but also because it provides a focus for Keynesian analysis of process within a capitalist system. The emphasis in much Keynesian analysis with accommodating credit creation has been on the stability of financial relationships. (See most notably Godley and Cripps, 1983. See also McCallum and Vines, 1981, for a parallel drawn between this type of analysis and orthodox treatment of financial relationships.) But interdependence between demand and supply is no guarantee of stability. By retaining a separate focus on demand and supply within financial markets (in spite of their interdependence), we can use Keynesian analysis to explain the active role of financial markets in the production cycle. The following section thus gives an account of the business cycle where credit creation is endogenous to the private sector to some extent, subject to public sector influence to some extent, and dependent fundamentally on the given degree of confidence, generated in the irretrievable past, in expectations about asset prices and in the robustness of the financial system.

MONEY SUPPLY ENDOGENEITY IN THE BUSINESS CYCLE

The monetarist theory of the business cycle takes an increase in the money supply as the starting point and thus as the causal agent in the business cycle (see Friedman and Schwartz, 1963b). A Keynesian theory has no starting point as such on the grounds that the norm for the economy is cyclical movement rather than stability; there is no need therefore to identify any one cause of cycles. However, the variable normally singled out as a starting point for *analysis* is the marginal efficiency of capital, on the grounds that a major determinant, the state of long-run expectations, is subject to periodic discrete shifts which cannot be fully explained within an economic model.

Consider, then, a discrete improvement in long-run expectations propelling the economy into an upswing. As economic activity picks up, banks extend more credit to investors whose projects now look creditworthy. At the same time, expectations of rising asset prices encourage a general switching out of liquid assets into less liquid assets with a view to reaping capital gains. Liquid resources are thus freed up to finance further activity; not only has the willingness of financial institutions to lend increased but their capacity has increased also. As the expansion progresses and ever-higher capital gains are anticipated, borrowing becomes more highly geared. There is a progression from hedge finance (where expected cash flow is sufficient to cover interest commitments) to speculative finance (where expected cash flow is insufficient to cover interest commitments in the shortrun, but sufficient in the longer run, requiring debt refinancing) to Ponzi finance (where expected cash flow is never sufficient to cover interest commitments, requiring increasing debt). (See Minsky, 1982, Chapter 5.) At the same time, lenders' perception of risk is lulled by the steady increase in asset prices, and new instruments and institutions emerge to generate additional sources of credit. Foreign capital is attracted by high returns, while domestic lenders overseas are encouraged to switch into domestic assets.

Along with this process goes a tendency for activity to be diverted from productive activity to speculative activity, as the expected returns on the latter continue to rise in a way which returns on the former cannot. Speculative activity is attracted particularly to those assets in inelastic supply (non-reproducible assets, and those whose production, like housing, has a long lead-time). As markets become more active in these assets, their liquidity increases relative to carrying costs, so that they come more close to satisfying the necessary attributes of money. The growing availability of close substitutes for money (albeit a function of temporary market conditions) further reduces the willingness to hold idle money itself.

The situation outlined above can be described as one of increasing availability of credit as well as a falling willingness, relative to planned expenditure, to hold money. Both supply and demand are interdependent, since they are both responses to the widespread expectation of rising asset prices. The money supply (generated by credit creation) is certainly endogenous, but moving in the opposite direction to demand. Further, the greater the responsiveness of the supply of money to asset price expectations, the more potentially destructive is the process; the more the speculative euphoria is fuelled by easy finance the greater the ensuing collapse. Highly-geared borrowing can only persist if asset price growth keeps up its pace. Any slackening means ever-increasing debt requirements which ultimately pose too great a risk for lenders. The situation is also highly sensitive to interest rate increases, which can turn hedge finance into speculative finance, and speculative finance into Ponzi finance. Attempts by the monetary authorities to curb credit growth once borrowing is already highly-geared may thus actually engineer a financial collapse. Once the defaults and bankruptcies start occurring in such a situation, they have multiple effects throughout the system.

Once the euphoria has peaked, because of a slackening of pace in asset price expectations, because of monetary authority intervention, or because of reduced tolerance of investment mistakes, the process goes into reverse. Financial institutions curtail lending for other than the most secure risks; some are forced to curtail overall activity by defaulting on loans. Other sectors also attempt to generate more liquidity to deal with the consequences of unexpectedly-low selling prices for assets. Capital returns overseas where expected returns are higher and default risk lower. The situation is seriously exacerbated if the collapse of the speculative bubble has been such as to undermine confidence in the entire financial system. Then liquidity preference may take the form of demand for a strong foreign currency. A foreign exchange crisis might then ensue.

Again the money supply process is endogenous, influenced by the same type of factors which are influencing the demand for money. Unexpectedly-low speculative asset prices start the process of downturn; meantime productive activity has already peaked and is put under pressure by the drying up of sources of finance. The accelerator effects of the turnaround in activity continually weaken effective demand, lowering the marginal efficiency of capital. These factors bring about not only a contraction in the willingness and capacity of financial institutions to supply credit, but also an increased demand for liquidity. Again the supply process is endogenous, and again operating in a direction counter to demand. In both the upturn and the downturn, individual actions which are rational in themselves generate outcomes which act against the collective interest.

Endogeneity of the money supply process thus by no means consigns money to a powerless role in the business cycle. On the contrary, the form which that endogeneity takes ensures that financial activity exacerbates the tendency for private sector activity to generate instability. This process impedes the proper functioning of a monetary economy. In an expansion, the supply of money may increase to such an extent that other assets appear moneylike, which further fuels the speculative expansion; the attractiveness of previous metals, foreign exchange, and antiques, for example, is enhanced. An extreme euphoria followed by collapse may even irrevocably destroy the confidence in the outside money (or outside backing institution) which had allowed the financial system to function as it did. In the aftermath of the bursting of the speculative bubble, the supply of credit is inelastic relative to demand. As long as the financial system continues to function as before, domestic money still performs the money function. But its inelasticity of supply with respect to demand is so great as to force bankruptcies and impede investment plans, thus contributing to the contraction of output and employment.

CONCLUSION

In reality, which is set in irreversible historical time, the only logical distinction between exogenous and endogenous factors is contained within the distinction between the past and the present. It is a matter of theoretical judgement how that general endogeneity is segmented for analytical purposes, the choice of designation as endogenous and exogenous defining the scope of each segment.

The case for defining the money supply as exogenous rests primarily on the capacity of the monetary authorities to influence, if not control it. The consequences of particular monetary policy strategies may then be analysed. But money is not like other commodities. Attempts to manipulate its supply may in some circumstances alter the moneyness of the asset concerned. The functioning of a financial system rests on confidence in an outside agency which backs and regulates that system; any action which runs counter to those functions diverts demand to alternative money-like assets, disrupting the system and frustrating the attempts at control.

Although it is the case that monetary authorities do have influence on the supply of any particular money asset under their *aegis*, it is necessary for monetary analysis to investigate the process of money supply creation several stages further back than that of monetary authority intervention. The initial impetus for money supply growth comes from credit creation, so the factors influencing the demand for and supply of credit require investigation. The actual endogeneity of the money supply process is then reflected in the analytical framework.

Endogeneity robs a variable of causal power within the orthodox framework. But a Keynesian process analysis of cycles shows money as playing an integral role. This role is one of reinforcing the instability of capitalist economies; indeed the two are inextricably linked. The endogeneity of the supply of credit, and thus of money, is not necessarily one of passively accommodating demands. Rather, in boom phases, excessively elastic supply of credit responding to expectations of rising asset prices fuels speculative activity and thus increases the danger of financial collapse once the cycle peaks. In contractions, supply contracts just when demand for liquidity is at its most urgent, enforcing a stronger contraction of output and employment than would otherwise be the case. The amplitude and timing of the production cycle is tied up with the behaviour of speculative markets. Even long-run trends in output and employment are determined by the feedback between productive and speculative markets determined by the availability of credit, and asset price expectations.

If the monetary authorities succeed in so regulating financial institutions and so stabilising interest rates that speculative booms are avoided, money is allowed to perform its proper functions. Without diversion of financial resources into speculative markets, output, employment and investment can continue to grow unimpeded. Further, without speculative bubbles to burst, there is no necessity for the rush for liquidity normally associated with the contractionary phase. Thus, if just the 'right' degree of responsiveness of credit creation to demand is maintained, there will be no tendency to seek alternative sources of liquidity.

Money never ceases to matter in the sense that it is the origin and the object of accumulation. The private sector collectively frustrates its own ends by generating credit supply endogeneity of a type which brings about cyclical instability. The aim of sustained growth is best served by monetary authorities influencing credit creation so that activity is concentrated in productive sectors. Money then is an integral factor in that it is allowed to perform its proper functions. Attempts to raise interest rates when a speculative boom is under way not only undermine the functioning of the financial system, but add extra impetus to the downturn in the production cycle. As Keynes put it:

> Thus the remedy for the boom is not a higher rate of interest but a lower

rate of interest! For that may enable the so-called boom to last. The right remedy for the trade cycle is not to be found in abolishing booms and thus keeping us permanently in a semi-slump; but in abolishing slumps and thus keeping us permanently in a quasi-boom.

(Keynes, *C.W. VIII*, p. 322)

4. Speculation and the Monetary Circuit with Particular Attention to the Euro-currency Market

This chapter is a slightly amended version of an article which was published in Economies et Sociétés, *20,* Monnaie et Production, *3, pp. 95-109, 1986. The original paper was presented to the ISMEA Seminar, Paris, 14-15 June 1985.*

INTRODUCTION

The starting point of this paper is a fact: credit is created to finance speculation, as well as to finance enterprise. Yet the account of endogenous money creation is usually expressed in terms of the financing of planned expenditure on new capital goods, hence the monetary circuit of credit money financing real economic activity which is planned in order to generate increased monetary value. Lavoie (1984) has suggested that the theory of the monetary circuit needs to be extended to deal with credit-financed speculation. This paper is an attempt to suggest how that extension be approached, employing a Post Keynesian theory of liquidity preference. In the process the prior question is addressed as to whether attention to credit-financed speculation is warranted in the first place; not all facts, by their existence, need be incorporated in theory.

We start by consulting Keynes and Marx for their views on speculation and its finance. In the process we explore the meaning and significance of speculation. The following section discusses the implications of incorporating credit-financed speculation in the theory of the circuit. In particular the possibility is considered that speculation might crowd out enterprise in the credit market, that is, that the supply of credit does not completely accommodate demand. The fourth section takes the Euro-currency market as a case-study. It is particularly interesting from two points of view. First, it is a source of information on the international allocation of bank credit, yielding some insights as to the degree to which credit creation accommodates demand. Second, it is to a large extent an interbank market: banks are engaged in credit demand as well as credit supply.

It is concluded that speculative credit creation is indeed important in its capacity to crowd out credit to finance economic activity. As such, it exacerbates the way in which the monetary aspect of production promotes demand deficiency and the potential for crisis.

SPECULATION: SOME TEXTUAL AND DEFINITIONAL ANALYSIS

What emerges from an exploration of both Marx's and Keynes' writing is that bank credit creation (as opposed to trade credit) is inherently speculative. Borrowers are speculating on the prospective yield of the borrowed money, while lenders are speculating on the credit-worthiness of the borrower. This applies to credit created for the purpose of financing production or investment, or for financing speculation. However, both Marx and Keynes do tend to discuss the monetary circuit in terms of entrepreneurial borrowing.

For Marx, credit money is 'fictitious capital'; it is created in anticipation of accumulation of monetary value. As long as this accumulation is realised, as under normal conditions, there is no problem. But if full employment is reached and speculative fever takes hold, more fictitious capital is created than can lead to actual accumulation. Some of this excessive credit creation is geared to unproductive assets which have no basis in actual production, that is, their purpose is purely the appropriation of revenues. The capacity for such excessive credit creation is enhanced by the growth of a distinctive capitalist class, the class of finance capitalists, who engage with the industrial capitalists in a struggle for the realisation of value.

The creation of excessive credit to finance speculation which is unwarranted by actual production contributes to the onset of crisis, and as such has real consequences for the economy. The shortage of commodity money is exacerbated, and thus the power of finance capitalists to appropriate revenue from industrial capitalists through high interest rates is enhanced. The cutback in production and the extent of takeovers of marginal firms are both greater as a result of the excessive speculative creation of credit.

Crucial to Marxian analysis of speculative credit creation is the labour theory of value. Normal conditions mean that fictitious capital is created in accordance with actual accumulation, whose value is objectively determined by the labour theory of value. It is only in crisis conditions that expected value diverges seriously from what is objectively determined by labour inputs. Even if we treat Marx's theory of crisis as a theory of business cycles, so that divergence of expected from actual value occurs at regular intervals, we are still left with the identification of normality with the absence of credit creation in excess of what is required to finance production; other than for the analysis of crisis, we can safely discuss the circuit as if all borrowing were done by entrepreneurs.

Sardoni (1987, Chapter 7) has pointed out this feature of Marxian analysis in terms of effective demand failure. He contrasts Marx's limitation of effective demand failure to the crisis with Keynes' more general view that firms may operate at less than full capacity for significant periods of time. In the same way, Keynes viewed the significance of financial speculation as applying more generally than simply to the point of crisis.

Keynes' views on speculative finance derive at the same time from Marx's theory of the circuit and from a rejection of the labour theory of value. In the 1933 draft of the *General Theory*, Keynes adopted the Marxian notation for the circuit in order to capture the essence of a monetary production economy (which he calls here an entrepreneur economy):

> An entrepreneur is interested, not in the amount of product, but in the amount of *money* which will fall to his share. He will increase his output if by so doing he expects to increase his money profit, even though this profit represents a smaller quantity of output than before.
>
> (Keynes, *C.W. XXIX*, p. 82)

and again

> The firm is dealing throughout in terms of sums of money. It has no object in the world except to end up with more money than it started with. That is the essential characteristic of an entrepreneur economy.
>
> (Keynes, *C.W. XXIX*, p. 89)

Further, the choice that this motivation implies as between purchase of new or existing assets is evident in the following passage:

> For the entrepreneur is guided, not by the amount of product he will gain, but by the alternative opportunities for using money having regard to the spot and forward price structure taken as a whole.
>
> (Keynes, *C.W. XXIX*, p. 83)

It is a short step from entrepreneurs considering using credit to purchase alternative assets to full-time speculators considering the full range of available assets. But nowhere in Keynes' thinking is there an objective measure of value by which to measure 'actual' accumulation in terms of production, relative to total credit creation. As is evident from the quotations above, Keynes envisaged the possibility of increased profits resulting from reduced product. Further, given the uncertainty attached to predicting profits from productive activity, there can be no presumption that, even under normal conditions, expectations as to increased profits will be fulfilled. In sum, entrepreneurial decisions are inherently speculative (albeit over a long time-frame), and there is no benchmark for a normal amount of entrepreneurial credit creation.

In Chapter 12 of the final, 1936, draft of the *General Theory*, Keynes draws a distinction between the speculation of entrepreneurs with respect to the outcome of investment projects in the longterm and the speculation of those trading purely in financial assets on a shortterm. Indeed he calls the latter speculators in contrast to the former entrepreneurs. The two are linked by the influence of speculators on the cost and availability of finance for entrepreneurs' investment activity. They are also linked by the entrepreneurs' consideration of 'alternative opportunities for using money' noted in the 1933 quotation above, suggesting that entrepreneurs with retained earnings are potential speculators. And indeed, in a letter to Joan Robinson in 1932, Keynes *C.W. XIII*, p. 269) has argued that 'in truth all holders of securities are potential speculators in [the sense of] ... calling those who sell securities in response to a change of price speculators'. What is important for the subject at hand is that, not only may speculators in the Chapter 12 sense obtain credit for the purpose, but entrepreneurs may also employ credit speculatively. Further, banks themselves, as holders of securities, are also engaged in speculation; they too may obtain credit for that purpose.

Further, Keynes (*C.W. VII*, p. 158) argued that, the more organised the financial market, the more speculation predominates in the valuation of assets. It is this valuation which is most influential in determining investment decisions:

> I have shown above (Chapter 12) that, although the private investor is seldom himself directly responsible for new investment, nevertheless the entrepreneurs, who are directly responsible, will find it financially advantageous, and often unavoidable, to fall in with the ideas of the market even though they themselves are better instructed.
>
> (Keynes, *C.W. VII*, p. 316)

It is clear that speculation is of fundamental importance to Keynes' theory of effective demand. Without the anchor of the labour theory of value, we find value determined by the juxtaposition of speculation with enterprise (as well as the activities of the public sector in the form of fiscal and monetary policy). The particular concern here is to consider the significance of credit created to finance speculation in the Chapter 12 sense. Keynes did explicitly consider speculation financed by credit, but he also argued that this credit was not limitless at the going rate of interest:

> Thus we must also take account of the other facet of the state of confidence, namely, the confidence of the lending institutions towards those who seek to borrow from them, sometimes described as the state of credit.
>
> (Keynes, *C.W. VII*, p. 158)

We will use the term 'speculation' in what follows in the Keynesian (*C.W. VII*, Chapter 12) sense of 'forecasting the psychology of the market', contrasted with enterprise which involves 'forecasting the prospective yield of assets over their whole life'. But, rather than associating the activities with two distinct sets of individuals or organisations, we will consider both activities as being open to firms, and also to banks (in the sense that their willingness to lend to firms on a long-term basis requires an assessment of credit-worthiness over a long period, as well as an assessment of short-term assets).

THE IMPLICATIONS OF CREDIT-FINANCED SPECULATION

If speculation as well as enterprise is financed by credit, what are the implications for output and employment? Is the speculative trading in financial assets simply an additional eddy in the circuit? The answers to these questions depend to some extent on whether or not we accept Keynes' statement that the supply of credit is limited.

Suppose, first, that credit is limitless at the going rate of interest established by the monetary authorities. Then, as long as entrepreneurs anticipate higher yields from investment, they may continue to borrow from the banks. But suppose speculators are also engaged in borrowing to finance purchase of financial assets. If their demand is directed towards shares, whose prices then rise, then firms will be more inclined to finance new investment by share issue than by bank borrowing. Bank credit is still financing the investment, but now indirectly. The major difference is the greater liquidity for firms of borrowing through the stock market than directly from banks, but treating the credit creation as entrepreneurial is a reasonable approximation.

However, if speculative demand favours existing assets over new issues, the outcome will be quite different. Not only will professional speculators continue to be attracted to existing assets in anticipation of further price increases, but so will firms and banks. All are in the business of accumulating money, and if buying non-reproducible assets appears to each to offer the best opportunity for accumulation, then that will be their choice, over new capital goods and loans to purchase new capital goods. The fund revolves between buyers and sellers of existing assets, but by-passes the productive sector. Indeed employment and output are discouraged, not because credit is not available, but because accumulation appears to be better served by non-productive transactions. The capacity for speculative bubbles to burst means that this strategy is highly risky; but then so is commitment to new capital if the expansion and bursting of the speculative bubble are accompanied by a contraction in final demand for output. Transactions in any asset are necessarily speculative; the consequences of transactions in physical assets are simply longer lived (in the absence of an efficient market in used capital goods) than transactions in financial assets.

The above presumes that the banks are prepared to lend indefinitely to finance speculative purchases of existing assets; the central bank supplies the necessary reserves. But banks must be concerned with the credit-worthiness of borrowers as well as with interest rates; their depositors in turn are concerned with the soundness of the banks' assets. If the fear of lack of credit-worthiness of some borrowers does not place an effective limit on credit creation, the actuality of failures among borrowers will do so. Indeed a properly regulated banking system will have prudential limits placed on its credit-creation activities. Speculative bubbles threaten the soundness of the entire financial system, so it is rational for central banks to attempt to limit their scope.

In fact, it is meaningless to say that, without central banks, credit creation would be limitless at a going rate of interest. Banking systems can only function with some kind of outside money, whose value rests on the confidence of the issuer (a central bank, government, or dominant firm or bank) or on its scarcity in the case of commodity money. If there were no limit to credit creation the system would self-destruct, not through excessive increases in aggregate demand due to entrepreneurial borrowing, but through excessive increases in speculative borrowing inflating the prices of non-reproducible assets to such an extent that confidence is eroded in whatever performs the role of outside money. Historically, a crisis of confidence in one outside money system leads to a switch to a different outside money system. This is evident in the periodic swings in international preferences as between the US dollar and gold as international outside money.

The observable fact that credit creation is not limitless cannot, therefore, simply be ascribed to effective demand failure, that is, limited demand for entrepreneurial credit. Rather the above line of argument suggests that limitless credit would *bring about* effective demand failure by making existing financing assets and non-reproducible real assets a more attractive vehicle for accumulation. Further, the consequence of an excessive diversion of activity to speculative trading is a speculative bubble which may erode confidence in the entire financial system. Experience of this fact has led to a set of prudential controls on domestic banking system which place some limitations on credit creation and possibly on its composition. This latter is a difficult area for regulatory control since it is not at all straightforward, particularly in overdraft systems, to identify and place limits on uses of credit. However, it is interesting to note that, in his Clearing Union plan for the international financial system, Keynes included controls on speculative trading in national currencies (see de Cecco, 1979).

Once we consider *de facto* limitations on credit creation, then the possibility of crowding out emerges. Thus even if entrepreneurial demand for credit is outstanding, the available credit may be diverted to finance speculative trading, that is as a result of lenders' choice rather than borrowers' choice. If in fact the central bank maintains a steady rate of interest, then preference for lending to finance speculative trading would reflect a pessimistic judgement about entrepreneurial credit-worthiness, and thus the likelihood of the need for refinancing at the term of the loan. If, further, speculative borrowing were shorter term than entrepreneurial borrowing, the preference would also reflect lenders' liquidity preference. Finally, if in fact interest rates are not stable, lenders' liquidity preference becomes of prime importance, regardless of entrepreneurial credit-worthiness. Taking these considerations together, then, a speculative boom will see banks diverting progressively more credit to speculative borrowers as both lenders and borrowers anticipate rising interest rates. In the retrenchment following the collapse of the boom, banks will cut back on credit to both speculators and entrepreneurs in order to place funds themselves directly in relatively safe, liquid, fixed interest assets such as government bonds and interbank deposits.

The scope for crowding out becomes greater the more open the financial system internationally. If the system is closed, so that banks' choice is limited to domestic entrepreneurs and domestic financial assets, then not only will the degree of crowding out of any one class of borrower be limited, but also the banks will identify their interests closely with the long-term viability of the domestic economy. But openness extends the range of choice so that liquidity preference may be satisfied more readily by purchasing financial assets issued in other countries, or extending credit to residents of other countries, where asset prices are still on a consistently rising trend. Indeed domestic entrepreneurial borrowing can be crowded out by non-resident entrepreneurial borrowing, far less speculative borrowing. We turn now to consider the Euro-currency market as a prime example of international credit creation.

THE EURO-CURRENCY MARKET

The first point of interest with the Euro-currency market is the information it yields on the international pattern of lending and borrowing. In particular it provides evidence of crowding out on an international scale. The pattern of lending is consistent with a ranking of borrowers from high-income developed countries through to lowest-income developing countries. In the 1960s, credit was concentrated in the developed countries, while effective demand continued to grow. Indeed a major factor in the market's growth was the excess demand for credit in the US as a result of domestic credit constraint. During the 1970s, and particularly from 1973-74, as effective demand in Western countries weakened, international credit was diverted to developing countries. It is well-documented that this credit was nevertheless limited to the higher- income developing countries (see, for example, Beek, 1977, and Sargen, 1976).

In fact, examination of the BIS data on the Euro-currency market shows a significant proportion of the low-income developing countries consistently net lenders to the market. This is evidence of a double-edged process at work. For the governments of low-income developing countries the potential yield on foreign exchange employed in domestic development projects must be high. Yet if adequate credit is not made available (except conditionally by international lending agencies) for these projects *or* for contingency purposes, liquidity needs require that relatively large deposits be held in foreign currencies. Indeed, for private sector investors in such countries, the accumulation motive may be better served by speculative activity in foreign currencies than by domestic entrepreneurial activity. Hence the net creditor position in the Euro-currency market for both the public and private sectors. Thus, although openness provides scope for accelerated development with imported capital goods by offering a wider range of credit opportunities, it can frustrate development by offering a wider range of lending opportunities too.

The resulting financial crowding out refers to availability of credit rather than its price; there is an established structure of interest rate differentials between developed - and developing-country credit, and among developing countries (see OECD, 1980, p. 160). Such differentials conventionally are a reflection of perceived risk differentials, although the identification is problematic (see Kenen, 1976; see also Feder and Just, 1977, for an econometric analysis of interest rate differentials in Euro-currency borrowing). Various studies confirm that international credit is highly correlated with per capita income and export performance (see, for example, Eaton and Gersowitz, 1980). Indeed, following the rapid diversion of credit to developing countries in the mid-1970s, the Federal Reserve Banks and the World Bank engaged in an exercise of establishing criteria for developing-country bank lending (see, for example, Sargen, 1977). This exercise explicitly recognised the failure of individual banks to arrive at objective estimates of country-risk and attempted to influence credit availability to particular borrowers, using such criteria as their current liquidity (as measured by outstanding borrowing, and holdings of international reserves).

The issue of developing-country borrowing came to a head in the early 1980s with the emergence of the international debt crisis. This crisis had 'real' roots in the contraction of effective demand on the part of developed countries for developing-country exports. But it can also be attributed to the actions of international banks in withholding, or threatening to withhold, credit. This arose partly from the employment of the objective criteria mentioned above for determining availability of credit, and partly from the growing credit needs of developed countries which, having higher priority with the banks than the developing countries, crowded the latter out. The outcome of the effort to avert the crisis has been an explicit determination by the banks to restrict credit availability to developing countries in the future. It should be noted that, the greater the speculative demand for a currency, the greater the country's foreign exchange reserves, and thus the better the credit-worthiness according to the objective criteria for bank lending. For most developing countries, however, speculative trading of currencies and financial assets in general is conducted predominantly in foreign currencies. Their foreign exchange borrowing on the Euro-currency market is thus as likely to be for the purpose of speculative trading as for financing imports.

The degree of speculative activity in the Euro-currency markets is reflected in the high incidence of interbank borrowing and lending. Indeed, while the discussion above applies as much to dollar credit issued by US banks in the US to non-residents, the Euro-currency market has its own special features which are particularly pertinent to discussions of speculation and the monetary circuit.

The very existence of the Euro-currency market is highly relevant to the discussion of the origins of credit endogeneity. The market owes its existence primarily to the absence of regulatory control of bank operations in currencies other than the currency of the country in which the bank is located. As such, a primary concern over the Euro-currency market has been the spectre of limitless credit creation. (This concern is generally expressed in terms of orthodox bank multipliers, whose size is in inverse proportion to the degree of reserve backing of deposits; see, for example, Friedman, 1971.) Certainly the market has expanded dramatically from its inception in the late 1950s; at end-1984 it stood at a gross figure of $2,153.5bn. The fact that this growth is not infinite is consistent with the argument outlined above: credit creation internationally is limited not only by effective demand failure but also by the need to preserve an outside money internationally.

In fact, the net amount of credit creation is much less than the gross value of assets; it is estimated at $1,265bn at end-1984, or 59% of the gross figure. The disparity is due to the high degree of interbank activity in the market. Euro-currency market activity thus diverges from the conventional view of banking as matching long-term loans with short-term non-bank deposit liabilities, that is, with 'money creation'. Even the net activity between banks and non-banks in the market involves a much lesser degree of maturity transformation than the traditional banking function. This trend towards financial intermediation rather than credit and deposit creation smacks of matching prior savings with the financing of investment. Indeed it is symptomatic of changes occurring within domestic banking systems towards greater reliance on interbank sources of funds, as reflected in the growing federal funds market in the US, and a 'securitisation' of credit, whereby banks trade their loans on the market. These trends are of potential importance to consideration of the monetary circuit, not least because they mark a change in banking practice from the times of Marx and Keynes.

The traditional banking function involved banks in issuing liabilities which are highly liquid to the lenders but which revolve sufficiently frequently that they are in aggregate rarely liquidated, that is, the depositors are content to use deposits as money. Deposits are created when banks extend credit in the form of a deposit liability which remains somewhere within the banking system; each bank relies on credit creation by other banks to ensure that its own deposits keep step with new credit. If banks are small relative to the national banking systems, then the redeposit ratio will be low, and individual banks may face net deposit loss on credit creation. Thus it is not surprising that a large federal funds market should have developed within the US unit banking system. But it is notable that it is the larger US banks whose portfolios show the highest proportion of federal fund liabilities. (Of these, the Chicago banks do in fact have the highest proportion, Illinois state legislation prohibiting all branch banking.) This might suggest that it is the largest banks which are more actively involved in credit creation and thus most in need of funding. But it might also suggest a greater propensity for speculative activity on the part of the larger banks themselves, borrowing from the federal funds market to finance their own purchases of securities. This latter hypothesis is more consistent with the evidence on the structure of their asset portfolios.

Similarly, the high degree of interbank activity in the Euro-currency market can be attributed to the large number of banks involved, each of which can expect to have a low redeposit ratio. Rather than relying on non-bank deposits to match loans, the Euro-currency market banks can go direct to each other to ensure immediate funding of their credit creation; the non-bank portion of the monetary circuit has been by-passed. It is the speculative activity, in turn, of banks willing to lend to other banks which funds the process. Indeed, since the borrowing bank may be engaged in employing the funds speculatively itself, the entire circuit may totally by-pass any entrepreneurial expenditure. There *may* be some 'net' expenditure at the end of the chain, but not necessarily.

In summary, the Euro-currency market offers more scope to banks for speculative lending *and* borrowing as an alternative to their traditional functions of entrepreneurial credit matched by short-term deposit liabilities. While entrepreneurs may enjoy increased credit availability from a wider range of sources, the competition for that credit is greater, as is the scope for ill-informed lending decisions or decisions not to lend due to geographical remoteness between borrower and lender.

CONCLUSION

The arguments presented here suggest a modification of the traditional account of the circuit as starting with credit created to finance entrepreneurial expenditure. Speculation is already inherent in this account in the sense that investment plans depend on speculative decisions arrived at under conditions of uncertainty. But the decision to buy new capital goods involves a decision not to buy existing capital goods and financial assets; even postponement of a purchase of new capital goods involves consideration of alternative uses of existing credit lines.

Further, the availability of credit to finance entrepreneurial activity is conditioned by alternative lending opportunities, either in the form of credit to speculators, or speculative activity by the banks themselves. The greater the opportunity for monetary accumulation in the markets for existing financial assets and non-reproducible real assets, the more credit will be channelled into these markets rather than into entrepreneurial activity (depending albeit on the regulatory environment). A speculative boom can thus be represented by a monetary circuit M-M′, which altogether by-passes productive activity. Intermediate conditions can be represented by a combination of purely monetary (speculative) circuits and the traditional M-C-M′ circuit. The two types of circuit interact in that credit expansion in speculative markets may discourage entrepreneurial investment plans and/or the availability of credit to finance them.

The growth of the Euro-currency market provides scope for extensive purely monetary circuits. The volume of interbank activity alone indicates the extent of speculative activity by banks, cutting out the redeposit aspect of the traditional circuit of credit and deposit creation. However, even without explicit regulation, credit creation within the Euro-currency market has not been limitless. Credit availability has been prioritised with crude estimates of country-risk employed to limit credit availability to developing countries, when it is not more directly crowded out by developed-country credit demand.

In summary, then, explicit incorporation of speculative credit creation in the account of the monetary circuit adds force to the precarious position of real expenditure and its vulnerability to speculative activity. The more sophisticated the financial markets the greater that vulnerability. Prudential controls may limit the scope of speculative bubbles, but credit limits may also contribute to crowding out of entrepreneurial borrowing. The only solution can lie in the direction of Keynes' proposal (for the international financial system) of regulating speculative transactions and, specifically, credit-financed speculation. Such a solution, it must be recognised, acts contrary to the aim of accumulation of monetary value which motivates entrepreneurial, speculative and banking activity.

5. Post Keynesian Monetary Theory for an Open Economy

This chapter is a slightly amended version of an article of the same title which appeared in the Journal of Post Keynesian Economics, 9(2), *pp. 237-59, 1986-87. It benefited from the helpful comments and suggestions of Paul Davidson.*

INTRODUCTION

Frenkel and Johnson (1976, p. 24) present their theory of the balance of payments as being monetary, rather than monetarist, on the grounds that it relies on a representation of the demand for money function which is generally accepted by monetary theorists. Indeed, no alternative approach emerged until Davidson (1982),[1] so that some form of global monetarism has become embedded in the neo-classical synthesis. While Keynesians in what Coddington (1976) calls the 'hydraulic Keynesian' tradition have de-emphasised the ability of monetary variables to influence output and employment in both the shortrun and the longrun; central to this approach is the instability of the demand for money. It seems a natural progression (and one advocated by Chick, 1983, pp. 357-8) to extend Keynesian theory to incorporate the monetary effects of economic openness, as an alternative to global monetarism. (Henceforth the terms Keynesian and Post Keynesian will be used interchangeably.)

The purpose of this paper, therefore, is to express Keynesian monetary theory in a form amenable to application to the open economy.[2] The approach is fully consistent with that of Davidson (1982) but places more emphasis on autonomous capital flows. The theory is presented alongside a brief account of the monetarist approach to highlight differences. The phenomenon chosen as the basis for analysis is the business cycle. The neo-classical synthesis was made possible by expressing different theories in a common, static framework. But both mainstream theorists[3] and Post Keynesians[4] have argued that it is in the analysis of an economy in a state of flux that the essentials of their theory may be found; it is thus a fruitful framework within which to explore differences.

Further, monetarists have maintained a strict dichotomy between the exogeneity of the nominal money stock (governments willing) in closed economies and in open economies with fully flexible exchange rates, on the one hand, and its endogeneity in open economies with fixed exchange rates, on the other. As Chick (1983) points out, Keynesian monetary theorists have occupied uneasily the middle ground between Keynes' *General Theory* assumption[5] of a fixed money stock and the position of the Radcliffe Report (1959) that the financial system was sufficiently flexible to expand in the face of rising demand. The approach developed here is an attempt to systematise the endogeneity of the money supply (in closed and open economies) in terms of the responses of financial institutions to differing economic conditions. Minsky (1976, 1982) provides much of the inspiration for this analysis.

The structure of the presentation is as follows. In the next section, the monetarist theory of the business cycle is presented briefly, first for a closed economy, then for an open economy. The Keynesian theory is set out for a closed economy in the third section and an open economy in the fourth, incorporating the main features of Keynesian monetary theory: the instability of expectations, the role of money as a refuge from uncertainty, the endogeneity of the money supply and the focus on historical, rather than mechanical, time, precluding the use of general equilibrium analysis.

THE MONETARIST AND GLOBAL MONETARIST THEORY OF MONEY AND THE BUSINESS CYCLE

To the monetarist, the short-run fluctuations in economic activity which constitute the business cycle are by and large a monetary phenomenon. (See, in particular, Friedman and Schwartz, 1963b.) Real sectors are viewed as being inherently stable, relying on a Walrasian market-clearing process, and the demand for real money balances to finance real activity is also stable. Barring other exogenous shocks, then, changes in the nominal supply of money are the only possible source of instability. An increase in the nominal money stock induces a temporary increase in output until inflationary expectations adjust in the labour market.

The process may overshoot, requiring several iterations before settling on the new long-run equilibrium position (identified by a higher price level), thus accounting for a cyclical rather than one-off adjustment process. Friedman and Schwartz (1963b) provide a range of reasons for such overshooting (see also Friedman, 1970a). First, the rate of price increase gathers force as output picks up, exceeding for a time the long-run equilibrium rate of inflation; this encourages a building-up of money balances which is excessive in the longrun. The resulting exaggerated cutback in activity is reinforced if money-holders have run down their holdings excessively as a result of failure to anticipate even the lower new equilibrium rate of inflation. Second, overshooting may occur for reasons connected with the operations of the financial system. If the initial increase in monetary growth refers to the monetary base, an even higher rate of increase in the money supply will occur in the catch-up phase, exaggerating the increase in demand for goods and other assets. This in turn is reinforced by the tendency for the cash-deposit ratio to fall, in line with the general diffusion of asset demand along the liquidity spectrum in response to the initial excess supply of money; the bank multiplier is higher the lower the cash-deposit ratio. Friedman and Schwartz explain persistent, rather than isolated, cycles by repeated alterations by the monetary authorities to the rate of growth of the money supply.

The rational expectations theory of the business cycle coincides with the monetarist theory in identifying changes in the rate of growth of the money supply as the cause, although limiting causal power to unanticipated changes, that is those which allow average short-run expectations to deviate from the long-run outcome. Being more explicitly micro-based than monetarist theory, rational expectations theory envisages economies as being in a perpetual state of flux as decision-makers adjust their expectations and behaviour in the light of new information about preferences and technology. What makes the money supply special is the monopoly of supply held by the monetary authorities. Misinterpretation of most market signals by decision-makers will tend to cancel each other out, preventing any systematic response. But actions by the monetary authorities affect the prices of all goods and assets (given gross substitution), so that there may be an economy-wide misinterpretation of signals which generates an economy-wide change in output which is not warranted by long-term supply-side considerations.

Additional explanations are required for the persistence of this misinterpretation in the form of a cycle, given that the rational expectations hypothesis rules out systematic error. First, information about the increase in demand for individual products and assets will be conveyed at different rates, producing a staggered response to the information. Second, producers' responses to this information will vary in terms of their consequences for other markets, and in the costliness and difficulty of reversal when the misinterpretation is eventually perceived. In particular, increased activity in the capital goods sector will have widespread repercussions, for example for the marginal physical product of labour in the consumer goods sector; unwinding mistaken capital expenditure also takes time.

The monetarist and rational expectations theories of the business cycle coincide because the money supply and the general price level happen to be two of the few truly macro-elements in the latter body of theory. The theories also coincide methodologically in two ways. First, each is expressed within a closed general equilibrium system in which exogenous shocks are necessary to initiate motion. While rational expectations theory allows for random shocks in a wide range of variables, it is only the money supply which can elicit an economy-wide reaction, that is, which allows macroeconomic analysis. Second, both theories are embodied in an instrumentalist methodology in the sense that predictive power is the ultimate criterion for theory appraisal. (See Friedman, 1953 and Lucas, 1980.) While in practice neither theory is purely instrumentalist, since each is justified in terms of general equilibrium microfoundations, nevertheless a direct correspondence is presumed to obtain between theoretical statements and observed reality. While general equilibrium theory in its pure form is expressed in terms of mechanical time, and therefore bears no direct correspondence to observations in historical time, the two are necessarily treated as equivalent in instrumentalist monetarist and rational expectations theory, so that there is a direct correspondence between the theoretical path of the business cycle and actual historical processes. But the tie to general equilibrium theory requires that historical time, to be consistent with mechanical time, must be reversible. (See Robinson, 1978, Termini, 1981, Carvalho, 1983-84, Dow, 1985, Chapter 5 for further discussion of the significance of different concepts of time.)

If we now consider an open economy, additional factors must be taken into consideration. First, the range of possible exogenous shocks is increased to include shifts in demand away from domestic products, for example. More importantly, a balance of payments surplus or deficit (with exchange rates fixed) causes a change in the domestic money stock. In the absence of a change in external conditions, the existence of a payments imbalance is interpreted by global monetarists as reflecting a domestic monetary imbalance: an excess demand for money in the case of a surplus and an excess supply of money in the case of a deficit. Economic openness thus diminishes the capacity of changes in the domestic money stock to cause cycles in activity. Consider again an increase in the domestic money stock. If capital is mobile internationally, any tendency for domestic interest rates to fall below international rates induces capital outflows, and a balance of payments deficit, until interest rates are returned to world levels. The excess money stock is thus eliminated before any plans to increase output can be put into effect. The cycle does not even have a chance to start.

If exchange rates are freely floating, then there is no payments imbalance and thus no external influence on the domestic nominal money stock. But outflows on the capital account bring downward pressure on the exchange rate, raising import prices. While output may rise in the non-tradeables sector as a result of excess money balances, rising import prices ensure that a high proportion of adjustment is immediately effected on the domestic price level, speeding up the adjustment of price expectations. The cycle is thus damped. If price expectations are rational, then no cycle occurs at all.

A KEYNESIAN THEORY OF MONEY AND THE BUSINESS CYCLE IN A CLOSED ECONOMY

Post Keynesian theory analyses economies out of equilibrium within historical time, that is, it analyses irreversible processes in the context of an unknowable future. Decision-making at any one time is the outcome of past actions, based often on unfulfilled expectations, combined with expectations about the future. Not only expectations, but the degree of confidence with which they are held, are subject to volatile shifts. While a complete analysis can only be context-specific, some regularities in changes in economic variable are conducive to generalised analysis. Keynes (*C.W. VII*, Chapter 22) thus tied his theory together in his 'Notes on the Trade Cycle', describing economies as moving along a cyclical path. (See Minsky, 1976, Chapter 3.) Under specific historical, institutional and political conditions cycles have greater or smaller amplitude, but always carry the potential for crisis.

A Post Keynesian business cycle theory must reflect the speculative nature of decision-making on the part of the household, business and financial sectors when decisions are made on the basis of expectations held with uncertainty.[6] Keynes held business decision-making as a variable of particular significance, because changes in investment and its financing influence the actions and expectations of the other two sectors. But the household and financial sectors also influence business activity and expectations by the ease or difficulty with which they make financing available for investment.[7]

The formation of expectations within the Keynesian framework differs from that in the monetarist framework: the differences are most evident in the context of the business cycle. As long as the cycle is, as in the monetarist framework, an aberration from a long-run steady state, then on average and in the longrun expectations will correctly anticipate the values of variables. Uncertainty with respect to the future is expressed as the probability of the deviation of actual values from expected values: what a Keynesian would call risk. There is no inherent reason for 'average' expectations to change, simply for the degree of risk to increase with the amplitude of the cycle.

Once the notion of a long-run steady state is removed, either as an actual outcome to be analysed, or as a basis for expectations formation, then uncertainty takes on a different meaning. Within Keynesian theory, uncertainty is distinct from risk; it reflects the degree of confidence with which expectations are held. (See Keynes, *C.W. VII*, pp. 148-50, 161 and *C.W. XIV*, pp. 113-14.) In particular, it reflects the limit to which probability analysis can be employed. Davidson (1982-83) shows that frequency distributions based (necessarily) on past experience can only be extrapolated into the future (in historical rather than mechanical time) if the market process in question is an ergodic stochastic process, which usually requires that it be stationary. The essence of historical time is that it generates, in general, non-ergodic processes; structural changes occur which invalidate the application of probabilities based on past experiments. Further, the experiments of investors, particularly, may not even be capable of yielding sufficient observations for a frequency distribution. The experiment of opening a new plant, for example, may be what Shackle (1955) calls a crucial experiment; the act of opening the plant changes the environment in such a way that the experiment cannot be replicated.

Since expectations are generally formed under the conditions of uncertainty associated with non-ergodic systems, they are inherently potentially unstable. Without a long-run steady state, the cycle has no starting point. Rather, groups of economic agents periodically adjust their expectations as their perceptions of the environment change. In the absence of any definitive basis for expectations formation, group conventions are employed (see Keynes, *C.W. XIV*, p. 114), but the scope for surprise is always present, requiring some behavioural adjustment. The account of the business cycle given here focuses on the consequences of shifting, collectively generated, expectations.[8]

An economic upswing is brought about by a change in expenditure which (aside from public sector activity) requires an increase in the marginal efficiency of capital (MEC). When businesses anticipate an increased return to new capital, relative to existing capital, new investment is planned and financing is sought from the banks or from securities markets. As long as the banks and securities markets share the business optimism, finance is made available and activity increases. As employment increases, consumers also seek financing for expanded expenditure plans, which again is forthcoming if lenders share households' expectations of income increase. The availability of finance depends primarily on the liquidity preference of financial institutions.[9]

The preceding downswing will have been characterised by a generally high degree of liquidity preference. While expectations of falling asset prices are prevalent, demand for liquidity rises relative to total wealth, or income. At the same time the liquidity of non-money assets falls as markets become less active, as capital losses become more likely. Since money is then the only remaining supplier of liquidity, demand for money increases even more than liquidity. The actual flow of money may fall short of demand, however, because of the unwillingness of banks to extend credit (high liquidity preference on the part of banks) and the unwillingness of non-money asset holders to accept the capital loss involved in adding to money balances.

During an upswing, however, liquidity preference falls as asset markets become more active and as capital gains are anticipated with confidence. As liquidity preference falls, the capacity of financial institutions to expand credit is enhanced, as is their willingness. Reserve requirements fall as deposit-holders switch from chequing deposits, to savings deposits, to certificates of deposit. The capacity of non-bank financial intermediaries to add a layer to the inverted pyramid of credit is enhanced as the public become more willing to accept their liabilities (fears of intermediaries' failure having subsided). Not only are financial institutions more willing to finance new activity, rather than trade in existing securities, but also individuals are more prepared to invest in the stock market rather than bank deposits.[10] At the same time, if expectations continue to develop of rising asset prices, decreasing liquidity preference reduces the degree of caution exercised in financing. Financial assets are bought on margin, while future capital gains and increased earnings are relied on for repayment of business and household debt. As Robinson put it:

> The improved prospect of profit counts twice over - once in promoting investment at a given cost of borrowing and once in lowering the cost of borrowing.
>
> (Robinson, 1952, p. 23)

Just as the downturn is characterised by rising liquidity preference and a falling supply of liquidity, the upturn is characterised by a willingness to expand finance running ahead of a falling relative preference for liquidity. Financial markets thus exaggerate the effects of swings in the MEC, further encouraging expansion in upturns, and contraction in downturns. But, given that both expansionary and contractionary phases are (generally) reversed, we must consider those factors which tend to stabilise cyclical movements.

The MEC may tend to fall as the capital stock rises. During an expansion, however, inflation can be expected to rise, since increasing wage claims can be expected to be passed on in increased prices as long as aggregate demand is expected to rise. As long as *nominal* returns to investment are expected to exceed the cost of financing, then new investment can be expected to go ahead. While, ultimately, some sectors will hit capacity constraints (full sectoral employment), Keynes did however suggest that activity would generally slow down before that point was reached because of financial factors. While the MEC need not actually fall,[11] it can be expected to fall short of expected returns on some assets in limited supply, notably real estate, gold and antiques. As more activity is diverted into these purely speculative markets, the returns (mainly capital gains) on those assets continue to rise relative to assets in productive markets and the demand for funds to finance this activity rises.[12]

While short-term interest rates normally fall during the upturn, reflecting an excess supply of funds, they can be expected eventually to rise. Central banks, in spite of Keynes' (*C.W. VII*, p. 322) injunction to the contrary, are often tempted to raise the cost of reserves to the banking system to curtail expansion. But, in any case, banks, now willing to increase their ratio of advances to reserves, raise deposit rates to attract interest-bearing deposits, in competition with alternative instruments holding the promise of capital gain. The credit market can bear an increase in loan rates because of the increasing returns expected from investments, particularly in purely speculative markets. Meanwhile, explosive market conditions, analysed graphically by Minsky (1976, 1982) cause carelessness.[13] Mistaken expectations are costly when financing is highly geared. The inverted pyramid of business and household financing is constructed upon the inverted pyramid of financial institutions. One default or bankruptcy can have multiple effects throughout the financial system. Any such hint that optimistic asset price expectations are unrealistic punctures confidence and encourages creditors to withdraw from markets, at the same time proving their expectation to be correct. A multiple contraction of asset prices and availability of funds follows with rising long-term interest rates, just as both debtors and creditors attempt to increase their liquidity.

The point at which financial constraints become operative depends partly on the actions of the central bank and of the banking system. The central bank can attempt to choke off interest-sensitive credit demand by putting upward pressure on interest rates, through open market operations or, more usually, through increasing the cost to banks of borrowed reserves. It can also curtail the capacity of the banking system to extend credit by prudential controls. To some extent banks themselves have voluntarily imposed their own control on portfolio structure because of the fragility of confidence in individual banks when they are seen to be overextended in risky assets. Continuing demand for financing in highly speculative markets may then direct available funds away from lower-return productive investment, causing an accelerated turnaround in output and employment. If financing is still plentiful enough to cover both unproductive and productive investment, then the turnaround in real activity will only occur once the collapse of confidence in highly speculative markets erodes the capacity of financial institutions to provide finance and, through income effects, erodes aggregate demand, and thus MEC. There is no reason why full employment should have been reached when employment begins to contract.

The factors which Keynes saw as preventing an indefinite contraction rely on the goods market rather than financial market. Because, for institutional reasons, money wages are sticky downwards, a downward wage-price spiral may be avoided, propping up aggregate demand. Second, when inventories are run down requiring increased production to replace them, and the fixed capital stock requires replacement if even current production levels are to continue, then, other things being equal, there is an additional inducement to invest. But if there is no expectation of a general turnaround, and indeed there is some expectation of continued contraction, then the risks attached to new investment may be perceived as being too great. In a closed economy, unless governments employ an expansionary fiscal policy, activity *can* stagnate indefinitely. Short-term interest rates fall somewhat, due to the collapse in the demand for money to finance high-return speculative activity. But the high demand for liquidity has forced the financial system to contract; deposits with institutions perceived to be risky are reduced, and relative demand for bank liabilities (requiring reserves) increases. Financial institutions themselves, caught with loans which they cannot call in without default or bankruptcy are extremely risk-averse in the choice of other assets for their portfolios. Only once some entrepreneurs perceive a relatively low-risk investment opportunity and a creditor finds the default risk acceptably low will economic activity begin to turn around.

In summary, then, financial markets tend to exacerbate cycles in nominal income by expanding the provision of credit during upturns and contracting it during downturns. Much of the upturn, in nominal terms, may however, be concentrated on speculative rather than productive activity; in general, the more feverish the early expansion of finance and thus the earlier the diversion of financial activity into speculative markets, the more quickly output and employment will peak. In turn, in general the more feverish the financial expansion, the more severe will be the ensuing contraction in finance and thus also in output and employment. Thus the more exaggerated the financial cycle, the lower the average level of output and employment.

Much, however, depends on the state of confidence in financial markets, which is vulnerable to historical accident. Thus financial expansion can be extended or curtailed, depending on the state of confidence. The potential is always present for a collapse in confidence which irrevocably erodes the functioning of the financial system. There is then an inevitability about financial cycles: on the one hand, new instruments, new perceptions of moneyness and new institutions which have emerged during the upswing may persist during a contraction, but, on the other hand, so will the erosion of confidence following a financial crisis. In neither case can the past be recaptured.

A KEYNESIAN THEORY OF MONEY AND THE BUSINESS CYCLE IN AN OPEN ECONOMY

Fixed Exchange Rates

Opening an economy extends the range of goods and assets among which domestic residents may choose, and extends the range of potential buyers of domestic goods and assets. The implications are more straightforward in the case of fixed exchange rates, which we consider first. If exchange rates are fixed, then the supply of finance is enhanced by a balance of payments surplus and diminished by a deficit (unless there is counteracting monetary authority action). Other things being equal, expected income growth, or profitability (relative to the rest of the world) encourages both domestic and foreign investors to sell foreign assets and buy domestic, increasing the domestic supply of finance. Not only does this increase the elasticity of supply with respect to expected returns but also any upper limit to the capacity of the financial system to supply credit may be eliminated or, at least, postponed to a later stage in the expansion. To the extent that domestic borrowers have direct access to foreign creditors, there is no reason for them to be constrained by the expansion capacity of the domestic banking system. In any case, that capacity is enhanced by an endogenous increase in monetary base effected across the exchanges. (See Miles and Davidson, 1979.) Further, demand for liquidity is less elastic with respect to expected returns than in a closed economy. A wave of pessimism about returns on domestic assets may be satisfied by an exchange of domestic non-money assets for foreign non-money assets, as well as for domestic money. Similarly, a wave of optimism may be satisfied by purchasing domestic non-money assets by running down foreign assets as well as idle balances of domestic money.

Compared with the case of a closed economy, then, a fixed exchange rate open economy is influenced more by the increase in the flow supply of money as income expectations improve relative to the rest of the world than by a reduction in flow demand. Further the theoretical limit on supply is the global, rather than domestic, capacity to generate finance, extending the theoretical capacity to finance expansion. (See Davidson, 1982, for example, p. 118.)

The operative word here is 'relative'. If expected returns on domestic investment are high relative to previous years, yet are exceeded by investment in other economies, then capital will flow out rather than in. In other words, the theory applies spatially as well as temporally. An economy with consistently higher returns than others will attract capital inflows at all stages of the cycle, although liquidity preference will be consistently lower than in other economies. Similarly, economies struggling with persistently lower returns will experience continuing outflows (forcing adjustment) while liquidity preference is consistently high. The demand for and supply of finance for any country, then, are contingent on alternative foreign rates of return. An increase in the alternative rate of return reduces the supply of finance without dampening demand.[14] The effect on the domestic economy would be to choke off an expansion. In a contraction, the reduced supply of money as capital flows out would be offset by a reduced demand for domestic idle balances as attractive foreign assets are substituted. But the effect of both of these factors in reducing foreign exchange reserves to dangerous levels would force the implementation of income adjustment measures which would worsen the downturn.

The net change in foreign exchange reserves and, *ceteris paribus*, the domestic money supply, is the outcome of the trade account as well as the short - and long-term capital accounts. Having said that higher domestic returns attract inflows of funds, we must now break those flows of funds down into their component accounts in order to make more specific application to particular types of economy.

Other things being equal, expected returns on physical investment and on long-dated securities are procyclical, so that the long-term capital account in general contributes procyclical additions to the supply of finance. The short-term capital account is influenced primarily by nominal interest rates (and somewhat by asset prices to the extent that they vary in the shortrun). Although financial markets are slack during the middle stages of the upswing and tight in the middle stages of the downswing, nominal interest rates start rising well before the peak and falling well before the trough because they reflect actual and expected changes in the price level. As the peak is approached, therefore, nominal interest rates will be high relative to those in countries experiencing less expansion, not only because financial conditions are tighter but also because inflation is higher. Similarly, as the trough is approached, nominal interest rates reflect falling inflation and encourage capital outflows, even though financial conditions are still tight. Short-term capital flows, then, while possibly dampening the early stages of an upswing or downswing, can be expected to prolong both.

The influence of the trade account upon the supply of finance depends on whether expansions tend to be internally or externally generated (following Whitman's, 1967, classification). For large, diversified economies where the foreign sector is relatively small, expansion is usually internally generated. The main effect of expansion, then, is to increase imports relative to exports. In this case, the trade account serves to modify procyclical money supply changes, thus modifying the amplitude of cycles.

For smaller economies dependent on exports, expansion is synonymous with export growth and thus further reinforcement in the form of foreign exchange inflows. While the expansion then will be all the stronger in the early stages, imports will eventually grow (particularly of capital goods), choking off the favourable trade account balance as well as reducing the export multiplier. The combined effect of curtailed net export earnings and income growth will raise prospects of a downturn (even if induced by the government to conserve foreign exchange holdings) and deter further capital inflows. While the early expansion will have been more dramatic than for the first type of economy, the turnaround will equally be more dramatic. For the export-oriented economy, the supply of finance will be at least as constrained after a period of expansion as for the closed economy.

These results are summarised in tabular form, along with those for flexible exchange rates, at the end of the section.

Floating Exchange Rates

With a pure system of floating exchange rates, the balance of payments has no direct effect on the nominal supply of money, the strain of adjustment being taken by the exchange rate itself. The exchange rate does however have an indirect effect on the supply of liquidity. First, an exchange appreciation reduces import prices and raises the real value of the money supply. Second, while the nominal values of flows across the exchanges must cancel out, there is no reason for the maturity structure of assets exchanged to be equal. Thus, foreign purchases of domestic long-term securities matched by domestic purchases of foreign bank deposits represent an easing of domestic liquidity. In both cases, expectations of expansion in the domestic economy increase liquidity; they encourage purchases of domestic medium - and long-term assets, which *ceteris paribus* cause an appreciation. For an open economy with floating exchange rates, then, the supply of liquidity would be more responsive to expected returns than for a closed economy (even if the supply of nominal money would not).

In terms of money, it is demand which is most affected. Expected exchange rate changes alter the liquidity of domestic money where liquidity refers to ease of exchange for an *international* standard of value. Thus, a given liquidity preference is satisfied by a smaller amount of domestic money when appreciation is anticipated. Thus, procyclical exchange rate movements can be represented by an increase in the elasticity of demand for money. At the same time, however, the demand to hold assets denominated in domestic money as an alternative to other currencies increases whenever exchange gains are anticipated. When exchange rates are freely floating, capital inflows attracted by expected exchange rate appreciation take the form of purchase of domestic currency with a view to purchasing securities; the domestic currency returns to circulation. Such currency purchases require a fall in the currency sold to induce the sale. Expectations are likely of a continued fall in the value of that foreign currency relative to the domestic currency so that the holder is likely to keep foreign currency assets liquid for a quick sale. In terms of the demand for money to hold, then, demand has risen for the depreciating currency. As soon as the domestic currency is expected to peak, demand for it rises as securities are sold with a view to exchanging currencies again.

Short-term capital flows are unlikely to be uni-directional over a phase of the cycle, even if exchange rates move steadily procyclically or counter-cyclically. Exchange speculation is undertaken by movement traders whose main task is correctly to anticipate turning-points. Thus short-term capital flows are most evident as inflows before a turning-point from depreciation to appreciation and as outflows when a switch to depreciation is anticipated. Demand for domestic money thus shifts down temporarily as the currency nears its trough and shifts up temporarily as it nears its peak, as traders go liquid in anticipation of profits in terms of foreign currency, and domestic currency, respectively.

Taking again the category of a largely self-sufficient economy with internally-generated expansion, the trade and long-term capital accounts tend to offset each other over the cycle so that there is no inherent tendency towards major exchange rate instability. The rise in nominal short-term interest rates in the later stages of the upturn to a peak in mid-downturn may attract short-term capital inflows, encouraging exchange rate appreciation; similarly the nominal short-term interest rate trough in mid-upturn may encourage outflows and depreciation. Initially, the J-curve effect ensures that an appreciation improves the trade account and a depreciation makes it worse. The medium-term effects may however be sufficient for the appreciation to prolong the income trough and the depreciation prolong the expansion. Otherwise, exchange rate instability elsewhere can induce short-term capital flows: inflows when the domestic currency appears strong relative to other currencies, and outflows when it appears weak relative to other currencies. The demand for liquidity increases relative to income, then, in the first case and falls in the second.

For an export-dependent economy, the trade account reinforces the long-term capital account, putting upward pressure on the currency in the upswing and downward pressure in the downswing. During the upswing, then, short-term capital moves in and out, taking exchange profits. When a weakening of the currency is anticipated, as imports rise relative to exports, a massive short-term capital outflow can be expected, helping to bring about the expected depreciation. Because of the J-curve effect, the depreciation itself worsens short-run income expectations, reinforcing the economy's turnaround; later in the downturn the depreciation may begin to improve the trade account. Similarly, an expected exchange rate improvement, as exports improve from trough levels, encourages massive capital inflows.

Unlike the fixed exchange rate case, the floating exchange rate case does not allow for an indefinite availability of finance, except in the sense that indefinite exchange appreciation would increase indefinitely the world value of the domestic money supply. Demand is more elastic than for a closed economy, except for low-return economies whose short-term funds are held in foreign exchange anyway, so that the supply constraint of domestic financial institutions does not become operative until later in the cycle, other things being equal. For self-sufficient economies with no strong cyclical exchange rate pattern, therefore, the expansion can continue longer unconstrained. It may also be aided by a depreciation induced by low interest rates in mid-upswing. For export-dependent economies, the exchange rate is strongly procyclical, subject to dramatic turnarounds induced by exchange traders; the timing of these turnarounds reinforces the income turnaround via the J-curve effect.

This summary of results, while taking effect through different channels from fixed exchange rates, bears a strong resemblance to the fixed exchange rate cases outlined above. Since, in practice, exchange rate regimes fall somewhere in between the fixed and the floating, actual experience will consist of some combination of the net capital flows mechanism and the exchange rate mechanism. The conclusions reached for both exchange rate regimes are summarised in Table 5.1.

	Fixed Exchange Rates	*Floating Exchange Rates*
Self-sufficient economy	Cycle as stable as for closed economy, because offsetting international payments. But capacity to prolong expansion further through continued capital inflows, and to limit strength of downturns, if expected returns still high relative to other countries.	Cycle as stable as for closed economy because stable exchange rate. But exchange rate depreciation (appreciation) may prolong the upturn (downturn). Demand for domestic money less cyclical.
Export-dependent economy	Supply of credit more strongly procyclical than in closed economy, increasing volatility of cycles. Volatility itself may cause a turnaround in capital flows which cuts off expansion and deepens contraction.	Cyclical exchange rate movements exacerbate volatility of cycle. Depreciation as upswing increases imports encourages capital outflows and cuts off expansion, only improving balance of payments eventually if demand price elastic.

Table 5.1 Demand for and Supply of Money

CONCLUSION

In the global monetarist model, it was shown that, while changes in the exogenous money stock are the major source of economic instability, economic openness diminishes the scope for that instability. Cycles are eventually damped by market forces in a closed economy; integration with broader international markets simply adds more power to that dampening process.

In a Keynesian closed economy model, the inherent instability of the economy is fuelled by market forces in general, and the activities of financial markets in particular. In expansionary phases, while finance motive demand for money rises in absolute terms, money is conserved relative to expected income as returns anticipated from alternative assets increase. At the same time, the capacity and willingness of financial institutions to extend credit accelerates. During contractionary phases, when the finance motive demand for money contracts, liquidity preference nevertheless rises as asset holders attempt to avoid capital loss. At the same time, the capacity and willingness of financial institutions to extend credit contracts. Financial ease thus fuels the upswing and tightness fuels the downswing. Financial markets may contribute to the curtailment of expansion by the limits placed by confidence and practicality on the expansion of the financial system in a closed economy and by the channelling of available finance into highly speculative markets at the expense of output-generating activity. The curtailment of the downswing is however dependent on a turnaround in expected returns to new capital assets; 'you cannot push on a string'.

Economic openness *may* increase the destabilising power of financial markets; it depends on the type of economy under consideration. Whether exchange rates are more or less flexible determines primarily the limitation put on the supply of finance during an expansion; the more fixed are exchange rates, the greater the scope for capital inflows to continue to finance an expansion. With fixed exchange rates, the responsiveness of supply to changes in expected returns increases; with floating exchange rates, it is demand which becomes more elastic. Since either of these increases the tendency towards financial ease in an expansion and tightness in a contraction, the general statement may be made that economic openness increases the scope for instability.

Instability in the form of steady expansion is not at all undesirable. Self-sufficient economies, relatively immune from external demand shocks, and particularly those with a history of higher-than-average returns, can enjoy more sustained expansions as a result of external sources of finance. For export-dependent economies, international financial markets are more of a mixed blessing. Export-led expansions are associated with high capital inflows and/or exchange appreciation; the turnaround as imports grow relative to exports and the debt servicing burden rises, however, prompts a rapid turnaround in capital flows and a sharp deterioration in foreign exchange reserves (or currency depreciation) as well as in income and employment. The further income adjustment required by the balance of payments deterioration, unless offset by international public sector inflows of funds, serves to exacerbate the downturn.

In the closed economy, financial markets worked in such a way that supply and demand moved in conflicting directions; the provision of liquidity diminished just as the need for liquidity rose. In an international context this dichotomy becomes even more marked. The time at which economies' needs for international liquidity are greatest, in order to avoid downward income adjustment, are those times when financial markets make the least available. For economies earning consistently low returns in international terms, the problem is a perpetual one.

In conclusion, then, just as Post Keynesians have sought to demonstrate that money plays a key role in all economic relationships within a closed economy, so it may be seen to play a key role in all economic relationships in the international economy. While access to world financial markets allows a greater capacity to finance expansion when expected nominal domestic returns are high on a world scale, it also allows capital, and thereby money, to seek higher returns elsewhere when domestic returns are expected to be low. Within a Keynesian framework, then, international money flows are a potential source not only of instability, but also of divergence between economies.

NOTES

1. The New Cambridge theory of the balance of payments, while put forward as a Keynesian theory, implicitly incorporated a stable demand for money function. The theory, based on national accounts identities, can in fact be viewed as a mirror image of the monetarist monetary approach. See McCallum and Vines (1981).
2. A similar exercise is conducted in the context of an open, regional, economy, using bank multiplier analysis, in Chapter 6 of this volume; the more general case of economies which are open either regionally or internationally was analysed in Dow (1981).
3. See, for example, Lucas (1980).
4. See Minsky (1976, pp. 55-64) and Keller and Carson (1982).
5. Keynes explicitly discussed the importance of overdrafts and the forms of endogenous money creation in his discussion of the finance motive, which in turn was a response to Robertson and Ohlin's criticisms of the *General Theory*. See Davidson, 1978, Chapter 7.
6. See Minsky (1976, pp. 133-6) and Davidson (1978, pp. 282-337) for analysis of the supply of finance in terms of the distribution of income between labour and capital.
7. See Kregel (1984-85) for a full exposition of the significance of liquidity preference among all sectors of the economy as a potential constraint on output and employment.
8. See Dow and Dow (1985) for an exploration of Keynes' theory of expectations formation among entrepreneurs, and of rationality in general, juxtaposed with the corresponding theory in a general equilibrium framework.
9. The term 'liquidity' is used throughout in the sense of ease of exchange for the medium of exchange, with some confidence in the expected price, that is there is a well-organised spot market in the asset. See Davidson (1978, pp. 62-3).
10. This capacity of the financial system to expand credit when their liquidity preference is low has led some Post Keynesians to adopt, as a stylised fact, the endogeneity of the money supply (in the sense of being determined primarily in the private sector). See Kaldor (1982) and Moore (1983, 1984b).
11. A falling MEC schedule has caused concern to those who find Keynes' microfoundations unsatisfactory. His theory of the firm appears to involve perfectly competitive firms with U-shaped cost curves. Further, if rising prices of capital goods following on increased investment plans are to be incorporated in the expected

value of MEC, then individual firms must correctly anticipate each other's behaviour in aggregate. Sardoni (1987, Chapter 9) suggests a Sraffian solution whereby Keynesian results are retained with firms in imperfect competition. An alternative way out is to take account of the *time* involved in formulating and implementing investment plans. By the time full capacity is approached towards the peak of the cycle, the escalation in value of non-reproducible assets reduces the availability of finance for further expansion in the producible goods sector, and the attractiveness of such a move for producers themselves.

12. The influence of actual or expected profitability on expectations and/or the liquidity premium which Mott (1985-86, p. 226) correctly identifies need not hark back to real forces of production, even in his non-neo-classical sense.
13. See Davidson (1978, Chapter 16) and Dow and Earl (1982, Chapter 11) for expressions, and extensions of, Minsky's theory.
14. This situation is exemplified by low-income developing countries which consistently hold net balances in foreign markets. Major economic agents hold most of their money balances in other currencies, minimising the responsiveness of the demand for domestic money to changes in liquidity preference.

6. The Regional Composition of the Bank Multiplier Process

This chapter is a slightly amended version of an article entitled 'The Regional Composition of the Money Multiplier Process' published in the Scottish Journal of Political Economy, *29(1), pp. 22-44, 1982. It benefited from the helpful comments of Tom Wilson, Max Gaskin, Paul Hare and Pauline Andrews.*

INTRODUCTION

A significant element of Keynes' macroeconomic theory which has received surprisingly little attention at the theoretical level is his recognition of the importance of the composition of national aggregates.[1] Regional economists have focused attention on the importance of that composition for the regional distribution of income and employment. But discussion of the relevance of that distribution for national developments has been conducted very much on the sidelines.[2]

In turn, while Keynes emphasised the crucial role of money at the national level, this role has not been transposed into the sub-national framework of regional economics. While much of regional economics is Keynesian in its use of multiplier analysis, little reference is made to a regional role for money, on the grounds that money supply is endogenous at the regional level.[3]

The purpose here is to address both of these questions together: the question of whether money does have a role to play in determining the regional composition of income and employment, and the question of whether regional financial conditions can affect national monetary aggregates, and thus national income and employment. In short, to borrow Friedman's epithet, does it matter regionally and/or nationally where exactly the helicopter drops its banknotes?

These questions have already been addressed in a very similar context, that is with respect to money creation and distribution among groups of countries. Thus, global monetarists argue that, *in the longrun,* money has no effect on output and that a money supply increase in one country has the same outcome in terms of the level and distribution of nominal international aggregates as would the same increase occurring in another country.[4] The Keynesian counter-argument refers to the short-run effects of monetary developments on individual countries, and the implications of the resulting changes in relative competitiveness for the distribution of income and employment in the longrun.[5]

In order to translate this debate into a regional context, a multiplier framework is employed here. This has the advantage of being a framework common both to monetary analysis and regional income analysis, allowing some basis for a regional monetary analysis. While bank multipliers are conventionally rejected by non-monetarists because they tend to conceal portfolio behaviour, portfolio analysis can be introduced into a multiplier framework.[6] This will be done to a limited extent when changing regional expectations are introduced. The resulting coefficient adjustments during the multiplier process also represent an attempt to avoid the pitfalls of 'timeless' income multipliers.[7]

The major difference between the international and interregional contexts is an institutional one. In particular, there is an institutional distinction between the banking systems of different countries, but not necessarily between those of regions within a country. With the growing international character of banking, the national distinction is becoming less marked, so that the differences are more of degree than of kind, the degree being less between, say, the US regional banking structure and the international than between the UK nationwide banking structure and the international. But these differences can be expected to be reflected in the portfolio behaviour of regional banks, and particularly the role of reserve assets. The implications of these differences will be drawn from the multiplier analysis.

In the second section, the use of bank multipliers in a regional context is discussed, while Tsiang's (1978) more general multiplier analysis is considered in the third section; Tsiang's analysis refers to financial sectoral composition, but may be adapted to regional composition. While Tsiang concludes that the compositional outcome of reserves diffusion is independent of the process of diffusion, a counter-argument is presented in the fourth section. On the basis of this argument that short-run processes are significant, the next section concentrates exclusively on alternative short-run reserves diffusion processes. By tying these short-run multipliers into an income multiplier framework, the influence of short-run regional financial developments on regional and national income is demonstrated in the following section. The multiplier models are all developed in a simple two-region context, where one region is developed or Central both in real and financial terms, and the other is under-developed or Peripheral in both terms.

The model refers primarily to banking systems where banks' portfolio structures are regionally separable. In the penultimate section, the theory is discussed in the context of national branch banking systems, and some tentative conclusions are drawn as to its applicability. Some policy conclusions are suggested in the concluding section.

BANK MULTIPLIERS

Conventional bank multipliers measure the relationship between monetary aggregates and some monetary base. They are definitional on the assumption that all financial institutions concerned can and do expand their assets to the extent allowed by their reserves constraint. In other words, there is an excess demand for loans at current interest rates. Leakages between groups of institutions whose liabilities make up the monetary aggregates occur according to stable ratios, as do leakages outside these institutions.

The simple M_1 multiplier, m_1, measures the volume of demand deposits (plus currency) generated by an injection ΔH of high-powered money into the banking system as a whole:

$$m_1 = \frac{\Delta M_1}{\Delta H} = \frac{1+c}{r+c} \tag{6.1}$$

where c is the cash-demand deposit ratio and r the reserve-demand deposit ratio. The multiplier is greater the lower the reserve requirement and the lower the cash-deposit ratio.

Similarly, the multiplier, m_2,[8] is defined as follows:

$$m_2 = \frac{1+t+c}{r_1 + r_2 t + c} \tag{6.2}$$

where t is the ratio of time deposits to demand deposits, c is the ratio of currency to demand deposits, and r_1 and r_2 the reserve requirements attached to demand deposits and time deposits, respectively. The multiplier is greater the lower the two reserve ratios, the lower the cash-deposit ratio, and the greater the ratio of time deposits to demand deposits if reserve requirements are higher on demand deposits than time deposits.[9]

The pattern emerging is one of higher bank multipliers the lower the liquidity of the portfolios of both the banks and the public. The pattern is preserved as multipliers are calculated for broader and broader monetary aggregates. By induction, the conclusion emerges that the money supply, by any definition, is higher for a given monetary base the less liquid are portfolios. (Liquidity is assumed to increase as we progress along the range of assets: currency, bank, reserves, demand deposits, time deposits and so on).

The preferred liquidity structure of portfolios may vary in two senses: on the one hand, a more or less liquid structure may be preferred with respect to a range of assets, each with a given liquidity premium (a movement along the liquidity preference function). On the other hand the liquidity premia themselves may change, prompting a change in portfolio preferences (the liquidity preference function may shift because of a change in the supply of liquidity from any given portfolio).

The first is the conventional case of Keynesian liquidity preference, whereby expectations of capital gains on non-money assets promote a reduction in liquidity preference and expectations of capital losses an increase in liquidity preference. For a given interest rate structure, then, the money multiplier increases with bullish expectations and decreases with bearish expectations. This difference is amplified to the extent that an excess demand for loans is more likely to be associated with a bullish market; if banks are unable or unwilling to lend up fully in a pessimistic market, the multiplier will correspondingly be reduced. Portfolio theory would suggest[10] that the multiplier change would be dampened by an interest rate fall in the market-rise case and a rise in the market-fall case. But in the case of strongly-held expectations of a continuing increase or decrease in asset values, the interest rate changes may be insufficient to reverse expectations and thus changes in liquidity preference.

Second, these changes may be associated with changes in the liquidity of assets themselves. Thus, trading activity tends to increase on a rising market, both for real and financial markets. (The housing market is a notable example of thinness when values fall.) Similarly real assets are more acceptable as collateral when their value is expected to rise than when it is expected to fall. In periods of optimistic expectations, then, the liquidity of many assets rises, further encouraging a movement toward the less liquid end of the spectrum, while the converse is true of periods of pessimistic expectations.

In the longrun, financial assets tend to acquire a greater degree of liquidity over time.[11] Thus, a major reason for the shift of attention to ever-broader measures of the money supply is the increasing 'moneyness' of financial assets during the process of financial development. As a result, the income elasticity of demand for any money aggregate tends to fall with economic development as demand shifts along the liquidity spectrum, and so the corresponding money multiplier is higher at higher levels of economic development.

Suppose it is possible to translate these arguments from a temporal to a spatial context. Then for contemporary economies with equal money bases, their money supplies will be higher the more optimistic are expectations regarding local asset prices, the more active are markets in local assets, and the greater is the degree of financial development.

While most regions occupy some middle ground, it is possible to identify regions which can be treated as polar cases: Central regions and Peripheral regions. The analysis here will concentrate on these polar cases in order to highlight the financial implications of their real economic differences. Thus, Centre, an archetypal central region, is characterised by prosperity which is expected to continue, active markets, and financial sophistication. Periphery, an archetypal peripheral region, has a stagnating economy, thin markets and a lesser degree of financial sophistication. Even within nations, financial innovations only extend to regions remote from the financial centre after a lag. The additional transactions and information costs associated with remoteness help to preserve a continuing differential in financial sophistication between the two regions. The liquidity of any given asset is thus less in Periphery than in Centre. In the long-run, then, Centre's bank multiplier is higher than Periphery's, a tendency accentuated in the shortrun by bullish expectations in the former region and bearish expectations in the latter. Other things being equal, then, the money supply is higher where liquidity preference is lower.

But one crucial difference between the temporal and the spatial contexts is the possibility of two-way transactions between economies. Thus, agents in each economy may hold assets and liabilities issued by other economies. As a result, not only is the liquidity of portfolios not confined to local financial conditions, but also the monetary base becomes endogenous, altered by net financial flows between the economies. In the next section, the conventional bank multiplier is modified to take account of these flows.

REGIONAL BANK MULTIPLIERS WITH INTERREGIONAL TRANSACTIONS

A model disaggregating bank multipliers to incorporate flows within a national financial system has been developed by Tsiang (1978). He disaggregates by function of financial institution rather than by region, and analyses the process of reserves diffusion among the different types of institution. Flows between institutions are determined by fixed proportionality relationships (subject to probability distributions). We have so far considered leakages for the entire banking system only in the form of currency and reserves as a fixed proportion of total assets. Tsiang further incorporates leakages in the form of purchases of the liabilities or assets of other financial institutions on the part of the customers of each financial institution or the institution itself, as a proportion of the turnover of that institution's deposits. The net leakage for each institution takes the form of an addition to or withdrawal from each institution's reserves.

Because each institution and its customers have different portfolio preferences, represented by different leakage rates to and from each other, each is subject to a different multiplier. The aggregate bank multiplier is the sum of all institutions' multipliers, weighted by their share of the national monetary base.

In-so-far as financial institutions can be classified on a regional basis, as for example in the US, Tsiang's model can be applied directly in regional terms. Within national branch banking systems, on the other hand, it cannot be assumed that bank portfolios are determined on a regional basis, in the sense that asset structure is determined by liability structure on a regional basis. But, the analysis will be conducted as if it were generally true that financial institutions are regionally separable. We will then consider what conclusions may be carried over to situations where portfolios are established on a national basis.

In adapting Tsiang's model to a two-region system, it eases exposition to restrict the range of assets. Suppose the public in the two regions may hold currency, C_c and C_p, or interest-bearing deposits, D_c and D_p, with the banks in Centre and Periphery respectively. The banks hold reserves, R_c and R_p, loans to local borrowers, L_c and L_p, and nationwide securities, S_c and S_p. The term 'loan' is used in the broad sense of 'advance', that is, including advances against overdraft facilities as well as fixed-amount advances. 'Securities' includes all marketable securities, not simply public debt.

It has already been suggested that liquidity preference is higher in Periphery on the part of the public and the banks. In this simplified model, this preference can be characterised by a higher cash-deposit ratio on the part of the public and a higher reserve ratio and ratio of national securities to local credit on the part of the banks. For banking systems where reserve ratios do not vary regionally as they do in the US (at least among state-registered banks), banks in a Peripheral region may be expected to hold reserves in excess of the required minimum for prudential reasons: where reserves requirements are applied to a national bank, they may be regarded implicitly as being an average proportion of deposits ranging from a high in Peripheral regions branches to a low in Central regions' branches.[12] Thus:

$$
\begin{array}{llll}
c_c < c_p & \text{where } c_c = C_c/D_c, & c_p = C_p/D_p &) \\
r_c < r_p & \text{where } r_c = R_c/D_c, & r_p = R_p/D_p &) \\
s_c < s_p & \text{where } s_c = S_c/L_c, & s_p = S_p/L_p &)
\end{array}
\qquad (6.3)
$$

Flows between the two regions on the part of the non-bank public may, in line with Tsiang's model, be expressed as a proportion a of transactions in each region, measured by the turnover of deposits, kD (k being a velocity measure). Gross non-bank flows out of Centre, designated $a_{cp}k_cD_c$, are made up of purchases of goods and services from Periphery. The net outflow, once reserve flows from Periphery are taken into account, is thus $(a_{cp}k_cD_c - a_{pc}k_pD_p)$. Other things being equal, this net flow determines the change in reserves of the banks in each region in each period, together with the net flows associated with the banks' purchases of national securities. Let α denote the proportion of security purchases involving a net outflow from the region (taking account of the location of the issuer's expenditure as well as the location of the security purchase). In any period, then, the change in the reserves of banks in the two regions, ΔR_c and ΔR_p, is:

$$- \Delta R_c = (a_{cp}k_cD_c - a_{pc}k_pD_p) + (\alpha_c\Delta S_c - \alpha_p\Delta S_p) = \Delta R_p \qquad (6.4)$$

Taking those net flows into account as well as the conventional cash and reserves leakages, suppose there is an injection, ΔH, of high-powered money somewhere in the banking system. Then the national money supply increases by a multiple m_n of ΔH:[13]

$$m_n = \frac{(1 + c_c)a_{pc}k_p + (1 + c_p)a_{cp}k_c}{(r_c + c_c)a_{pc}k_p + (r_p + c_p)a_{cp}k_c} \qquad (6.5)$$

The regional components of the national money supply increase by multiples, m_c and m_p, of ΔH:

$$m_c = \frac{(1 + c_c)a_{pc}k_p}{(r_c + c_c)a_{pc}k_p + (r_p + c_p)a_{cp}k_c} \qquad (6.6)$$

$$\text{and } m_p = \frac{(1 + c_p)a_{cp}k_c}{(r_c + c_c)a_{pc}k_p + (r_p + c_p)a_{cp}k_c} \qquad (6.7)$$

Where $c_c = c_p$ and $r_c = r_p$, the national multiplier collapses to the conventional multiplier in equation (6.1).

But once differences in reserve ratios and cash-deposit ratios are considered, the regional composition of financial aggregates, as determined by interregional financial flows, determines the scale of the national aggregate. Any change in the regional portfolio ratios r and c will change the scale of the national money supply increase. Further, given assumptions (6.3) a higher rate of non-bank outflow of Periphery to Centre (a higher $a_{pc}k_p$) increases the national multiplier, increases the Centre multiplier and reduces the Periphery multiplier. (The reverse is true for a higher rate of non-bank outflow from Centre.) This outcome is the result of the greater concentration of monetary base, by reserves inflows, in the region with the lower rate of leakage into reserves and currency.

The simple regional versions of Tsiang's multipliers confirm two important conclusions of his analysis:

(1) the regional and national multipliers are independent of the regional location of the injection of high-powered money,[14]
(2) they are also independent of the banks' portfolio behaviour other than the reserves requirement, or decision (except in the case where that behaviour prevents a stable approach to equilibrium).

Both conclusions are in fact inherent in conventional multiplier analysis. Multipliers measure changes between one equilibrium position and another. In the context of regional flows, where leakage rates vary between regions, the national aggregate money supply is only in equilibrium once all net regional flows have ceased. A consequence of this requirement that regional reserve holdings become stationary, is that the banks' portfolios do not change, so that there are no new security purchases. In terms of equation (6.4), then:

$$\Delta R_c = \Delta R_p = \Delta S_c = \Delta S_p = 0 \quad (6.8)$$

and the equilibrium condition becomes:

$$a_{cp}k_cD_c = a_{pc}k_pD_p \quad (6.9)$$

No matter how or where the injection occurs, and no matter how banks adjust their portfolios to the injection, then, reserves will flow back and forth between the regions until deposits in each region reach a level where the condition given by equation (6.9) is satisfied. Thus the regional distribution of the money supply is fully determined by the non-bank balance of payments condition, while the scale of the money supply is jointly determined by this condition together with the regional reserves and currency leakage rates.

These results are highly significant in themselves. National monetary base increases have a relatively greater impact on the money supply of regions with low liquidity preference and low rate of outflow to other regions. To the extent that regional money supply increases set a ceiling on regional investment, the former type of region will experience higher-income growth. Further, this tendency cannot be counteracted by deliberate attempts to direct money supply increases at high liquidity preference regions with high rates of outflow, if the predetermined final equilibrium distribution is taken to be the end-point of the process.

The analysis can however be taken several steps further, along the lines of the portfolio critique of multiplier analysis which postulates endogenous changes in the various asset ratios. In the next section the possibility is considered of an endogenous form of the stock equilibrium condition given by equation (6.9). Then in the following section we look in more detail at the multiplier process in the shortrun, where banks' portfolio behaviour affects monetary flows and levels.

THE LONG-RUN STOCK EQUILIBRIUM CONDITION

The balance of payments condition has so far been described as a trade balance condition, with regional import propensities, a_{cp} and a_{pc} fixed in relation to the volume of transactions k_cD_c and k_pD_p respectively. Because of the greater degree of financial sophistication in Centre, deposit turnover is higher than in Periphery, that is $k_c > k_p$.[15] While Peripheral economies may be expected to have a higher propensity to import, that is $a_{pc} > a_{cp}$, the net payments balance will be determined by the combination of import propensities and velocities of circulation.

The import propensities themselves may be viewed as endogenous to the money creation process. Thus, depending on the expenditure associated with the initial injection, the marginal propensity to import may vary from the average, changing the average at the new equilibrium. An injection of new money, for example, to finance a government project employing local resources would reduce the import propensity relative to the financing of a project involving imported capital goods and other factors. The new equilibrium deposit level for that region would be higher in the former case than the latter.

But the balance of payments condition can be extended to include non-bank capital flows. Suppose the non-bank public can hold securities as well as bank deposits and currency. Then balance of payments equilibrium takes the form of net flows on trade account plus net flows on capital account.

Analysing the determination of net regional capital flows is not a simple matter. Capital is attracted by high financial returns, high real returns, and low risk, suggesting a tendency for net flows into Centre. On the other hand, finance is relatively scarce in Periphery both for these reasons and also because of the lower rate of growth of local bank credit suggested by the earlier multiplier analysis. The expected market response would be an increase in interest rates or a reduction in security prices which would redress the balance, to some extent at least.[16]

Whitman's (1967) analysis is helpful in this regard. Translated into the present context, Central economies tend to have internally-generated expansion which attracts capital inflows, offset eventually by increased imports; similarly, downturns involve capital outflows but also reduced imports. In contrast, Peripheral economies are more dependent on export-led expansions which also attract capital inflows, but are more likely to be choked off at an early stage by a high marginal propensity to import. In summary she postulates a much smaller tendency to variance in payments for Central economies than for Peripheral economies. In a two-region model, Periphery's payments deficit equals Centre's surplus, but this is not inconsistent with different *ex ante* tendencies towards payments imbalance. The position may be approximated by representing the Centre total outflow propensity, a_{cp}, as being stable and low whereas the Periphery total outflow propensity, a_{pc}, is high and rises when expectations of a deterioration in the Periphery economy cause capital outflows as Periphery residents purchase Centre securities.

If the location of the high-powered money injection alters expectations, then it will alter the rate of capital flows between the regions and thus alter the stock equilibrium condition. Suppose, conventionally, the injection occurs in the financial centre in Centre region, filtering through to Periphery as counterparts of increased imports and security purchases on the part of Centre residents. It seems plausible to suggest that, if an injection were to occur instead in Periphery, then expectations with respect to the value of Periphery assets might be altered.

The nature of the injection would of course be significant. If it were to finance a local development project, it would be accompanied by expectations of economic development on the real side, discouraging capital outflows on the financial side. If the new money were to finance imports from Centre, expectations would not be significantly affected. However if the fact of a large initial boost to Periphery banks' liquidity itself discourages net capital outflows, then a_{pc} will be lower for an injection in Periphery than the same injection in Centre. Referring back to the multipliers in equations (6.5) - (6.7), the consequence of a lower a_{pc} would be a lower national and Centre bank multiplier, but a larger Periphery multiplier.

Much of course depends on the portfolio behaviour of the banks, as well as the non-bank public. If the Periphery banks' liquidity preference also were to fall if the injection occurred in Periphery, this would take the form of increased local lending relative to national security purchases (a higher s in condition (6.3)). While not itself entering into the long-run equilibrium condition, the consequence of this increased credit could alter expectations about asset prices in Periphery and further reduce non-bank purchases of Centre securities. Indeed, for regionally-separable banks whose profits are constrained by deposit levels, the Periphery banks would gain by a policy which thus increased the regional money multiplier.

Tsiang (1978) gives bank portfolio behaviour an important role only in terms of the stability of the multiplier process. If the rate at which banks increase lending is a sufficiently large multiple of excess reserves in each round of the multiplier process, then net interregional flows will grow progressively larger rather than tend towards zero. He dismisses this possibility on the grounds that regional financial flows are observed to be stable.

Rather than pursue this point further it seems more fruitful to concentrate instead on the short-run multiplier process itself, on the grounds that conditions never stay static long enough for systems either to converge on equilibrium or diverge from it. In the next section, therefore, we look at the round-by-round multiplier process, over the first few rounds, using numerical examples.

THE MULTIPLIER PROCESS IN THE SHORTRUN

The various parameters ascribed to each region will now be given numerical values in order to demonstrate how the regional location of the injection and also the banks' portfolio behaviour, play an important part in the scale and distribution of monetary aggregates following the injection.

In line with the conditions set out in (6.3), the cash-deposit ratios, the reserve ratios, and the securities-loans ratios are given the following values:

$$\left.\begin{array}{ll} c_c = 0.05 & c_p = 0.1 \\ r_c = 0.1 & r_p = 0.2 \\ s_c = 0 & s_p = 0.5 \end{array}\right\} \quad (6.10)$$

Further, assuming a higher non-bank rate of outflow in Periphery, and a higher deposit velocity in Centre:

$$\begin{aligned} a_{cp} &= 0.1 \qquad & a_{pc} &= 0.25 \quad) \\ k_c &= 2 & k_p &= 1 \quad) \end{aligned} \qquad (6.11)$$

Further, it is assumed that banks in both regions fully employ any excess reserves in each period, Centre banks entirely in local loans and Periphery banks half and half in national securities, that is:

$$\beta_c = 1 = \beta_p$$

Finally, it is assumed that, while Periphery banks purchase these securities in Centre, one half are issued by Periphery businesses or are issued by the government for the purpose of financing expenditure in Periphery. Thus half of the value of security purchases results in a net outflow from Periphery: $\alpha_p = 0.5$.

The dynamic process may be expressed as follows, in symmetrical form, with the subscripts i and j referring to either Centre and Periphery or Periphery and Centre respectively. (The i and j subscripts are employed for complete generality and may be replaced by 'c' and 'p', or by 'p' and 'c', respectively.)

$$\begin{aligned} D_{i_t} - D_{i_{t-1}} &= (L_{i_t} - L_{i_{t-1}}) + (S_{i_t} - S_{i_{t-1}}) + (R_{i_t} - R_{i_{t-1}}) \quad) \\ L_{i_t} - L_{i_{t-1}} &= (1 - s_i)\beta_i E_{i_{t-1}} = (1 - s_i)\beta_i (R_{i_{t-1}} - r_i D_{i_{t-1}}) \quad) \\ S_{i_t} - S_{i_{t-1}} &= s_i \beta_i E_{i_{t-1}} = s_i \beta_i (R_{i_{t-1}} - r_i D_{i_{t-1}}) \quad) \\ R_{i_t} - R_{i_{t-1}} &= A_{j_{t-1}} - A_{i_{t-1}} - c_i (D_{i_{t-1}} - D_{i_{t-2}}) \quad) \\ A_{i_t} &= a_{ij} k_i D_{i_t} + \tfrac{1}{2} (S_{i_t} - S_{i_{t-1}}) \quad) \\ &= a_{ij} k_i D_{i_t} + \tfrac{1}{2} s_i \beta_i (R_{i_{t-1}} - r_i D_{i_{t-1}}) \quad) \end{aligned} \qquad (6.12)$$

where
D_{i_t} = deposits in region i, period t
L_{i_t} = loans in region i, period t
S_{i_t} = securities purchased by banks in region i, period t
R_{i_t} = bank reserves in region i, period t
E_{i_t} = excess bank reserves in region i, period t
A_{i_t} = reserves outflow from region i, period t

Tables 6.1 and 6.2 show the application of this multiplier process with the assumed coefficient values and initial values for the various components of the banks' portfolios which give an initial payments equilibrium ($A_c = 20 = A_p$). In the first case, depicted in Table 6.1, banks in Centre acquire an increase of 10 units in their reserves. By increasing local lending in Centre, increased outflows to Periphery are generated, allowing an increase in local lending there and thus an increase in outflows to Centre. In Table 6.2, by way of contrast, the initial injection occurs in Periphery.

$\Delta H_c = 10 \quad \Delta H_p = 0$

CENTRE						PERIPHERY						
Assets			Liabs	Reserve Outflows		Assets				Liabs	Reserve Outflows	
(E_c)	R_c	L_c	D_c	C_c	A_c	(E_p)	R_p	L_p	S_p	D_p	C_p	A_p
0	10	90	100			0	16	32	32	80		
				0	20						0	20
9	20	90	110			0	16	32	32	80		
				0.5	22						0	20
6	17.5	99	116.5			1.5	18	32	32	82		
				0.5	23.5						0	20.5
2	14	105	119			4	21	32.5	32.5	86		
				0	24						0.5	22
0	12	107	119			4	22.5	34.5	34.5	91.5		
				0	24						0.5	24
0	12	107	119			3	22	36.5	36.5	95		
				0	24						0.5	24.5
0.5	12.5	107	199.5			1.5	21	38	38	97		
				0	24						0	25
-	-	-	-	-	-	-	-	-	-	-	-	-
-	-	-	-	-	-	-	-	-	-	-	-	-
-	-	-	-	-	-	-	-	-	-	-	-	-
0	12.5	113	125.5	0	25	0	20.5	40	40	100.5	0	25

Table 6.1 Regional Bank Multipliers: Injection into Centre

The long-run outcomes, shown in the bottom line of each table, are the same in both cases since the rate of outflow from each region is treated here as being fixed and exogenous. But even without any portfolio response to the location of injection, it is clear from these tables that the scale effect of that location significantly alters the distribution of bank deposits between the two regions, as well as the national totals, in the shortrun. Total deposits (D_c+D_p) are about 3 units higher on average during the first six rounds in Table 6.1 than Table 6.2. In the long-run position, Centre is favoured in both cases, with an addition of 25.5 units in deposits and 23 units in local lending, compared with 20.5 units and 8 units in Periphery, respectively. The difference is the direct result of the different portfolio preferences of the banks and their customers in each region.

$\Delta H_c = 10 \quad \Delta H_p = 0$

CENTRE						PERIPHERY						
Assets			Liabs	Reserve Outflows		Assets				Liabs	Reserve Outflows	
(E_c)	R_c	L_c	D_c	C_c	A_c	(E_p)	R_p	L_p	S_p	D_p	C_p	A_p
0	10	90	100			0	16	32	32	80		
				0	20						0	20
0	10	90	100			8	26	32	32	90		
				0	20						1	22.5
2	12.5	90	102.5			3.5	22.5	36	36	94.5		
				0	20.5						0.5	25.5
6.5	17.5	92	109.5			-1.5	17.5	37.5	37.5	92		
				0.5	22						-0.5	24
7	19	98.5	117.5			-2.5	15.5	37	37	89.5		
				0	23.5						0	22
5	17	105.5	122.5			-1	17	36	36	89		
				0	24.5						0	22
2	14.5	110.5	125			1.5	19.5	35.5	35.5	90.5		
				0	25						0	22.5
-	-	-	-	-	-	-	-	-	-	-	-	-
-	-	-	-	-	-	-	-	-	-	-	-	-
-	-	-	-	-	-	-	-	-	-	-	-	-
0	12.5	113	125.5	0	25	0	20.5	40	40	100.5	0	25

Table 6.2 Regional Bank Multipliers: Injection into Periphery

Suppose now we consider the banks' portfolio reaction to the location of the injection. In particular, suppose expectations regarding the value of Periphery assets became more optimistic when the injection occurs in Periphery. The Periphery banks' response is to increase local lending relative to security purchases, out of the reserves increase. This situation is depicted in Table 6.3, with the value of s_p down from 0.5 to 0, that is all excess reserves are devoted to local lending. This has the consequence of increasing local lending more rapidly than in Table 6.2, but also of reducing the rate of capital, and thus total, outflow. Periphery deposit levels stay higher, longer and excess reserves do not run out as fast as in Table 6.2. As a corollary, Centre deposits do not grow as rapidly; because of the higher rate of leakage into cash and reserves from Periphery deposits, this has the further consequence of reducing the average level of total deposits (D_c+D_p).

$\Delta H_c = 10 \quad \Delta H_p = 0$ Endogenous S_p

CENTRE						PERIPHERY						
Assets			Liabs	Reserve Outflows		Assets				Liabs	Reserve Outflows	
(E_c)	R_c	L_c	D_c	C_c	A_c	(E_p)	R_p	L_p	S_p	D_p	C_p	A_p
0	10	90	100			0	16	32	32	80		
				0	20						0	20
0	10	90	100			8	26	32	32	90		
				0	20						1	22.5
2.5	12.5	90	102.5			3.5	22.5	40	32	94.5		
				0	20.5						0.5	23.5
4.5	15.5	92.5	108			0	19	43.5	32	94.5		
				0.5	21.5						0	23.5
5.5	17	97	114			-1.5	17	43.5	32	92.5		
				0	23						-0.5	23
5	17	102.5	119.5			-1	17.5	42	32	91.5		
				0.5	24						0	23
3	15.5	107.5	123			0	18.5	41	32	91.5		
				0	24.5						0	23
-	-	-	-	-	-	-	-	-	-	-	-	-
-	-	-	-	-	-	-	-	-	-	-	-	-
-	-	-	-	-	-	-	-	-	-	-	-	-
0	12.5	113	125.5	0	25	0	20.5	48	32	100.5	0	25

Table 6.3 Regional Bank Multipliers with Endogenous Expectations: Injection into Periphery

Numerical examples have been used here in order to highlight the different paths which the reserves diffusion process might take. The attendant cost is however the necessarily arbitrary nature of examples chosen. In order to show how far the results are dependent on each numerical assumption, a sensitivity analysis is set out in Table 6.4, with respect to the results in Tables 6.1 and 6.2. Thus the values of the deposit and local lending multipliers and in each region in the longrun and shortrun are shown first for an injection, H, of 10 units into Centre alone (as in Table 6.1) and then into Periphery alone (as in Table 6.2), neutralising each assumption in turn, and then neutralising all assumptions together. ('Neutralising' in this context means removing any difference between Centre and Periphery values by setting Periphery values equal to the Centre values of conditions (6.10) and (6.11).)

Coefficient Values	*Longrun*				*Shortrun (6 round average)*			
Table 6.1	Centre		Periphery		Centre		Periphery	
	m_c^D	m_c^L	m_p^D	m_p^L	m_c^D	m_c^L	m_p^D	m_p^L
(a) Initial values	2.56	2.31	2.05	0.82	1.72	1.25	0.86	0.23
(b) $c_p = 0.05 = c_c$	2.86	2.57	2.29	0.91	1.73	1.25	0.87	0.26
(c) $a_{cp}k_p = 0.2 = a_{cp}k_c$	2.22	2.00	2.22	0.89	1.69	1.24	0.94	0.24
(d) $r_p = 0.1 = r_c$	3.23	2.90	2.58	1.03	1.78	1.28	0.96	0.28
(e) $\beta_p = 1 = \beta_c$	2.56	2.31	2.05	1.64	1.67	1.23	0.94	0.50
(f) (b)+(c)+(d)+(e)	3.33	3.00	3.33	3.00	1.63	1.22	1.13	0.64
Table 6.2								
(a) Initial values	2.56	2.31	2.05	0.82	1.28	0.78	1.09	0.37
(b) $c_p = 0.05 = c_c$	2.86	2.57	2.29	0.91	1.36	0.67	1.18	0.40
(c) $a_{cp}k_p = 0.2 = a_{cp}k_c$	2.22	2.00	2.22	0.89	1.22	0.70	1.18	0.40
(d) $r_p = 0.1 = r_c$	3.23	2.90	2.58	1.03	1.33	0.64	1.20	0.43
(e) $\beta_p = 1 = \beta_c$	2.56	2.31	2.05	1.64	1.12	0.66	1.24	0.83
(f) (b)+(c)+(d)+(e)	3.33	3.00	3.33	3.00	1.13	0.64	1.63	1.22

Table 6.4 Sensitivity Analysis Summary: Deposit and Lending Multipliers, Tables 6.1 and 6.2

The first four columns show the deposit and lending multipliers for each region, reflecting the total change in deposits and lending once equilibrium has been restored. The multipliers are the same for the 'Table 6.1' and 'Table 6.2' situations, reflecting the earlier conclusion that the equilibrium position was independent of the location of any high-powered money injections. The long-run multipliers are sensitive to regional differences in the values of coefficients.[17] Comparing row (f) where all coefficients in Periphery are set equal to those in Centre with row (a) which incorporates the initial values of conditions (6.10) and (6.11), the deposit and lending multipliers are at least 30% higher. Rows (b) to (e) show the multipliers, for Periphery at least, increasing when any one of the Periphery coefficients is given the Centre value.

The second set of four columns shows the short-run multipliers, where the shortrun is defined as six rounds beyond the initial position. They are calculated as averages over these rounds to reflect the significance of the length of time over which higher deposit and loan levels occur; other events may supercede the multiplier process after a small number of rounds so that it is important how rapidly totals approach what would be their long-run equilibrium levels if they were ever reached.

In the shortrun, the coefficient value changes for Periphery do alter the values of the multipliers, consistently raising Periphery's multipliers. Comparing row (f) (all differences removed) with row (a) (initial values), the deposit multiplier m_p^D is higher by 31% and the loan multiplier m_p^L by 178% when all coefficient differences are eliminated and the initial injection occurs in Centre; when it occurs in Periphery the multipliers are higher by 50% and 230% respectively. In percentage (though not percentage point) terms, then, the short-run multiplier sensitivity is similar to the long-run.

But, over-riding this sensitivity is the multiplier impact of the location of the initial injection. Even without any differences in financial structure or behaviour at all, represented by row (f), Periphery's deposit multiplier is 44% higher if the injection occurs in Periphery than if it occurs in Centre and the lending multiplier 91% higher. The ranges within which the multipliers vary are completely distinct for Centre as between the 'Table 6.1' and 'Table 6.2' situations; they overlap somewhat for Periphery, primarily because of the power of the $s_p = 0.5$ assumption and its effect on Periphery lending. Abstracting from this assumption, as in row (c), the multipliers are still sensitive to differences in cash-deposit ratio, rates of balance of payments flow and reserve ratio differences. This sensitivity is measured by the difference between rows (e) and (f), but is still overshadowed by the sensitivity to location of injection, measured by the differences between the rows (e) in each half of the table and the rows (f) in each half of the table.

THE BANK MULTIPLIER IN THE SHORTRUN WITH INCOME ADJUSTMENT

The short-run bank multiplier process is only important in-so-far as it impinges on real activity. To construct the multiplier with only veiled reference to real forces has been partial, although no more so than income multiplier analysis without reference to financial constraints. The purpose of the analysis so far has been to reach a point at which the interdependencies of the real and financial sectors may be made explicit.

In this section, the bank multiplier is interlocked with an income multiplier. The feedback between the two multipliers operates through the financial flows arising from export and import demand (now a function of income), and the finance of investment, and the financial expectations associated with difference types of real expenditure. In fact, since this income multiplier process is fed by induced change in investment demand, it really represents the income *supermultiplier*.[18] Once the accelerator is added to the conventional multiplier to form the supermultiplier, the question of financial constraints on investment demand must be faced; the simple income multiplier in contrast starts with a given investment expenditure after all financial constraints have been taken into account.

As in the previous numerical examples, the role of non-bank portfolio behaviour is not highlighted. If savings can be held in the form of securities or bank deposits (currency is dropped from this form of the model for simplification), then an increase in liquidity preference takes the form of a shift into deposits. This has a direct effect on the finance available for investment and on capital flows. But since bank portfolio behaviour already captures this effect with shifts between local lending and securities issued outside the region, attention will be concentrated on the banks. For simplification, therefore, it is assumed that the public hold all their savings in bank deposits.

The particular model of the real sector is as follows, employing the conventional national accounts symbols:

$$Y_{i_t} = C_{i_t} + I_{i_t} + G_{i_t} + X_{i_t} - M_{i_t} \tag{6.13}$$

$$C_{i_t} = 0.8Y_{i_{t-1}} \tag{6.14}$$

$$I_{i_t} = \text{ the smaller of } \begin{matrix} I_{i_o} + (Y_{i_{t-1}} - Y_{i_{t-2}}),\ t > 2 \\ L_{i_t} + \delta_i\,(S_{p_{t-1}} - S_{p_{t-2}}) \end{matrix} \tag{6.15}$$

$$G_{i_t} = H_{i_t} \tag{6.16}$$

$$X_{i_t} = M_{j_t} \tag{6.17}$$

$$M_{i_t} = a_{ij}Y_{i_{t-1}} \tag{6.18}$$

where $\delta_c = 1\ \ \delta_p = 0\quad when\, H_{c_1} > 0\ \ H_{p_1} = 0$

$\delta_c = 0\ \ \delta_p = 1\quad when\, H_{c_1} = 0\ \ H_{p_1} > 0$

H_{i_t} = injection of high-powered money in region i, period, t

The investment function given by equation (6.15) is based on a simple accelerator process, with additions to investment equal to income changes in the previous period. But availability of finance puts a potential ceiling on investment demand; actual investment is constrained by financing by local banks and by the stock of securities issued. The earlier assumption of a continued excess demand for bank credit is now relaxed; credit demand is now equated with investment demand and may exceed or fall short of credit availability.

$H_c = 10 \quad H_p = 0$

Centre											Periphery											
C_c +	I_c +	G_c +	X_c −	M_c =	Y_c	(E_c)	R_c +	L_c =	D_c		C_p +	I_p +	G_p +	X_p −	M_p =	Y_p	(E_p)	R_p +	L_p +	S_p =	D_p	
										A_c												A_p
						0	10	90	100								0	16	32	32	80	
440	110	0	55	55	550					55	176	44	0	55	55	220						55
						9	20	90	110								0	16	32	32	80	
440	110	10	55	55	560					56	176	44	0	55	55	220						55
						7	19	99	118								1	17	32	32	81	
448	119	0	55	56	566					56.5	176	44	0	56	55	221						55
						5	17.5	106	123.5								2	18.5	32.5	32.5	83.5	
453	126	0	55	56.5	577.5					58	177	44.5	0	56.5	55	223						56
						3	15.5	111	126.5								3	20.5	33.5	33.5	87.5	
462	131.5	0	55.5	58	591					59	178.5	45.5	0	58	55.5	226.5						57.5
						1	14	114	128								3.5	22	35	35	92	
473	136.5	0	56.5	59	607					60.5	181	47	0	59	56.5	230.5						59
						-0.5	12.5	115	127.5								4	23.5	36.5	36.5	96.5	
485.5	139	0	57.5	60.5	621.5					62	184.5	48.5	0	60.5	57.5	236						60.5
-	-	-	-	-	-	-	-	-	-	-	-	-	-	-	-	-	-	-	-	-	-	-
-	-	-	-	-	-	-	-	-	-	-	-	-	-	-	-	-	-	-	-	-	-	-

Table 6.5 Regional Bank Multipliers with Income Adjustment: Injection into Centre

In this particular example, the extreme assumption is retained that Centre banks have such low liquidity preference that all free assets are made available for local lending ($S_c = 0$). Periphery banks devote half of their free assets to security purchases, but the location of issuers depends on the state of expectations. Thus, if an injection of government spending of 10 units financed by new money is made in Centre, only Centre securities are purchased. However, a money-financed injection of government spending in Periphery of the type to offset pessimistic expectations encourages local banks to purchase only Periphery securities. The bank multiplier operates as before (with the exclusion of a currency drain).

Table 6.5 depicts the situation of the injection in Centre, and Table 6.6 of the injection in Periphery, with the attendant differences in expectations about future asset-values in Periphery. Both cases start off in payments equilibrium, and with savings equal to investment *ex ante*. Investment demand is triggered by the government spending, setting off both the income supermultiplier and the bank multiplier as banks are confronted with demand for their excess reserves. The process is exported to the other region in each case by the impetus to imports given by the income increase.

The outcomes are markedly different in the two cases, with income growing faster in Centre in the first case and in Periphery in the second. This is a combination of the scale effects of the location of the initial injection, combined with the changed portfolio behaviour of Periphery banks in the second case which allows a greater proportion of investment demand to be financed and also reduces capital outflows. It is a central feature of this model that it is availability of finance which constrains income supermultipliers rather than availability of savings. In Table 6.5, Centre is prevented from making investment demand effective in four rounds, with one-half of demand met by the end of the sixth round. Periphery is similarly constrained in four periods, making two-fifths of investment demand effective in total. But savings fall short of actual investment in Centre while exceeding investment in Periphery, reflecting the role of capital flows (in purchase of securities or in payment for imports) as a means of satisfying excess demand in one region.

Similarly, in Table 6.6, investment demand is constrained by lack of finance in four rounds in Periphery, although only in two rounds in Centre. Periphery is only able to make a quarter of its investment demand effective over the entire period, compared with three quarters in the case of Centre. But in this case Periphery savings continually fall behind investment, a lack made up by excess savings from Centre.

The difference in short-run effects on income in the two cases can be measured by the average income supermultiplier over the six periods.

$H_c = 0 \quad H_p = 10$

Centre											Periphery											
C_c +	I_c +	G_c +	X_c −	M_c =	Y_c	(E_c)	R_c +	L_c =	D_c		C_p +	I_p +	G_p +	X_p −	M_p =	Y_p	(E_p)	R_p +	L_p +	S_p =	D_p	
										A_c												A_p
						0	10	90	100								0	16	32	32	80	
440	110	0	55	55	550					55	176	44	0	55	55	220						55
						0	10	90	100								8	26	32	32	80	
440	110	0	55	55	550					55	176	44	10	55	55	230						57.5
						2.5	12.5	90	102.5								4.5	23.5	36	36	95.5	
440	110	0	57.5	55	552.6					55	184	52	0	55	57.5	233.5						58.5
						5	16	92.5	108.5								1	20	38	38	96	
442	112.5	0	58.5	55	558					56	187	56	0	55	58.5	239.5						60
						8	20	97.5	117.5								-2.5	16	38.5	38.5	93	
446.5	117.5	0	60	56	568					57	191.5	57	0	56	60	244.5						61
						10	24	106.5	139.5								-5.5	12	37.5	37.5	87	
454.5	125.5	0	61	57	584					58.5	195.5	55	0	57	61	246.5						61.5
						12	27	116.5	152.5								-7	9	35	35	79	
467	135.5	0	61.5	58.5	605.5					60.5	197	50	0	58.5	61.5	244						61
-	-	-	-	-	-	-	-	-	-	-	-	-	-	-	-	-	-	-	-	-	-	-
-	-	-	-	-	-	-	-	-	-	-	-	-	-	-	-	-	-	-	-	-	-	-

Table 6.6 Regional Bank Multipliers with Income Adjustment: Injection into Periphery

When the injection occurs in Centre, the average Centre income multiplier is 3.7, the average Periphery multiplier is 0.6, and the average national multiplier is 4.3. When the injection occurs in Periphery in such a way as to ameliorate expectations, the Centre and Periphery multipliers are equal at 2, giving a national multiplier of 4.

This example serves to demonstrate that income supermultipliers are incomplete without reference to financial constraints. The nature of these financial constraints, as a function of financial conditions in the two regions, derives from financial flows mirroring flows of goods and services, but also from capital flows and portfolio decisions based on expectations regarding asset values in the two regions. These expectations in turn are liable to change in response to both real and financial developments.

Once consideration is given to the possibility of different financial constraints in different regions, many of the conclusions of regional analysis conducted in real terms must be qualified. Injections of expenditure into backward regions may not achieve their full income supermultiplier potential if financial constraints specific to those regions inhibit induced investment.

REGIONAL BANK MULTIPLIERS WITH A NATIONAL BANKING SYSTEM

The type of regional banking structure denoted above involves regionally-based banks, as in the US. Banks are constrained by the availability of reserves, although the nationwide securities market cushions the system from short-term regional payments imbalance.

For a national banking system, as in the UK, the constraints apply at a national, rather than regional, level. Certainly there is still a degree of regional differentiation in the form of the Scottish and Irish banks, and the relevance for bank multipliers of lower reserve requirements for the Scottish banks before 1971 has indeed been discussed by Gaskin (1965, pp. 192-200). Further there is a degree of regional separability among the non-bank financial intermediaries.[19]

While we have concentrated here on bank behaviour, we could instead have put more emphasis on non-bank portfolio choices. Even without any reaction from the banks, or the branches of national banks, asset-holders (particularly businesses) in each region are constrained by their holdings of liquid assets in the same way as a bank. Any factor causing a bearish switch into Centre assets from Periphery assets has the consequence of reducing borrowers' deposit levels in Periphery and prompting further attempts to increase liquidity. How these effects are multiplied still, of course, depends on the asset-preferences of financial institutions.

It is important to consider the asset behaviour of a nationwide bank not only for the UK but also because the trend, in the US for example, is towards wider branching and closer relationships between different banks. A rather different approach is required from that used here, but some tentative conclusions may be drawn.

Even with a national banking system, there is a strong tendency (noted for example by Morgan, 1973) for capital to flow to the financial centre. The greater this tendency, the lower are deposit levels in peripheral bank branches. This reinforces any tendency (institutionally regulated, or otherwise) for decisions on large loans to be made centrally.

The bank multipliers for particular regions in this type of situation depend crucially on the loan allocation decisions at the centre. Without delving into the many complex issues involved, it is reasonable to suggest that a nationwide bank has less vested interests in lending in a particular area than one whose profit base is the local economy. While the higher liquidity preference of a local bank in such an area relative to a national bank will encourage a lower proportion of loans to total assets, nevertheless there would be that stable proportion reserved in effect for that area.

Thus a national banking system may exacerbate net capital outflows from a region. Such behaviour is efficient to the extent that the assessment of relative returns is correct and also because it increases the national money multiplier (and thereby the banks' profit base). But the judgement as to relative returns may be self-fulfilling if the supply of credit is sufficiently low to discourage investment. The earlier multiplier analysis in the sixth section demonstrated that availability of finance is an effective constraint on investment and income,[20] and thus may contribute to depressing the value of local assets which are dependent on local markets.

A full analysis of regional bank lending allocation is called for. Suffice it to say that the role of finance in influencing the size and composition of national income multipliers *could* be even more effective in a nationwide banking system than one which is regionally based. This could result from the greater ease with which outflows from Peripheral regions could be effected.

CONCLUSION

The foregoing represents a Keynesian analysis of money at the regional level. In showing that financial variables can change regional income levels, it has also been shown that regional financial developments can also alter national aggregates.

While the analysis applies directly to banking systems which are regionally separable, it seems that the general principles developed here can be carried over into a nationwide banking system; how far such a system moderates the forces identified for separable systems and how far they accentuate them cannot be answered here.

But, within the institutional structure studied here, in line with aggregative Keynesian analysis, the income supermultiplier is constrained by availability of finance. The goods and financial markets are interdependent primarily through the role of expectations about the value of all assets, both real and financial. Thus, for example, government transfer payments to inhabitants of declining regions return to the Centre, to finance investment there, if the fact of the transfer does nothing to alter expectations.

Further, for a given monetary base, changes in expectations which increase liquidity preference in Periphery have the consequence of reducing its supply. Similarly an associated reduction in liquidity preference in Centre has the consequence of increasing liquidity there. In this way, financial responses exacerbate the effects of changes in expectations regarding the economic future of a region.

Finally, there is a strong implication of the effect of regional composition on national aggregates. As Keynes (C.W. XXI) pointed out, an increase in aggregate demand caused by government expenditure in a stagnant sector or region increases output more and prices less than the same expenditure in a fully-employed sector or region (as long as the import propensity of the stagnant sector or region is not too high). Similarly, an increase in the monetary base in declining regions increases the aggregate money supply by less than if the monetary base increases in fully-employed regions, less in the fully-employed regions, and less in total.

NOTES

1. See Keynes (*C.W. VII*, Chapter 24) and Keynes (*C.W. XXI*, pp. 109-23).
2. The regional composition of the labour market has been suggested as determining the position of the Phillips curve. See for example Schofield (1974).
3. See Dreese (1974) for a survey of the role of money in the regional economics literature.
4. See, for example, Mundell (1961).
5. This position was set out in the UK 1978 Green Paper on the European Monetary System.
6. See Goodhart (1975, pp. 129-36) for a discussion of the relationship between the multiplier and portfolio approaches.
7. See Robinson (1964, p. 75) for a discussion of Keynes' multiplier concept in a temporal context.
8. The definition of M_2 employed here, bank demand and time deposits, corresponds

broadly to the aggregate defined in the UK as 'M_3'.

9. The precise condition for $\frac{dM_2}{dt} > 0$ is that $r_1 > r_2 - (1-r_2)c$.
10. See Goodhart, op.cit.
11. This phenomenon received attention recently when the overprediction of US money demand suggested a downward shift in the money demand function. This has been explained by the introduction of a variety of banking innovations designed to increase the liquidity of interest-bearing assets and increase the return on liquid assets. See for example Porter *et al.* (1979).
12. Reserve requirements in the US are in fact higher on large banks than smaller banks (and pre-1972 on central reserve city, than other reserve city, and than country banks). The rationale presumably incorporates not only the possibility of greater absolute variability of higher deposit levels, but more importantly the fact that smaller banks hold relatively larger additional operating reserves with larger banks. Nevertheless, the smaller the bank the larger the proportion of assets held in excess reserves. Also the smaller the bank, the larger the proportion of assets held in the form of currency. In practice, then, variability of cash withdrawals may coincide with high liquidity preference, because of the greater instability of payments into and out of a small, open economy. See Board of Governors of the Federal Reserve System (1976) for evidence on the portfolio behaviour of US banks of different classes.
13. The multipliers are calculated using the following equilibrium conditions:
    $(c_c + r_c)\Delta D_c + (c_p + r_p)\Delta D_p = \Delta H$
    $a_{cp}k_c\Delta D_c - a_{pc}k_p\Delta D_p = 0$
    and solving for ΔD_c and ΔD_p, where $m_n = \frac{\Delta D_c + \Delta C_c + \Delta D_p + \Delta C_p}{\Delta H}$,
    I am grateful to Adriana Amado for pointing out an error in the original footnote.
14. The 'location' of the high-powered money injection is most clearly identified in the case of money-financed government expenditure which itself has a regional location. Payment may of course be made into an account of a bank, or head office, in another region. While these variations can be incorporated by separating the real and financial effects of government expenditure, attention is confined here to situations where the money injection is clearly identified regionally.
15. This proposition is confirmed for the regions of the US by Garvy (1959).
16. Useful insights into the relationship between rates of return on physical capital and on financial capital in economies at different stages of development are provided by Khatkhate (1980).
17. Marginal sensitivity may be calculated using the bank multiplier equations (6.5) and (6.6), using the following relationships between bank multipliers and deposit and lending multipliers for each region:
    $m_c^D = \frac{m_c}{1 + c_c}$, $m_c^L = (1 - r_c)m_c^D$, $m_p^D = \frac{m_p}{1 + c_p}$, $m_p^L = (1 - r_p)\, m_p^D$
18. The supermultiplier concept was introduced into regional income multiplier analysis by Wilson (1968). The significance of the savings requirements of induced investment is also pointed out in this chapter.
19. Regional separability of financial institutions is assumed by Goodhart (1975, pp. 278-9) for his model of regional portfolio adjustment.
20. See Gaskin (1960) for a discussion of the structural effects of unavailability of finance for new borrowers attempting to set up business in peripheral regions, who also are treated as marginal relative to established borrowers.

7. The Treatment of Money in Regional Economics

This chapter was published as an article of the same title in the Journal of Regional Science, *27(1), pp. 13-24, 1987.*

INTRODUCTION

Periodic attempts have been made to incorporate financial variables into regional economic models. Four recent attempts have appeared in the pages of the *Journal of Regional Science*: Beare (1976), Fishkind (1977), Roberts and Fishkind (1979) and Moore and Hill (1982). These articles are representative of the progression in thought on the subject, and it is our first aim here to survey that progression. The second aim is to add a further step to the existing analysis, with particular reference to the questions of regional money supply endogeneity or exogeneity, and the independence of the regional supply of and demand for money, or for credit.

Most of the literature refers to the US regions which, historically, have experienced a considerable degree of regional financial separability, not least because of state restrictions on bank branching within and outside home states. This separability has gradually been broken down *de facto* with the development of regional interactions under holding companies, and by means of the correspondent system between banks. Now, regional separability is further breaking down *de jure*, with the gradual elimination of interstate branching restrictions. We will bear these developments in mind in the discussion which follows, not only to ensure the relevance of the US literature to contemporary conditions, but also to consider its relevance to other countries which already have nationwide branch banking.

FROM BEARE TO MOORE AND HILL

Beare's (1976) work is an attempt to assess the monetarist-Keynesian debate in a regional setting. The debate is expressed in the terms of the

Friedman-Meiselman (1963) controversy: is nominal income determined more by the money supply or by autonomous expenditure? In the regional context, Beare specifies the two possibilities as follows: is regional income externally generated by national monetary policy, or internally generated by autonomous expenditure, which is accommodated by capital inflows? Beare tests for the two possibilities by regressing income (nominal and real in turn) of the three Prairie provinces of Canada on the national money stock and provincial farm income (the autonomous expenditure variable).

As Beare himself concludes, this type of reduced form test is unsatisfactory; its fundamental shortcomings were well rehearsed at the time of the Friedman-Meiselman debate (see Ando and Modigliani, 1965 and Chick, 1977, pp. 44-6). However, although the Friedman-Meiselman test itself cannot discriminate between the two hypotheses, Beare's verbal expression of them provides a useful starting point for our analysis. Is regional activity influenced more by exogenously-determined national monetary conditions (so that regional monetary conditions are unimportant for analytical purposes) or is it influenced more by highly elastic interregional capital flows responding to relative changes in regional rates of return? The second hypothesis certainly reflects accurately the absence of monetary variables in standard Keynesian multiplier analysis, which necessitates the assumption that the supply of credit fully accommodates the multiplier and supermultiplier processes. But it is not in fact incompatible with Beare's first hypothesis; it is intersectoral financial flows which constitute the process by which exogenous monetary changes generate monetarist results at both the regional and national levels. All Beare's analysis can hope to discriminate between is whether regional income is influenced more by changes in (national) aggregate demand or by changes in relative regional demand. In fact, Beare's empirical results that *real* regional income is influenced more by national aggregate demand than by relative changes in demand is a very non-monetarist result (contrary to the conclusion drawn by Beare).

A perfectly elastic regional supply of money is central to Fishkind's (1977) analysis of the regional impact of monetary policy. This enquiry requires a more thorough investigation of the relationship between national monetary variables and the regional economy. Fishkind uses the Mundell small open economy model as the basis for analysis; specifically, this model specifies a fixed interest rate, determined outside the economy, which is maintained by inter-economy capital flows. The external balance relationship is thus a horizontal line, at that interest rate, superimposed on the economy's IS-LM relationships. Any tendency for the trade balance to deviate from exactly offsetting the capital account would cause the internal rate to move (down, in the case of an overall balance of payments surplus, and up, in the case of a deficit). Any slight deviation from the national interest rate, however, attracts capital flows (out, in the case of a surplus, and in, in the case of a deficit), which restore interregional payments to balance and the interest rate to the national rate.

Although Fishkind does not explicitly do so, a restrictive national monetary policy would have to be represented by an upward shift in the external balance line, so that it is horizontal at the new, higher, national interest rate. In terms of the Mundell analysis, this would force the regional balance of payments into deficit; capital flows out, reducing the regional money supply until internal interest rates are driven up to the national level, and equilibrium is restored at a lower level of income. As Fishkind shows, using the Indiana economy as a case study, the downward effect on income depends on the interest elasticity of the IS curve.

The Mundell analysis would have to be amended somewhat, however, to apply to national monetary policy and its effects on regions. Clearly, not all regions can simultaneously experience capital outflows. (If the 'national' interest rate is high, these regional outflows cannot correspond to a net national outflow.) The process must rather be expressed as follows. Restrictive national monetary policy pushes up the national interest rate *at the same time as* reducing regional money supplies. Regional interest rates thus move immediately to the higher level. To pursue this further, we must specify more carefully the process by which the regional money supply is determined.

The standard specification of the money market in Mundell-type models involves a money supply made up of an exogenous component determined by the monetary authorities and an endogenous component corresponding to imbalance of regional payments; a surplus involves additions to the regional money supply, and a deficit, reductions. For national economies, with separate currencies and a monetary authority, an exogenously-determined component of the money supply is defensible, although not at all indisputable. Monetary authorities may choose not to control the money supply, and, even if they do so choose, what constitutes money may change as a result, eluding control. (See Moore, 1979a and Kaldor, 1983a.) If in fact the monetary authorities choose to maintain a given interest rate, then the LM curve and the external balance curve collapse into one, horizontal, line at that interest rate. The domestic component of the money supply may still, however, be distinguished from the component corresponding to changes in foreign exchange reserves.

For regions the distinction between the two components of the money supply is more difficult to identify. Certainly, Federal Reserve Districts allow precise identification of interdistrict flows. But the smaller the region, and the more financial institutions operate across regional boundaries, the more blurred the distinction becomes. However, if in fact capital flows are not perfect interregionally, then there is more scope for identifying regional financial markets and thus something corresponding to a regional money supply.

This is the possibility explored by Roberts and Fishkind (1979), inspired by L?sch's (1954) analysis of regional differentials in the cost of credit. They use a choice-theoretic model whereby individuals select portfolios which equalise marginal rates of return on all assets, not of transaction costs, and adjusted for risk. Because of regional patterns in transactions costs, risk and attitudes to risk, it is possible to identify distinct regional markets in each asset, such that the market rate of interest can diverge from the national rate. In particular, regional demand for and supply of an asset will be less elastic, over a wider range of interest rates, the higher are information costs, risk and risk aversion. If the LM curve for a region is derived, as Roberts and Fishkind suggest, from an aggregation of all asset markets within the region, its elasticity and its propensity to shift will vary regionally, as will the equilibrium interest rate. (Unfortunately, the exact formulation of the LM curve is not specified.) Roberts and Fishkind suggest, as a result, that national monetary policy can have differential regional impacts not only because of different interest elasticities of the regional IS curve, but also because of different elasticities and positions of the regional LM curve.

These regional differences are ascribed by Roberts and Fishkind to market imperfections, although financial markets must in fact be efficient if interest rates adjusted for risk and transactions costs are equalised. Moore and Hill (1982) take much further the analysis of market imperfections, in the form of institutional impediments to arbitrage among assets of different regions. They choose to portray the differential between the cost of credit from small, local financial institutions and that from the national market (in the form of large institutions in the financial centre) as a mark-up charged by the former. The national financial market is thus depicted as being segmented between small and large institutions. The national interest rate is determined by the demand for and supply of loanable funds within the large institutions. Interest costs for borrowers from small, local institutions are determined by the demand for and supply of credit within the local market with two important qualifications: if the local credit base is too small to meet demand, local institutions must borrow nationally, charging a mark-up on the national rate (this borrowing is subject to a ceiling determined by the local institutions' capital base); but if the local market only supports a rate much lower than the national rate, the local institutions' assets (other than a politically-necessary minimum) will be invested in instruments outside the region. In other words, strong local credit demand relative to the local credit base faces a higher rate of interest than the national rate, and ultimately a credit ceiling, while weak credit demand relative to the deposit base will go largely unmet. These possibilities of unsatisfied demand for credit capture more satisfactorily the market imperfections associated with regional differences than do the interest rate differentials of Roberts and Fishkind's analysis.

Moore and Hill's use of the bank multiplier as the determinant of the local credit base is helpful for understanding the regional money supply process. Total deposits are shown to be a multiple of primary deposits, which are either regional 'outside money' being liabilities of the monetary authority, or a net inflow from a balance of payments surplus. The multiplier is greater the lower the reserve ratio of local banks, the lower their propensity to invest in assets outside the region and the lower the non-bank public's propensity to make payments outside the region. The desired deposit total, they suggest, is determined by personal income. By implication, excess deposit holdings would lead to leakages which would restore holdings to the desired level, while inadequate holdings would lead to reduced leakages. (Like Roberts and Fishkind, Moore and Hill do not fully specify their diagrams. As a result there appears to be a difficulty in that investment in outside assets is shown in the diagrams as the residual of the local credit base, once local demand has been met. Yet the multiplier analysis shows that this residual in turn must constitute a leakage from local bank reserves and thus reduce the overall size of the credit base, and the local deposit total.)

Referring back to the Mundell model, dividing the regional money supply into an exogenous component and a balance of payments component now appears to take on a particular character for regions. The money supply is made up of a stock of reserves, grossed up by the multiplier. Thus all endogenous components of the balance of payments (systematic propensities to import and to buy outside assets, for example) are incorporated in the multiplier. Exogenous components of the balance of payments (an increase in export demand, or a changed preference for outside assets, for example) would be reflected in a change in reserves. But not all reserves may be treated as exogenous. If the local demand for credit is strong, so that local banks borrow on the national market in order to meet this demand, there is an inflow of reserves (possibly, ultimately from the monetary authority) in response to the demand for credit.

The typical Mundell specification of the money supply is:

$$M^s = \overline{M^s} + \Delta R \tag{7.1}$$

where $\overline{M^s}$ is the exogenous, domestic component of the money supply, an dΔR is the change in reserves. What the multiplier analysis suggests is, rather (using Moore and Hill's notation):

$$M_r = mB \tag{7.2}$$

where M_r is the regional money supply, m the bank multiplier and B the monetary base, where:

$$m = m(r, i_o, F_r) \tag{7.3}$$

where r is the reserve ratio, i_o the propensity of banks to invest outside the region, which in turn is a function of the regional demand for credit, and F_r the propensity of the non-bank public to spend in the region. But, in addition, what we are suggesting here is that:

$$B = B\,(H_r, \overline{F}_r, C_r^d) \tag{7.4}$$

where H_r is liabilities of the monetary authority, the vehicle for monetary policy, $\overline{F}_r$ is the exogenous component of the balance of payments, and C_r^d is the regional demand for credit. Thus the regional demand for credit influences both the multiplier and the multiplicand. Once it is accepted that both the multiplier and the multiplicand are partly endogenous, however, multiplier analysis loses some of its analytical appeal (a point originally expressed by Tobin, 1963).

In the next section, we will pursue the implications of the influence of the demand for credit on the regional money supply. But at the same time we will return the analysis to the context of the money market. Both Roberts and Fishkind, and Moore and Hill, in their different ways, analyse the interest rate as the cost of credit, determined in the market for loanable funds. The LM curve, in Roberts and Fishkind's analysis, is derived from an (unspecified) aggregation of all asset markets. For Moore and Hill, money is, implicitly, demanded for transactions purposes only, excluding the possibility of an asset demand for money. In other words, both sets of authors set their analysis within loanable funds theory, thus excluding Keynesian liquidity preference theory. The following analysis will be couched instead in Keynesian terms. This involves retaining the emphasis on the cost and availability of credit, but deriving these credit conditions from the state of liquidity preference.

A KEYNESIAN THEORY OF REGIONAL FINANCIAL MARKETS

Beare characterised Keynesian models as deriving output from demand rather than supply conditions; changes in output result from changes in autonomous elements of demand, amplified by the multiplier process. Supply constraints are thus regarded by Keynesians as being of limited importance for regions, if there is a high degree of interregional factor mobility.

While this accurately reflects much of the Keynesian regional literature, it is not necessarily in the spirit of Keynes' own theoretical perspective, particularly as it concerned financial markets. The importance of finance in *The General Theory* derived from its capacity to inhibit productive activity. The provision of finance for both productive and unproductive activity was generated within markets serving the goal of financial accumulation. In particular, the rate of interest was a monetary variable, equating the supply and demand for money, not a real variable, equating saving and investment. A rate of interest set too high would cause output to settle below the full employment level.

At the national level, the demand for money is not only a transactions demand, but also a speculative demand. Demand increases when expectations are strong of rising interest rates (and falling capital values) or when confidence in expectations in general is weak. The supply of money is determined by the behaviour of those institutions whose liabilities are conventionally regarded as money. New deposits are created as a counterpart to credit creation. But financial institutions are not simply passive in the face of demand for credit; they too are influenced by their own liquidity preference in general, and by their expectations as to their borrowers' credit-worthiness in particular. A general, economy-wide increase in liquidity preference, then, reduces the willingness of financial institutions to extend credit. If the rise in liquidity preference is the result of a generalised fall in asset values that is an economic downturn, then demand for credit to fund highly-geared asset purchases and for working capital may not be satisfied, further fuelling the downturn.

In order to assess the relevance of this argument for regional economies, let us take the state of theory as set out by Moore and Hill as our starting point. We assume, therefore, that regional financial markets are segmented in such a way that small businesses in regions distant from the financial centre do not have access to the national financial market, only to their local financial institutions. When these institutions want to lend beyond their capacity, they borrow on the national market on behalf of their clients, up to a limit imposed by their capitalisation, charging a mark-up on the national rate. Local demand for credit is strong during periods of regional expansion, to finance investment, but also to finance working capital when the regional economy is weak.

In such conditions, where availability of credit is never assured, liquidity preference will be high. For the non-bank public, this means not only a relatively high preference for holding bank deposits, but also a preference for any longer-term investment to be in national securities rather than local regional assets. This latter preference is manifested both in a lowering of the price of regional assets, and in the value of the regional bank multiplier. For the banks, high liquidity preference will also be manifest in a preference for national over local assets, that is in a reduced bank multiplier together with a reduced local supply of credit (which reinforces the non-bank public's liquidity preference). Together, these two sets of reactions will make more likely Moore and Hill's case of unsatisfied local demand for credit.

This situation may be depicted in Figure 7.1 which is an adaptation of their Figure 4. Moore and Hill start in the North-East quadrant, with regional personal income, Y_0 determining demand and time-deposit holdings $(D_r + T_r)$. These in turn, in the North-West quadrant, determine, after the retention of required reserves, the assets available for placing as local credit (CR_r) or outside investment (I_o). The particular level of regional income therefore places a ceiling on local credit availability which, in this case, is below local credit demand (in the South-West quadrant) at the interest rate determined in the national credit market (plus mark-up), as portrayed in the South-East quadrant. The difference, AB, is made up by funds borrowed from outside the region.

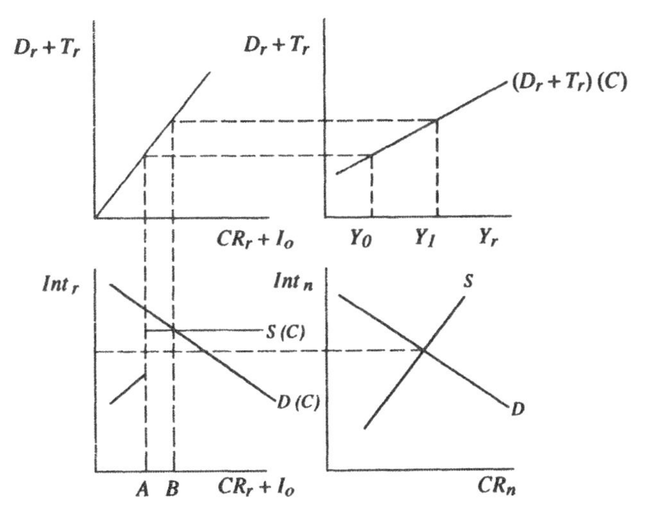

Figure 7.1 The Determination of Regional Credit, Deposits and Income

Here, we show the demand for deposits, the demand for credit and the supply of credit as being a function of C, confidence in the expected value of local assets. A Keynesian interpretation of the process would start in the South-West quadrant. The vertical portion of the supply of credit curve is determined by the previous period's behaviour. The short-fall in local credit is made up by borrowed funds, AB, so that the total deposit creation is thereby increased to a level which is consistent with regional income Y_1. If I_o were to represent net outward investment, regional deposit creation would be reduced accordingly. Thus, $(D_r + T_r)$ is determined by the intersection of the local supply and demand curves for credit in our model.

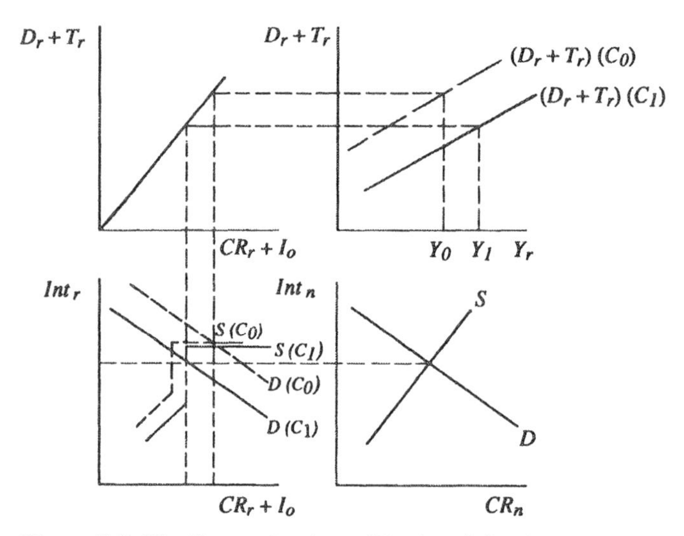

Figure 7.2 The Determination of Regional Credit, Deposits and Income with a Shift in Confidence

The significance of the dependence of the supply and demand for credit and liquidity preference on the state of confidence may be seen from the following comparison. The higher the propensity on behalf of either or both of the non-bank public and the banks to invest in outside assets rather than local assets, the lower the bank multiplier *and* multiplicand. Thus, a wave of pessimism about the local economy will shift the vertical portion of the supply curve to the left, as shown by the hatched line in Figure 7.2. (The new, more pessimistic, stock of confidence is denoted C_0, as compared with C_1). At the same time, it shifts to the left the overall supply of credit function, because of higher expected default risk at any given interest rate. The demand for credit function will also, initially, shift to the right as demand for working capital and for credit to fund earlier short-term loans increases. (Eventually, bankruptcies will reduce this demand for credit.) The interaction of the two curves comes perilously close to the maximum supply allowed by the local banks' capitalisation (represented by the right-hand, terminal point of the supply curve). The interest charge on credit, as long as it is available, continues to be determined by a mark-up on the national interest rate.

Meanwhile, moving round the figure in a clockwise direction, the amount of local credit which the banks decide to extend determines the level of local deposits. But a higher level of liquidity preference, shown by an upward shift in $(D_r + T_r)$, means that this deposit level is now compatible only with a lower level of regional income, Y_0. The process by which income is reduced is the multiplier-accelerator effects of a reduced willingness of local businesses to invest, given their reduced confidence in the region's prospects, coupled with the increasing difficulties they experience in maintaining existing employment as working capital becomes more inaccessible.

This adaptation of Moore and Hill's analysis, reversing the direction of causation and introducing the state of confidence in the region's assets as a determinant of the level of credit, deposits and income thus provides a theory of regional finance more compatible with Keynesian monetary theory. Let us now consider the relevance of the financial institutional structure. In particular, does a higher degree of financial integration between regions, in the form of branch banking, alter these conclusions? A major consequence of interregional branching is that local branches can finance local credit beyond their own capacity, as measured by the bank multiplier, by borrowing from Head Office rather than the national market in general. Lending beyond strict capacity, therefore, should not carry a penal interest rate. In fact, the national rate structure, across branches, would normally be uniform. Does this suggest a horizontal supply curve, in all regional markets, at the national interest rate, that is a perfectly elastic supply of credit?

First, the uniform nationwide interest rate structure allows for a regional pattern in rates charged within that structure. In particular, rates will be higher the higher the perceived default risk. Therefore the position of the horizontal supply curve will vary among regions, depending on the banks' confidence in returns within each region. Second, the rate of leakage of reserves from each region (and thus each branch's bank multiplier) does not generally act as a constraint on any branch's credit creation. Nevertheless, weak deposit growth relative to credit expansion is an indicator of the state of the local economy. A low bank multiplier for a particular branch may thus result in limitations on credit creation imposed by Head Office. Certainly, no branch could expand credit indefinitely, within the normal practice of branch banking, if there are doubts about local credit-worthiness. For regions caught in a low credit growth/low income growth vicious circle, therefore, the horizontal supply curve will have a relatively low terminal point.

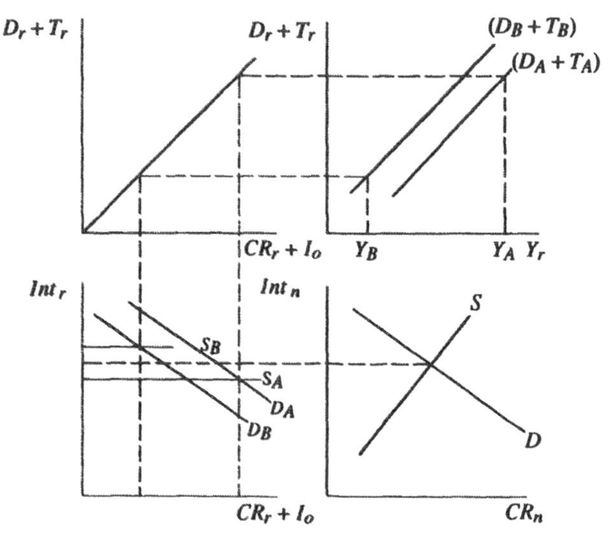

Figure 7.3 Interregional Comparison of Credit, Deposits and Income Determination, with Branch Banking

The case of a prosperous region, *A* (with a high state of confidence, in the value of local assets) is compared in Figure 7.3 with the case of a depressed region, *B* (with a low state of confidence). Region *A* is characterised by a higher demand for credit, because of the high level of perceived local investment opportunities, a supply of credit lower than average on the interest-rate structure (because of low perceived default risk) and low liquidity preference (low $(D_A + T_A)$ relative to Y) because of optimism about high yields on longer term assets. Region *B*, in contrast, is higher than average in the interest charge structure because of high perceived default risk, and is also subject to a low credit ceiling (S_B has a terminal point close to the vertical axis). Liquidity preference, however, is high. As a result, region *A*'s income is much higher than that in Region *B*.

Note that the positions of the curves are based on conventional perceptions of expected yields and default risk. As both Roberts and Fishkind, and Moore and Hill, point out, spatial remoteness of small rural communities is subject to information problems regarding assessment of yields. To the extent that reference must now be made to Head Office, outside such regions, for credit expansion beyond a particular level, these information problems could bite harder than within a unit banking system. For prosperous remote regions there will be benefits from having access to a nationwide pool of bank funds, rather than being subject to the limited borrowing capacity, on their behalf, of local unit banks. But for depressed, remote regions, the lack of availability of credit could become even more severe.

CONCLUSION

The literature dealing with the relevance of financial variables for regional economies has tended to follow the lead of monetarist theory as applied to small open economies. This was understandable, given the conventional assumption of Keynesian regional economics that the supply of funds to a region is perfectly elastic at a nationally-determined interest rate. This juxtaposition of monetarist and Keynesian theory was the basis of Beare's analysis.

Within a Mundell-type open economy framework, then, as employed explicitly by Fishkind, and Roberts and Fishkind, regional economic differences take the form of regional interest rate differences, and different interest elasticities of regional expenditure. These interest rate differences in turn are the consequence of regional patterns in portfolio preference. These theoretical developments contribute an explanation of regional diversity which is more realistic than the apparent homogeneity of monetarist macroeconomics. It is also consistent with the trend in macroeconomics to deal specifically with microeconomic diversity, and makes some sense of this diversity by suggesting that it conforms to a regional pattern.

Moore and Hill go further than Roberts and Fishkind in introducing market imperfections as an explanation of differences in regional financial conditions. Rather than simply causing differential price responses, the Moore and Hill imperfections actually segment markets, so that the differential availability of credit becomes more significant than its price. The theoretical framework, however, is still monetarist in the chain of causation: income levels determine deposit levels which in turn determine the local credit base, which is apportioned to local credit and outside investment predominantly on choice-theoretic grounds.

The adaptation of Moore and Hill's diagrammatic presentation developed here retains their account of market imperfections and suggests a common variable on which both the supply of credit and its demand are dependent: the state of confidence in the value of local assets. The resulting local credit availability determines how much money, or liquidity, is available relative to the current state of liquidity preference. A shortage of liquidity raises the demand for credit and reduces its supply, pushing up interest rates and further reducing the level of credit. The interest rate is thus determined by monetary conditions, but influences the level of output and employment through the cost and availability of credit.

Branch banking rather than unit banking was shown to render the credit supply curve horizontal, as in the standard Keynesian model. But its position and length are still variable regionally, generating results similar to those for a unit banking system. The main difference would be in reducing the credit availability constraint on prosperous regions, but strengthening it on depressed regions.

Finally, the above analysis allows further consideration of the question of the exogeneity or endogeneity of the regional money supply. The Mundell representation suggests a strict dichotomy between the exogeneity of the domestic money supply and the endogeneity of changes due to a net imbalance of payments. For regions without monetary authorities or separate currencies, the dichotomy is more difficult to define. The regional money supply is made up of an existing stock of bank reserves, grossed up by a multiplier whose parameters are partly endogenous and partly exogenous, plus changes in reserves due to action by the national monetary authority, and to net imbalance of interregional payments (partly endogenous and partly exogenous). The implications of the resulting confusion were evident from Moore and Hill's argument in terms of their diagrams where no feedback was allowed for from the decision to invest bank assets outside the region. The distinction between endogeneity and exogeneity becomes even more clouded in the case of a branch banking system, where an important component of interregional capital flows consists of book entry debits and credits between bank branches and their Head Offices.

Roberts and Fishkind, and Moore and Hill, were on the right track in looking at credit rather than money. That, after all, is the significant variable for expenditure in the regional economy. But they were on the wrong track in deriving credit, then, from the regional money supply (whose function is shown as fulfilling only a transactions demand). Money rather than credit is indeed important, but as a satisfier of liquidity preference. In the tradition of the Radcliffe Report (1959), it is more satisfactory analytically to focus on the interest rate as the price of liquidity, than on some notion of a stock of liquidity. The importance of liquidity preference is in determining the interest rate charged on credit, and the availability of credit.

8. Incorporating Money in Regional Economic Models

This paper was originally published in F. J. Harrigan and P. G. McGregor (eds.), Recent Advances in Regional Economic Modelling, London Papers in Regional Science, *vol. 19, pp. 208-18, 1988, Pion Ltd., London. It benefited from comments from the editors and from Philip Arestis.*

INTRODUCTION

Why should money be incorporated into regional economic models? That is by no means an empty question. Theorising and modelling inevitably involve simplification, and the argument for climbing Everest need not apply: just because money is there we are not obliged to include it in our theories and models. The judgement of most regional economists, to go by the literature, would appear to be that abstracting from money in a regional context is a useful simplification.

The purpose of this chapter is to discuss the role of money in the process of regional economic development, and how that might be incorporated into regional economic models. I start with a general discussion of the arguments for and against the inclusion of money in macroeconomic theories and models. The differing approaches inherent in these arguments are then related to the specific field of regional economics. The four approaches identified are: Walrasian general equilibrium theory, non-Walrasian general equilibrium (or disequilibrium) theory, post-Kaleckian monetary theory, and Post Keynesian monetary theory. The last of these approaches will be considered in greater depth in the fourth section, and the possibilities of using a modelling technique to capture it are discussed in the penultimate, fifth section.

THE MACROECONOMIC SIGNIFICANCE OF MONEY

Much of macroeconomic theory is conducted in real terms: variables are expressed in real rather than nominal terms, the demand for money (if considered at all) is a real transactions demand, and the interest rate is a real variable, bringing about equality between saving and investment. The justification for this can be found in Walras' law, which states that, if $(n-1)$ of n markets are in equilibrium, the nth market too must be in equilibrium. If we classify the money market as the nth market, then in equilibrium analysis of all other markets we can simply assume equilibrium in the money market without analysing it. (The same argument could be applied equally to any market or markets.) Indeed, as long as all markets are presumed to clear in the Walrasian manner, the very rationale for the existence of money is open to question (for example, see Hahn, 1981, pp. 17-18). Its only macroeconomic role lies in the relationship (via the quantity theory of money) between the exogenously-determined money stock and the general price level.

Non-Walrasian general equilibrium theory (also referred to as disequilibrium theory or neo-classical theory) accepts the Walrasian results, but only as applying to longrun equilibrium. The mechanism by which the quantity theory result obtains is one of short-term disequilibrium. Thus it is important to include money in theory and modelling in order to understand this disequilibrium process. Exogenous changes in the money supply can move the economy away from its full-employment equilibrium state, and indeed cause cycles. This approach can be represented by an IS-LM system, whereby the particular impact of a money-supply increase can be determined by reference to the interest (and income) elasticities of demand for money and for final output. But, when combined with an aggregate demand-aggregate supply framework, to generate the full-employment long-run general equilibrium solution, financial variables cease to have any real significance, just as in the Walrasian system. (The practical relevance of long-run equilibrium is, however, doubted by many neo-classicists, not least on the issue of the capacity of the system to adjust to such equilibria.)

Money appears to be given a stronger role in these neo-classical models, in disequilibrium, than in what might be called post-Kaleckian models (following Arestis, 1987), in spite of Keynes' own emphasis on money. This difference in fact stems from a different view of the process of money creation; whereas in neo-classical theory the money supply is presumed to be exogenous, in post-Kaleckian theory it is regarded as endogenous. Kaldor (1970a; 1970b; 1981; 1982) and Moore (1979b; 1983; 1984a) see the lender-of-last-resort function of the monetary authorities as being a necessary feature of advanced financial systems, which allows the supply of bank reserves to be demand determined. They argue further, that attempts by the monetary authorities to discourage demand for reserves (by raising their price) simply encourages the emergence of new forms of money and new ways of economising on its use. The role of the monetary authorities is to set the discount rate, which then influences the whole structure of interest rates, and thereby influences total expenditure. The only modelling of the money market is required since the price is set by the authorities. The chain of causation from expenditure plans to credit creation (given the set interest rate) to deposit creation focuses attention on the expenditure plans rather than on the money market.

Post Keynesian theory approaches the question of 'incorporating' money in theory and models rather differently. Keynes (*C.W. XXIX*) explicitly discussed the significance of analysing monetary production economies, as opposed to barter or cooperative economies (see Rotheim, 1981). In particular, if the primary motivation within a modern economy was monetary accumulation, then money should be at the heart of theorising, not an optional addition. The primary determinant of output and employment is effective demand, of which investment is a key component. If the demand for finance for purchasing new capital goods and the supply of finance are both subject to liquidity preference, given the fundamental nature of the uncertainty surrounding investment planning, then liquidity preference should be central to any theory of output and employment (see Shackle, 1974, p. 28). Thus to the beginning of the post-Kaleckian chain of causation is added the state of liquidity preference; this is prior to decisions about expenditure on new or secondhand capital goods, new or secondhand financial assets, all of which can engender new credit.

We have, then, identified four different approaches to the question of theorising with or without money. Of these, the Walrasian approach supports simplification to real analysis; the post-Kaleckian approach regards credit as being important, but in almost passive response to expenditure plans; disequilibrium and Post Keynesian theory regard monetary variables as actively important, but for very different reasons.

Where these last two differ most significantly is in their use of the concept of equilibrium. For disequilibrium theory, market-clearing equilibrium is the benchmark, which applies in a theoretical longrun and, possible in an historically temporal longrun; in this longrun, financial variables cease to have significance. For Post Keynesian theory, equilibrium is used in a partial sense, or as a process of gravitation in historical time, but without any requirements of market clearing, or indeed any form of simultaneity. (See Dow, 1985, Chapter 5 for a full discussion of these distinctions.) The endemic short-run importance of money, then, extends to the longrun in Post Keynesian theory. This distinction is crucial in an analysis of the factors contributing to persistent (that is, long-run) regional economic disparities. In the next section, these two approaches which suggest the importance of incorporating money in national models will be discussed explicitly in terms of regional economics (with aspects of post-Kaleckian thought incorporated into the Post Keynesian account).

MONEY AND REGIONAL ECONOMICS

Regional economics is concerned both with micro - and with macro-questions. Into the first category would fall questions about location of establishments, the relative performance of different firms and industries, demographic patterns, and so on. But questions about the state of regional economies as a whole are macro-questions; it is on these that we will focus our attention here. In particular, regional economics in this sense focuses on regional differences: in rates of unemployment, in percapita incomes, and in rates of growth of percapita income.

The nature of these differences severely limits the relevance of Walrasian general equilibrium theory, since involuntary unemployment is ruled out by market clearing, factor mobility between regions eliminates differences in factor returns (for given endowments of skills, etc.), and the rate of growth of real income is uniform nationwide, in equilibrium. Courchene (1981) insists that regional differences in income and employment are the equilibrium responses to differences in the public-sector presence in each region. But this explanation leaves unexplained the historical evidence of regional differences before the emergence of the public sector as a significant macroeconomic force.

The disequilibrium neo-classical approach offers more promise of relevance to regional problems which can in fact be classified as disequilibrium problems. Indeed, disequilibrium analysis at the macrolevel gains from regional analysis, in that regional differences in money illusion and expectations formation, and in factor mobility, can impede the return to market-clearing equilibrium (for example, see Archibald, 1969; Lipsey, 1960). Within this framework, the most obvious model for incorporating money into regional analysis is the small open-economy model associated with global monetarism. With the assumption of fixed exchange rates and perfect capital mobility (which is seen as paralleling the uniform currency situation of regions), this shows that small open economies lose all monetary independence. The supply of money is completely endogenous at the internationally set interest rate, in the case of national economies, or the national rate in the case of regional economies. If there is an excess demand for money in a region, it can be met in the national money market at the going rate; similarly an excess supply of money corrects itself as the excess flows out in payment for imported goods or securities. The region has no monetary identity.

There is still scope for disequilibrium analysis of monetary conditions in the region. The first possibility of regional differences, in spite of uniform national monetary conditions, is a regionally distinct interest elasticity of demand for expenditure (see Fishkind, 1977). Then changes in national monetary conditions can be seen to have different regional impacts, depending on whether demand in any region is or is not interest elastic. If long-run equilibrium is reached, however, either factor mobility eliminates any differences in factor markets, if the monetary shock reflected an event which altered the long-run equilibrium, or the differences are reversed when the short-term effects of the monetary shock are eradicated as money illusion disperses.

The second possibility is that the assumption of perfect capital mobility is unwarranted, that is, there is some regional segmentation in financial markets (for example, see Roberts and Fishkind, 1979). Regional segmentation implies the possibility of regional differences in interest rates and/or rationing. This segmentation would affect credit availability and cost for those firms dependent on local financial institutions, although not necessarily for those with access to national financial markets. Regional financial segmentation can also be extended to the demand-for-money side, with different patterns of demand for money and non-money assets determining the regional pattern of capital flows, and thus the cash base of regional financial institutions.

Partial equilibrium analysis, which allows for general disequilibrium in the (theoretical or temporal) shortrun, can demonstrate the differing regional consequences of segmentation. In particular, regional differences in loan charges and/or credit rationing will constrain expenditure in some regions, causing income and wealth differentials (see Chapter 7 of this volume; Harrigan and McGregor, 1987; Moore and Hill, 1982; Roberts and Fishkind, 1979). But, if these models were to be extended into a general equilibrium framework, the interrelationship between real and monetary variables would be eradicated. In equilibrium, all expectations would be realised, so that interest-rate differentials would reflect objective risk. To the extent that rationing constrained expenditure in any region, factor prices in that region would fall, encouraging demand for their services either in that region or elsewhere, restoring their returns to parity. Regional income and wealth per capita would therefore be restored also to parity. To the extent that the theoretical longperiod and the temporal longrun are interchangeable concepts, historically persistent regional differentials cannot be explained by financial variables within a general equilibrium framework. (It is in fact not clear how anything can explain persistent differentials in such a framework.)

If the break is made from a full-employment long-run equilibrium, then an analysis of institutional determination of credit availability, of price and wage-setting, etc., accords sufficiently closely with post-Kaleckian analysis to be absorbed under that umbrella. The focus of post-Kaleckian analysis on effective demand, given an endogenous supply of finance, has been applied explicitly in the regional context by Kaldor (1970a; 1970b) and Thirlwall (1980). The national rate of interest is taken as given by the monetary authorities, and all demand for credit (and money) is met at that price. The rate of interest is important in that it may limit effective demand to a level below that which ensures full employment. But more important is the process of cumulative causation, whereby the rate of return on investment in regions which happen (because of old wealth) to start with an advantage increases as a result of increased investment. In other words, there are dynamic economies of scale, whereby growth generates productivity growth. Correspondingly, regions which start with a productivity disadvantage attract less investment, and the disadvantage becomes entrenched. There is no need within such a framework to model financial markets explicitly, because they are not seen as contributing significantly to this unstable process. The modelling framework, however, is one of partial equilibrium and trends, in that the focus is on instability rather than stability. Unrealised expectations are not ruled out, therefore, or the role of liquidity preference in the face of uncertainty, both of which are given a high profile in Post Keynesian theory.

Post Keynesian theory regards money as being endemically important to the economic process, whether at a national, international, or regional level. There is no readily identifiable Post Keynesian regional economic theory as such, although both cumulative causation theory and dependency theory have elements in common with Post Keynesian development theory in general (see Chick and Dow, 1988). There is a potential conflict between the two, however, in that cumulative causation theory suggests growth of prosperous regions at the expense of poor regions, whereas dependency theory analyses the dependence inherent in the growth of poor regions. Both do have in common the fact that they are theories of dynamic process, with no concept of static equilibrium. To the extent that they involve a concept of dynamic equilibrium, it is an equilibrium defined in historical time (which is irreversible). Neither, therefore, can be captured by a general equilibrium system, where equilibrium is defined in mechanical time, and processes are reversible. As far as the role of financial variables is concerned, the notions of credit rationing, market segmentation, and liquidity preference can be outlined in the partial equilibrium frameworks of Chapter 7 of this volume and Harrigan and McGregor (1987). The question arises therefore as to how far this type of analysis is adequate to the task, and how far shunning the concept of general equilibrium poses modelling problems.

What is suggested by this brief consideration of modelling money according to the four macroeconomic approaches, with a regional framework, is that money has a significant regional role to play only outside the constraints of general equilibrium, whether Walrasian or non-Walrasian. Otherwise its significance is that of an input to production, where regional elasticities of demand differ, as they may do for any other input. The question remains as to how money should be incorporated in a modelling framework without general equilibrium. The discussion above of money in a regional model using a Post Keynesian approach was very brief. In the next section this case is considered in much more detail, since it is the only approach explicitly to allow the short-run real effects of financial variables to extend into the longrun. (The same is true, but much more implicitly, for post-Kaleckian theory.)

MONEY IN A POST KEYNESIAN REGIONAL MODEL

The importance of money in Post Keynesian models arises from the importance for investment expenditure of liquidity preference, of which the availability of credit is but one manifestation. If we define money in its broad sense (that is, including interest-bearing deposits, as long as they are readily accessible for financing expenditure), the demand for it at a given level of income is determined by a preference not to hold less liquid assets. Such a preference might arise from expectation of capital loss from non-money assets, or from uncertainty as to what to expect, that is, a lack of confidence.

Keynes (*C.W. VII*, p. 166) expressed liquidity preference, for expositional purposes, as a choice between money and a much broader range of assets; households, firms (to a markedly growing extent), and financial institutions all hold a range of assets: physical assets (or title to them in the form of shares or collateral), securities of various kinds, and money. A rise in liquidity preference, which increases the demand for money, depresses the price of all other assets. In particular, a rise in liquidity preference encourages capital outflows to the financial centre, where the most liquid assets are issued. This reduces the redeposit ratio in the financial institutions of the peripheral region, reducing their ability to extend credit, just as the increase in their own liquidity preference reduces their willingness to commit their assets to advances to local industry (see Chapter 6 of this volume). The reverse process applies to a region experiencing increasing confidence in expected returns on assets, which reduces liquidity preference among asset holders and suppliers of credit. (See Dow and Dow, 1988, for an analysis of this process at the national level, and Chapter 5 of this volume for an international treatment.)

In terms of the money market, then, there is an interdependence between demand and supply. As soon as the supply of credit is analysed endogenously, then demand and supply may be interdependent in the sense that both respond to the interest rate. It is conventional at the macrolevel to show demand for money as a negative function of the interest rate, and supply as a positive function of the interest rate. Within a national banking system, it is still possible to show the supply of credit to a region as a positive function of the national rate of interest for the same reasons (portfolio choice of financial institutions being a function of the interest rate). But the interdependence suggested above refers to shifts both in the demand schedules and in the supply schedules, whatever they are, in response to changes in liquidity preference (or confidence in expectations as to the value of relevant assets). The specific interdependence arises from the fact that asset choices of the non-bank public directly affect the capacity of banks to extend credit, at the same time as banks themselves will be subject to similar influences in their asset choice.

Interdependence of demand and supply causes modelling problems of various kinds. First, there is an identification problem, as well as one of observational equivalence. If an increase in liquidity preference is unlikely to be satisfied because the same underlying forces reduce the supply of liquidity, then observed holdings of liquidity will not significantly change; the same applies to a reduction in liquidity preference coinciding with an overabundant supply of liquidity. Demand and supply functions are both difficult to identify. The resulting apparent stability of observed holdings of liquidity would be equally consistent with a theory based on perfectly elastic regional supply of money and a stable pattern of demand (see Cooley and LeRoy, 1981).

The identification problem is less serious, econometrically, if there is a discriminating variable, which shifts one of the two curves, but not the other. Then there is some chance of estimating the other curve by the shifts caused by this variable. But this procedure requires the possibility of specifying the interdependent shifts also. If the interdependence arises from the common effects of a shift in confidence, then some measure of confidence is required. Proxies for the state of confidence are possible: investment intentions, share prices, new credit, all specific to the region. But these proxies are also variables which are the outcome of the effect of changes in confidence on the demand for liquidity and its supply, thus adding to the analytical difficulties involved.

Further, it was suggested that the increase in liquidity preference of financial institutions in declining regions might be manifested in rationing credit as well as in increasing its price. Thus observed credit creation may reflect a position on the supply curve, but not on the demand curve. To the extent that rationing occurs, the identification problem is exacerbated.

The final issue refers to the interest-rate variable. It is legitimate to use one interest rate as being representative of the entire structure of interest rates, if that structure has some deterministic basis. In particular, it is legitimate to use a national interest rate in regional analysis if any regional differentials exactly offset regional differences in objective risk. Then the expected return across regions is the same. But as soon as uncertainty is recognised as being inherent in any process of risk assessment, then regional differentials in loan rates in particular may provide a clue to regional differences in liquidity preference. Thus an increased risk premium in a particular region could be identified as resulting from increased liquidity preference on the part of both borrower and lender. The difficulty first of obtaining actual loan-rate data, and then of establishing an estimate for 'objective risk' (to eliminate the 'objective risk' premium from the interest-rate differential) may however prove intractable.

It may seem from this discussion of problems with modelling the interdependent supply and demand framework of the Post Keynesian approach that the prospects are bleak. This would only be a reasonable conclusion, however, if the modelling technique were to require a general equilibrium benchmark. But the Post Keynesian approach does not accord with general equilibrium theory, since the emphasis is on evolutionary change in historical time, with an irreversible past and an uncertain future.

This is not to suggest that there is no notion of equilibrium in Post Keynesian theory. There is the related notion of norms, which are the conventions by which uncertainty is handled by economic agents (see Keynes, *C.W. XIV*, pp. 109-23). Thus, if the norm is one of regional balance, assured perhaps by active regional policy on the part of central government, then the reaction to diverging regional trends in asset prices would be an equilibrating one, with capital attracted by falling asset prices, thereby reversing the fall. But if there is no such norm, or if such a norm is challenged by actual events, then behaviour will be disequilibrating. Since these norms are the result of social convention, and subject to discrete shifts, a theoretical focus on equilibrium as an organising concept may be seriously misleading.

The alternative modelling approach, then, is to use a partial rather than a general concept of equilibrium, in an attempt to capture aspects of a complex historical process, without tying the system down to simultaneity. Although this limits the apparent explanatory power of the theoretical framework, it enhances its empirical application. Since actual economic relationships are not simultaneous, and do not normally arrive at a state of general equilibrium (where all expectations are realised) it is not at all clear how the theoretical notion of general equilibrium corresponds to observations (see Dow, 1985, Chapter 8). Even temporary equilibrium has a correspondence problem, since it is also couched in mechanical time (thereby also excluding the notions of uncertainty and liquidity preference). The correspondence problem is much less serious for a theory expressed in terms of historical rather than mechanical time.

In considering the role of the financial sector in regional development, then, it would be quite reasonable to combine the type of partial model of credit creation and liquidity preference suggested by Chapter 7 of this volume and Harrigan and McGregor (1987) with empirical estimation of partial relationships, such as the determinants of credit creation in different regions. (Foster's, 1987, study at the national level provides an excellent example.) Particularly useful in this respect would be the development of data series reflecting states of regional confidence, regional differentials in loan charges, and the general price level of regional assets. Then, the relationship between credit creation, investment, income, and employment can be estimated in a partial way to explore the significance of any regional financial constraints implied by the credit-creation analysis. But the cumulative nature of the process, as analysed theoretically, the interdependence between the determinants of credit creation and liquidity preference, on the one hand, and the outcome in the form of income, employment, and wealth on the other, and the significance of the historical evolution of institutions and conventions, all preclude the combining of the different steps in the process into one large deterministic system.

CONCLUSION

From an investigation of the theoretical underpinnings of different possible approaches to the issue of incorporating financial variables in theories of regional economic performance, it becomes clear why so much of the literature ignores the issue. The approaches which suggest that money has an active role to play in regional development are disequilibrium theories on the one hand, and Post Keynesian theory on the other. Both approaches are internally consistent, in that their scope for modelling and its relationship is clearly defined as partial. It is the essence of the active macroeconomic role of money that there should be uncertainty, disappointed expectations, market imperfections, differing regional rates of return, and so on. Indeed, since these factors are central to most perceptions of the nature of regional disparities, it seems only natural to give due weight to the role of money in relation to these factors.

But macroeconomic theory and monetary theory in their most common form are not very helpful in this respect. Both fields are currently dominated by the imperatives of general equilibrium theorising; the conditions of general equilibrium are antithetical to the factors, outlined above, which underlie the active role of money in the economy. But they are by the same token antithetical to the predominant concerns of regional economics, notably to explain the emergence and persistence of real economic disparities. What is required is a theoretical approach which focuses explicitly on evolutionary processes. This in turn requires a modelling approach which focuses on partial relationships and historical trends, rather than on simultaneous relationships.

In conclusion, money and financial variables in general play an important part in the emergence and persistence of regional disparities. So any theory without them is missing an important element. But it has to be accepted that the process of which money is a part can only be modelled in a partial framework, albeit part of a more general theory.

9. The Capital Account and Regional Balance of Payments Problems

This chapter is a slightly amended version of an article of the same title which was published in Urban Studies, *23(2), pp. 173-84, 1986.*

INTRODUCTION

The distinction drawn within economics between regional and international questions seems in many ways to be an artificial one. Not that this distinction has always been present. Indeed some of the classic early contributions to the modern theory of international trade, such as Ohlin (1933), dealt jointly with interregional and international trade. But the current situation is characterised by two quite distinct specialist fields of regional and international economics, each with its own coterie of specialists and its own literature. There are of course important differences, primarily of an institutional nature, between regional and national economies. But international institutional arrangements vary enormously from country to country; in addition, inter-country groupings like the European Community occupy some middle ground between the conventional institutional characteristics of nations and regions.

The purpose of this chapter is to apply to the regional context a concept which is central to international economics: the balance of payments. Given the factors in common between international and interregional economic relationships, it is hoped that useful insights may emerge from the resulting cross-fertilisation of ideas. The balance of payments framework is particularly useful, since it can also highlight the significance of those important institutional features of (most) national economies which still differentiate them from regions: separate currencies and sovereign governments with fiscal, monetary and regulatory powers.

In the next section, we discuss the meaning of the balance of payments of a region. The traditional issues within regional economics can in fact be expressed in terms of the major conventional balance of payments categories. These issues relate to what are perceived to be regional problems, and yet there is almost never any discussion of regional balance of payments problems. The third section explores what we might mean by a regional balance of payments problem, and the associated adjustment mechanisms. Attention is focused in the following section on the capital account (referring to portfolio and direct investment); this is the one major balance of payments category which does not correspond to an issue addressed by the regional economics literature. The possibility is explored that the regional capital account is what prevents the emergence of regional balance of payments problems. The alternative possibility is then explored that the capital account may add to regional problems and as such warrants as much concern as other aspects of regional economies. This latter conclusion illustrates the value of taking a fresh look at regional economies in terms of the balance of payments. Finally, since the foregoing discussion is conducted at a theoretical level, attention is focused in section five on the availability (or otherwise) of data which would allow empirical application of the theory.

THE BALANCE OF PAYMENTS OF A REGION

The balance of payments is an accounting convention which measures payments into and out of a particular unit, with these payments categorised according to various sub-accounts. While the term is used almost exclusively to refer to national economies as the relevant unit, there is no reason why it should not be applied to other units. We could, for example, talk about a household's balance of payments; the information contained in these accounts would tell us about the household's economic relationship with the rest of the economy. Here we will consider the balance of payments of regions as a framework for discussing interregional economic relationships.

At this general level of discussion, the term 'region' is being used in the sense of any subnational spatial unit which has some economic homogeneity. Balance of payments accounts can be envisaged for any such category, and can thus be applied to economic analysis of either large regions or smaller sub-regions. The choice of regional breakdown will vary with the type of question being addressed by means of the accounts. For many purposes the ideal unit may be smaller than existing administrative boundaries suggest, but there would be attendant problems regarding data gathering. We return to this question in the fifth section.

The general structure of the balance of payments is set out in Table 9.1. The major sub-accounts are the current account and the capital account and such items as transfers, in the case of the current account, and direct investment, long-term portfolio investment and short-term portfolio investment, in the case of the capital account. For a national economy, there is a further item 'below the line' measuring the change in official reserves, which corresponds to the overall balance of payments surplus or deficit. Since regions do not have their own currencies, or reserves of foreign exchange, this item has no regional equivalent.

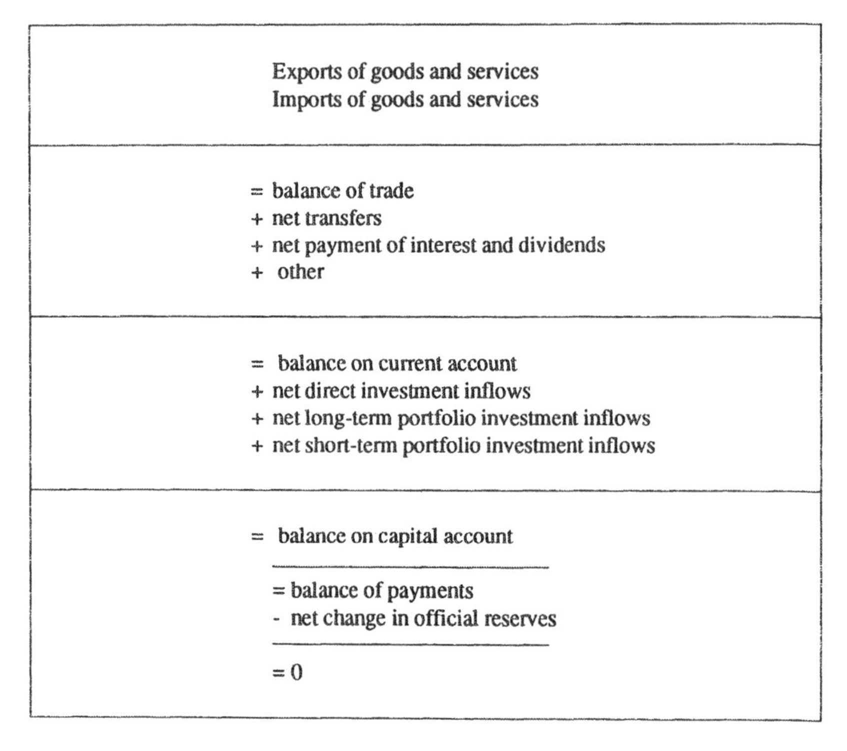

Exports of goods and services Imports of goods and services
= balance of trade + net transfers + net payment of interest and dividends + other
= balance on current account + net direct investment inflows + net long-term portfolio investment inflows + net short-term portfolio investment inflows
= balance on capital account = balance of payments - net change in official reserves = 0

Table 9.1: The General Structure of the Balance of Payments

Similarly, the national balance of payments is expressed in terms of the national currency. If the exchange rate is allowed to fluctuate, then the market for foreign exchange may be cleared (payments will balance) without any change in foreign exchange reserves.

We will now discuss each of the items, other than official reserves, as they apply to regions, and relate these items to the major concerns of regional economics. Perhaps the major concern in regional economics is with the regional pattern of output and employment. Under this heading would come such areas as location theory, which discusses the regional location of establishments, regional income multiplier theory, which discusses the consequences of expenditure changes in a region, and regional growth theory, which discusses the regional pattern of particular types of expenditure regarded as capable of inducing growth, notably investment and exports. The two balance of payments sub-accounts most relevant to these concerns are the trade account and the direct investment account.

The trade account measures payments for goods and services exported from the region allowing comparison with payments for goods and services imported. Location theory determines the type of goods and services which different regions specialise in, and therefore the types of goods and services exported and those imported (see, for example, Richardson, 1978, Chapter 3). Export expenditure is one multiplicand of multiplier theory, while the marginal propensity to import influences the size of the multiplier. Regional growth theory is concerned further with the dynamic effects of changes in export expenditure. (See, for example, Kaldor, 1970b.) By considering the trade account, therefore, much can be learned about the production specialisation of different regions, and about the relative strength of exports and imports.

Although deficits on trade account *may* suggest poor locational advantage for export-based industry, low-income multipliers and poor growth potential, they are not necessarily a sign of regional backwardness. Whitman (1967) suggests rather a categorisation according to whether the impetus for economic change (whether growth or decline) is internal or external to the region. Internally-generated growth has its main impact on imports in the shortrun, causing a deficit to emerge; only in the longer term, if the dynamic effects of growth boost export productivity, may the trade balance improve. Externally-generated growth, however, has its immediate impact on exports, with only a longer-term effect on imports as the export multiplier works through. Conversely, internally-generated decline is associated with a balance of trade surplus, while externally-generated decline is associated with a trade deficit. The source of impetus in turn depends very much on economic structure; it is much more likely to be internal in large advanced economies with a developed local market in manufactured goods. External impetus is more characteristic of economies dependent on exports of primary products.

Finally, the concern with the regional pattern of investment relates to the direct investment component of the capital account. This account measures the value of new plant and equipment installed by external interests, compared with direct investment effected elsewhere by interests within the region. The transfer of profits resulting from this investment is included in the current account. Thus, a net deficit on the direct investment account *may* mean a net surplus on repatriated profits. But, since it is expenditure rather than income as such which is important for generating income and employment *growth*, a direct investment deficit would not augur well for the region's growth prospects relative to other regions.

As far as regional policy is concerned, there is interest not only with incentives to alter the private sector behaviour captured in the trade and direct investment accounts, but also with more direct government involvement, in the form of direct transfers to local government or regional government bodies and also direct government expenditure. Against this must be set the regional pattern of taxation. In terms of the balance of payments, this fiscal activity is spread through several sub-accounts. Government expenditure on goods and services (from outside the region) would form part of the exports total, regional (as well as corporate and household) transfers appear in the transfers component of the current account, offset by taxes transferred out of the region, while public sector capital expenditure (financed from outside the region) contributes to inflows of direct investment. By studying net government flows in the various categories, the scale and composition of government involvement in the regional economy may be assessed.

The regional balance of payments, as described so far, differs more in degree than in kind from the national balance of payments. Regional economies are in general more open than national economies, in that the proportion of expenditure on exports and imports, and thus vulnerability to trade imbalance, is correspondingly greater. Further, the incidence of multi-regional corporations is greater than that of multinational corporations, so that private sector direct investment flows can be expected to be relatively more significant for regions than for nations. The most noticeable difference perhaps is the large fiscal presence in regions of a national government. Conceptually, however, transfers between the regions and the national government are not fundamentally different from international transfers and transfers between national and international bodies.

But we have already noted that there is a difference in kind relating to the absence of regional currencies and foreign exchange reserves. The remaining question is whether there is a (possibly related) fundamental difference between regions and nations with respect to the portfolio investment components of the capital account which would justify the relative absence of attention devoted to them in the regional literature; this lack of concern with regional capital flows is in marked contrast to their central role in international economics. Long-term portfolio investment refers to purchases and sale of long-term securities issues outside the region, or by non-residents of the region of securities issued within the region. Short-term portfolio investment refers to transactions in short-term securities, including balances on bank accounts. Now, clearly, residents of regions engage in this type of investment, and they do so across regions. It is not at all straightforward to identify what is meant regionally by transactions involving national institutions - deposits with a bank which operates across several regions, for example. But the same may be said of international capital flows involving multinational financial institutions, and those which do not involve changing currencies (as is the case with transfer of a Euro-currency deposit from one European country to another, for example).

The special significance of the capital account can be seen by referring back to the general format of the balance of payments in Table 9.1. If there is no official reserves component, then, in order for the balance of payments to sum overall to zero, the capital account must exactly offset the current account; if there is a deficit in the current account, then there *must* be a surplus on capital account. This feature of the regional balance of payments raises the whole question of whether or not regions actually experience balance of payments problems and, if so, of what nature.

REGIONAL BALANCE OF PAYMENTS PROBLEMS

We have seen that most regional economic problems can be analysed in terms of components within the balance of payments. But a balance of payments problem as such relates specifically to the constraint that payments into and out of a region must balance. The manifestation of balance of payments problems at the national level is a change in foreign exchange reserves or in the exchange rate, if by a 'problem' is meant a tendency towards imbalance of payments. But either of these indicators of problems is in turn the short-run solution to a tendency towards imbalance. Changing reserves or exchange rates, therefore, allow payments to balance, and also act as signals that there may be a persistent tendency towards imbalance. An indefinite reduction or increase in reserves or in the exchange rate, in the case of persistent imbalance, is generally regarded as a problem rather than a solution in the longterm (and indeed, in the case of reductions in reserves, would be impossible). A balance of payments problem, then, can be defined as a persistent tendency for payments to be in imbalance. The accounts can be used to highlight particular aspects of that imbalance, for example that a capital account surplus is insufficient to offset a persistent current account deficit.

A tendency towards imbalance can occur between regions just as between nations. A decline in competitiveness in one region will cause a deterioration in the trade account for that region, for example, just as it would between nations. But regions do not have changing reserves or exchange rates to act as indicators of problems. In addition they lack these means of ensuring balance of payments in spite of an underlying tendency towards imbalance. Yet payments must balance between regions so some other form of adjustment must take place. If this adjustment takes the form of, say, income deflation in the region with declining competitiveness, then the solution to the underlying payments problem in turn constitutes a problem in itself. Further, that deflation is enforced by financial (balance of payments) constraints; there is no regional equivalent of national fiscal or monetary policy to effect the deflation in a planned manner. Nations have a choice between adjustment to remove an imbalance of payments, and letting the imbalance be manifested in a change in reserves or the exchange rate. Regions, not having separate currencies, do not have that choice. The constraint of payments balance may thus have more serious consequences for regions than for nations.

It is an important consideration therefore whether there are features of regions which nevertheless limit the scope for imbalance of payments, and therefore the need for adjustment in the first place. Here the relevant literature is that which addressed the question of what is an optimal currency area; that is what conditions warrant eschewance of the exchange rate mechanism? This literature discusses not only the likely incidence of payments imbalance, but also the scope for automatic correction of imbalance. Kenen (1969) argues that trade imbalance is more likely to arise the more specialised the economy. Should one sector of a highly diversified economy become relatively uncompetitive, then the overall impact on the balance of payments will be much more limited than if this is a dominant sector. Even with a demand-induced trade imbalance, income changes will have a more marked effect on imports in a specialised economy, since it will be more open than a diversified economy. This diversification criterion militates against regions, which are likely to be more specialised than nations; it would seem that regions would have an even greater need of a separate currency whose value could be altered to counteract changes in relative competitiveness.

McKinnon (1963) in turn looks at those factors which would prevent a separate currency successfully correcting a trade imbalance in any case, focusing on the relative size of the tradeables sector, and with particular reference to the labour market. If money wages are determined by parity with workers in the same tradeables sectors in other economies, an exchange depreciation would simply encourage money wages in the tradeables sector to increase until their real value was on a par with those elsewhere, with spread effects on the rest of the labour market; this would counteract the beneficial effects on competitiveness of the depreciation.

This consideration has direct application to the national/regional comparison; because of the greater openness of regional economies, regional wages are more susceptible to comparisons with other regions than national wages with other nations. Thus, if a separate currency is judged in terms of its ability to offset divergence in competitiveness, then it would be relatively powerless for regions of one country.

The Mundell (1961) criterion for optimal currency areas has more general application, in that it deals with trade imbalance due to divergence both on the supply side (relative competitiveness) and on the demand side (relative income growth), as well as imbalance on the capital account. He argues that an area does not need a separate currency to correct payments imbalance if there is factor mobility with other areas. Then, if relative competitiveness in one region should fall, because of declining labour productivity for example, labour would move to other regions, reducing the marginal product of labour there and restoring balance. Similarly, if income growth in one region increased the demand for imports from another region, their price would rise, and so would the value of the marginal product of labour there; labour would be encouraged to move out of the growing region, restoring equality in the value of marginal product across regions, and at the same time reducing the demand for imports into the first region. Further, if there should be a divergence in the relative return on capital in different regions, capital would flow to where the return was highest, thus restoring equality in returns across regions. (The argument in the case of both labour and capital mobility rests on the assumption that the marginal product curves are downward sloping.) Since factors are in general more mobile between regions than between countries, it would therefore seem that factor mobility can be relied upon to correct any tendency for payments imbalance more between regions than between nations.

To summarise what emerges from the optimal currency area literature, the greater specialisation of regional production may make regions relatively vulnerable to trade imbalance, but the extra facility of a separate currency would not be very effective in equalising competitiveness because of the national character of wage settlements. Nevertheless, factor mobility may automatically correct imbalance, not only that arising from the trade account, but also from the capital account. It is useful, then, to analyse regional economic problems in terms of the balance of payments, in order to understand how regions adjust without separate currencies. The manifestation of a balance of payments problem, then, would be accommodating regional flows of capital and labour, rather than of foreign exchange or an exchange rate change.

However, the overwhelming emphasis throughout this literature is on imbalance arising from, and corrected by, the price mechanism, requiring all the neo-classical assumptions about the nature of production functions, and so on. If we depart from the assumption of downward-sloping marginal product curves, factor mobility has quite different consequences. Suppose labour moves out of a declining region, reducing the market for non-tradeable goods, requiring the fixed costs of infrastructure to be spread over a declining population and not in fact causing the marginal product of labour to rise, then there will be further incentives for labour to move out of the region, with the consequences of cumulative decline. In the shortrun, adjustment is effected by falling incomes and rising unemployment, which automatically curtails imports in line with exports.

The concept of cumulative causation is one developed by Myrdal (1964) and developed further by Kaldor (1970a) and Thirlwall (1980), emphasising the factors promoting output and employment divergence between regions. Here, the emphasis is on income adjustment rather than price adjustment, and on the significance of differences in economic structure which determine whether the region is on a growth path or one of decline. Myrdal distinguished between spread effects, by which growth in one region spills over into other regions (through increased import demand, for example) and backwash effects, by which growth in one region inhibits growth in other regions. The major source of backwash effects on which Kaldor focuses attention is productivity growth, which he argues is itself a product of output growth. Thirlwall relates Kaldor's thesis specifically to the regional balance of payments, by identifying the export sector as the key element of regional demand. Indeed he identifies regional problems with balance of payments problems because a weak export sector means weak income growth, given the constraint that interregional payments must balance.

Kaldor also points out a feature of regions which does tend to counteract the divergence produced by market forces: the fiscal role of central government. Just as there are automatic stabilisers which operate to counteract cyclical movements in the economy as a whole, the automatic stabilisers of increased transfers and lower taxation when income falls operate across regions. This provides an automatic process which tends to balance trade deficits, where these are associated with relative income decline. (In the case of deficits resulting from internally-generated growth, the effect is perverse in terms of payments balance, although corrective in terms of modifying the income growth advantage of the region.) Further, governments can make discretionary payments to deal with particular problems, or purchase goods and services or make capital expenditures in the regions experiencing payments problems. Indeed some American studies have highlighted the offsetting nature of government payments and private sector payments between Federal Reserve Districts in the US. (See in particular Hartland, 1949 and Bowsher, Daane and Einzig, 1958). But, given that payments deficits are not always associated with relative income decline, and given the lags in discretionary expenditures, and indeed in tax payments, following relative income decline, it is not obvious how the government sector could inject funds in exactly the right amounts to offset private sector payments imbalance. Certainly, central government has the capacity to assist in correcting regional payments imbalance, and indeed in using measures which deal with the underlying problems of disparities in income growth and competitiveness. In this sense, regions have an adjustment mechanism which nations lack. But this mechanism cannot be the final explanation of the apparent lack of regional balance of payments problems.

How does a regional balance of payments deficit manifest itself if there is no stock of foreign exchange reserves whose changes can be monitored? What is the immediate effect of a shortfall of export receipts, even if relative price adjustments and factor mobility *do* automatically correct the imbalance eventually? What processes are put in train by such a shortfall, and how do they contribute to, or detract from, the process of payments adjustment? We must turn now to look more closely at the capital account; since a shortfall of receipts has an immediate financial effect, it is the capital account in which the first effect must be felt. In addition, the determinants of the capital account must be explored further to see whether there is scope for payments imbalance to have its origins in this quarter, as well as in the trade account.

THE CAPITAL ACCOUNT

The distinction is drawn with respect to a country's balance of payments between autonomous and accommodating transactions. Autonomous transactions are those effected without regard to the balance of payments, while accommodating transactions are those designed to offset the effect on the balance of payments of autonomous transactions. The distinction cannot however be applied categorically. Transactions will take place as a result of policies designed to correct the balance of payments, like income deflation to reduce imports, or a tight monetary policy to increase interest rates and thus attract capital inflows. Although econometric estimates can be arrived at which show the effect of each policy, the estimates can only be of limited accuracy. The only truly accommodating transactions are reflected in the changes in foreign exchange reserves. The corollary would seem to be that all transactions are autonomous in regions. But then how do these autonomous transactions happen always to sum to zero?

There are some who see the short-term capital account as automatically accommodating autonomous changes in the trade account and the direct investment and long-term portfolio investment components of the capital account. This role of the capital account is therefore seen as explaining the absence of regional balance of payments problems. The short-term capital account can perform this function in regions, but only to a much lesser extent among nations, because of the high degree of integration of a national financial system. Suppose the region's payments start in balance, and then an additional import is ordered. This import must be paid for in some form; money from stocks, money acquired by sale of assets, or borrowed money. Between regions, there is no additional step required of converting domestic money into the currency of the exporter. If the latter were necessary, and in the absence of any offsetting movement in the capital account, there would be a corresponding fall in the region's foreign exchange reserves, or a fall in the value of the region's currency to induce a sale. But without a separate currency, all the action must be confined to the capital account.

Suppose the payment is made in cash, drawn from the importer's bank account. Suppose further that the bank has branches also in the exporter's region, and the payment is made entirely within that bank. Herein lies an initial difficulty in identifying a region's capital account. Is there any sense in which there is a capital flow offsetting the additional import payment? Are there any consequences for bank behaviour with respect to the two regions? Other things being equal, the branch in the importing region would require a 'loan' from head office, while the exporting region's branch would have a corresponding credit. Unless there is a direct connection between each branch's deposit liabilities and its asset portfolio, there may be no further repercussion of the transfer of funds. Practice varies from country to country, and from bank to bank, but generally a branch's lending capacity is not strictly limited by its deposit liabilities. Increased lending can be balanced against increased liabilities to head office as much as increased local deposits. In fact, if we view credit creation as the moving force of bank expansion, deposit increases follow from increases in advances, rather than vice versa.

But one of the features of branch banking is the capacity to reallocate existing assets regionally, or sectorally, to maximise returns, so that there would seem to be an automatic capital account inflow (through the bank's head office books) to offset the import payment. In turn, even if the import payment is made between two different, nationwide banks, there is no automatic mechanism whereby the fall in deposits of one bank and the rise in the other's should have direct consequences for the regions of the branches in question. We can nevertheless treat the transfer as being from the exporting region to the importing region, through the capital account; the branch in the importing region 'borrows' from its head office while the branch in the exporting region 'lends' to its head office. (The head office transactions cancel out if they are located, as is usual, in the same region.)

While at the margin, there is unlikely to be any regional repercussion of a net transfer from one branch to another, or from one bank to another, cumulative transfers require a different response. If autonomous payments out of the region consistently exceed receipts, because of a declining export sector, for example, then there will be a corresponding re-evaluation of returns within the region on the part of the local bank manager. In other words, the conditions which brought about the cumulative outflow of short-term capital also discourage bank advances, or encourage interest charges which squeeze out demand. (While nationwide banks tend to have uniform nationwide interest rate *structures* the position within that structure of a particular borrower will depend on the default risk perceived to attach to the advance.) In the case of a persistent trade deficit brought about by a weak export sector, then, there will be relatively limited capacity to offset payments out of the region with bank borrowing.

In a situation of export-led decline, bank credit will be sought primarily to meet income shortfalls on the part of consumers and firms, that is as a stop-gap measure, which alleviates without solving the underlying problem. This situation may be contrasted with a region experiencing internally-generated growth, whose trade balance may be in deficit. Even if long-term capital flows, attracted by the region's good prospects, are insufficient to balance interregional payments, consumer credit and working capital are a more attractive prospect for a bank in such a region than one in the declining region. Thus, a sufficiently strong long-term capital account will tend to make the short-term capital account favourable, just as the reverse is also the case (regardless of the current account position). A region unfortunate enough to have an export sector whose weakness causes a trade deficit and also poor investment prospects, is likely also to suffer from a growing reluctance on the part of financial institutions to provide the necessary inflow of short-term capital to balance interregional payments. Payments may alternatively have to be balanced by sales of long-term assets rather than short-term borrowing. If the assets to be sold to raise money to pay for imports are regionally based, then their value will be weak if the prospects of the regional economy are weak. The required capital inflow to finance the import payment therefore involves the importer in capital loss.

Now the assets to be sold need not be regionally based; if they are national securities, they are what Ingram (1959) calls 'generalised claims'. They are almost as good as money in the sense that they trade at nationwide prices. The import payment is balanced by a capital outflow corresponding to a change of ownership of the national asset. Ingram was in fact writing in the context of the American banking system which is much more regionally specific than the British banking system. Banks until recently could not branch outside their home state, and in some states (notably Illinois) they could not have more than one outlet. In fact, various institutional arrangements (such as holding companies overseeing several banks, and correspondence arrangements between banks) to overcome the branching limitations, and now inter-state branching is gradually being legalised. Until recently, transfers between banks in different regions could not be neutralised through the books of a national head office. But, since each of these banks holds a proportion of its portfolio in generalised claims, the net payment between banks resulting from the additional import payment could be financed by sales of these national securities. In fact, Ingram argues, banks used their stock of generalised claims as a buffer stock to avoid adjusting loans every time there was a change in deposit liabilities. Traditional bank multiplier theory implies that any change in bank reserves has a multiple effect on the bank's loans. But if banks meet reductions of deposits with sales of generalised claims, and increases in deposits with purchases of generalised claims, then there need be no impact on local credit at all. Indeed, since Ingram put forward this view, there has been a tremendous increase in the interbank market in the US which, in the case of many banks, has meant that borrowing from this market is as much a source of funds as direct deposits.

But again, this argument, which implies an automatic offset between the current and capital accounts of a region, refers exclusively to marginal transfers from bank to bank. As Pfister (1960) and Whitman (1967) pointed out in response to Ingram, if there is a continual drainage of deposits, sooner or later the bank's stock of generalised claims must run out (as must any individual's or firm's holdings). The bank then must respond by calling in loans and/or seeking credit from other financial institutions. Even in the latter case, the bank's credit-worthiness depends on the value of its assets. If this depends largely on loans to producers and workers in a declining region, the bank's own credit-worthiness is correspondingly reduced, and loans may not be forthcoming. The outcome of credit contraction in the trade deficit region will be downward income adjustment which will reduce imports, thus correcting the deficit. The regional economy's adjustment is in a sense simply an aggregation of the adjustments that individual firms and households must make when payments exceed receipts, when assets are run down (or when their sale would involve massive capital losses), and when credit is not forthcoming. Expenditure must fall. Since within a national currency area there is no necessary distinction between expenditure on local or imported goods from a financial point of view, expenditure on local factors and products will fall along with imports. (An exception is local expenditure which can be financed by trade credit, but even that may be limited if many sectors of the economy are interdependent, and experiencing financial constraints.) The result is further cutbacks in local incomes, reduced credit-worthiness, further falls in asset values as forced sales occur at reduced prices, and so on in a cumulative process. In other words, without the capacity to shield an economy in payments deficit by running down foreign exchange reserves or depreciating the currency, reliance must be placed on income adjustment which actually reinforces the difficulty of acquiring accommodating finance through the capital account.

A similar argument applies to a payments deficit arising in the long-term capital account. Further, it follows that payments problems can be initiated in the short-term capital account, even when the other components of the balance of payments are in balance. Expectations as to returns on tradeable assets are potentially unstable; short-term capital flight can itself cause payments difficulties which have knock-on effects on asset prices and long-term investment prospects.

The neo-classical view of the interdependence between the current and capital accounts is quite different. The view of Scitovsky (1957) which has found more recent expression among the global monetarists (see, for example, Frenkel and Johnson, 1976) is that the balance of payments is an expression of asset preferences. A trade deficit therefore reflects a wish to run down assets (in the case of global monetarists, money), while a surplus reflects the wish to accumulate financial assets. The function of an integrated capital market is to channel assets and liabilities accordingly, via the price mechanism. If there is an excess demand for credit in a region, therefore, the interest rate will rise and the price of local assets will fall, and the necessary funds will be attracted. The more integrated the capital market, the less resort must be made to income adjustment as an interim adjustment mechanism. According to this view, the increasing integration in international capital markets reduces the extent to which payments imbalance constitutes a problem internationally. As with the general neo-classical analysis of the balance of payments, the argument relies on static schedules expressed in terms of price which ensure the general equilibrium results. Further, actual configurations of the balance of payments reflect preferences. In this case, the demand for and supply of loanable funds are functions of the rate of interest, promoting an optimal allocation of credit. But if a region is on a cumulative path of decline, where an excess demand for capital does not raise its marginal product and adjustment is primarily by relative income decline which exacerbates the situation, the neo-classical theoretical framework cannot apply.

In practice, regions are not observed to decline (or grow) cumulatively in the inexorable sense implied by cumulative causation theory. As Myrdal pointed out, there are spread effects of regional expansion which benefit other regions. In addition, the automatic stabilisers of government fiscal activity, combined with active regional policy, serve to counteract the tendency for disparities to increase which is the product of market forces. Nevertheless, if we ignore the capital account of the regional balance of payments, we miss an important force for increasing regional divergence. Not only may capital flows fail to accommodate trade deficits, but payments problems may be initiated within the capital account, as a result of the assessment elsewhere of the region's asset values and its residents' credit-worthiness. The capital account has been given so little attention in the past because the orthodox view has been either that it automatically accommodated the current account, because of the integrated nature of the national financial system, or that the current and capital accounts were the mirror image of each other, representing a particular (satisfied) set of preferences.

Even Keynesian regional theorists who reject the neo-classical framework of analysis and use instead a cumulative causation framework fail to address the significance of the capital account. It so happens that a leading figure of this group, Kaldor, is also a leading figure among those Keynesians who regard the supply of credit as endogenous in any case. Their view is that, where credit demand arises, financial institutions are adaptable enough to find some way of meeting it, even in the face of monetary controls. Implicitly they bring this view to regional economics, assuming that the supply of bank credit to a region is determined at the national rather than the regional level. A notable exception, however, is Myrdal, who analysed productivity growth as being self-enhancing, not only in production but also in the financial sector. Increasing returns to scale in the financial centre inevitably create a disparity in expected returns there and in other regions quite independently of expectations about the returns to production in the sectors requiring finance. This pull of financial resources from the Periphery to the Centre has been noted in Britain by Morgan (1973).

DATA CONSIDERATIONS

The argument may be accepted in theory that it is important to consider a region's balance of payments in order to understand the forces of adjustment at work in any particular case. But data availability may be an effective stumbling block. Indeed, the area of regional balance of payments analysis has for long been caught in a vicious circle. Resources have not been devoted to collecting data because the area has not attracted theoretical attention, while theorists dismiss the topic on the grounds of poor data availability. (See Richardson, 1978, p. 95, for example.) It is certainly the case that the data problems are serious; with so many multi-regional production, financial and government institutions, there is no clear-cut way of allocating many items regionally. It cannot be overemphasised, however, that international data suffer from similar limitations, and do so progressively more the more transactions occur within multinational institutions. Even the net change in official reserves does not provide a foolproof 'fix' on the national balance of payments when international transactions are conducted without currency conversion. (It has long been understood that the UK and US balance of payments figures are difficult to interpret given the widespread use of sterling and the US dollar as third currencies.)

The balance of payments provides a useful framework within which to discuss general economic problems; this in itself constitutes a case for providing regional information in this form. Data availability has been improving in recent years for the Scottish region for example. Although there is no definitive set of regional accounts for Britain, it is possible to piece together a picture from different sources. Regional accounts are subject to particular technical scrutiny not least because of the political sensitivity of the data. Thus, at the time of the devolution debate in Scotland in the 1970s, attempts were made to estimate the net flow of public sector funds between Scotland and the rest of Britain. But the proponents of particular political viewpoints were able to focus on the technical shortcomings of others' versions of the accounts, and it is inevitable that any set of accounts will have shortcomings.

The Industry Department for Scotland (1984) has recently published the results of their input-output study of the Scottish economy in 1979. Inevitably such studies date very rapidly, but this one contains detailed export and import information by sector, which allows an aggregated measure of Scotland's trade balance. The aggregated data for an isolated year do not assist conventional types of analysis of changes in the trade balance over time, but the sectoral data are very instructive in indicating Scotland's trading structure and indicating how it would affect the outcome of economic events in the future.

The most comprehensive study of regional accounts for the standard regions in Britain is provided by Short with Nicholas (1981). They survey the various possible ways of constructing regional accounts and settle on a flow of funds approach which reflects an interest in the capital transactions between regions. In addition to the existing Central Statistical Office regional data gathered so far, they add detailed data on flows of funds associated with different types of financial instruments.

But the discussion here has focused on the significance of the balance of payments constraint itself for the other components of the balance of payments, and indeed for the regional economy itself. For this purpose we require an indicator of the operation of that constraint which would convey information equivalent to changes in foreign exchange reserves, or in the exchange rate at the national level. (Such an indicator is necessarily partial in that it misses adjustments to the balance of payments constraint which have occurred through, for example, deflation.)

The closest regional equivalent to the change in official foreign exchange reserves would be the change in deposits with banks within the region, which would in fact appear in the short-term capital account. For regional accounts then, changing bank deposits, or some broader measure of the money supply, should be shown separately 'below the line'. American regional economists have been in the forefront of analysing regional banking data (see, for example, Miller, 1978). The fact that US banks are regionally-specific, and that there are aggregated banking data by Federal Reserve District has been of considerable importance in facilitating this type of analysis. The choice of regional unit, however, is tied to Federal Reserve Districts, which may not be the appropriate units for regional economic analysis. For nationwide branch banking systems, economists are dependent on the willingness of the banks themselves to publish regional data (a willingness displayed by the Canadian banks, for example). For Scotland and Northern Ireland there is some scope for generating the relevant data given the regional structure of the banking system. (See in particular Gaskin, 1965, on the Scottish banking system.) The data however are not split according to branches inside and outside the relevant region. Further, ideally, since most regional analysis is conducted at the sub-regional level, it is for those units that balance of payments accounts should be constructed.

Given the fact that financial institutions are regionally-specific in terms of location (at least with respect to branches), the financial data required as indicators of the short-run effect of the balance of payments constraint are the most amenable part of the balance of payments to sub-regional breakdown. If financial institutions were so willing, it should be possible to identify deposits by branch and by degree of liquidity, thus allowing a compilation of money stock data by locality, according to different definitions of the money stock (including building society deposits, or not, for example). Deposits by residents of one locality in an institution in another locality would constitute a capital outflow, reducing the local money stock, while borrowing from such an institution, or net borrowing by a local branch of a financial institution from its head office would constitute a capital inflow, increasing the local money stock.

Short with Nicholas (1981) list current availability of regional financial data, in terms of the standard regions, covering the full range of public and private sector financial institutions. Unfortunately, the key institutions for translating financial flow accounts into balance of payments accounts are the banks; it is their deposits (among others, possibly) which need to be shown 'below the line'. But Short with Nicholas could only impute banking data for the standard regions (proportionately to regional income) in the absence of data from the banks themselves. Their experience strikes a note of pessimism with respect to compiling 'below the line' estimates for standard regions, far less for smaller regions.

It is to the banks, too, that one would look for the most pertinent information required to interpret the data on net money flows between regions. The composition of bank assets would indicate the reasons for net payment imbalance. The weaker credit growth is, and the more it is concentrated in business lending for working capital, the more serious the problem. If corporate credit for new investment is relatively strong, however, then the payments imbalance may be expected to be temporary. (Attractive investment prospects would normally be associated with net capital inflows, including net inflows on the part of the banks. But the initial import content of the expansion may be so high as to produce net monetary outflows.) The level and composition of the portfolios of other financial institutions would similarly be informative of underlying conditions, but bank data would be the key.

Even if full regional balance of payments accounts were available then they would be open to a wide range of interpretations. The standard neo-classical interpretation would regard the data as reflecting the fulfilment of preferences (albeit on an optimal adjustment path). The type of interpretation favoured here would involve exploring the forces underlying static balance of payments observations. For example, capital outflows may be the product of a situation of economic decline which at the same time creates an excess demand for credit. Imports may fall, not because of a desire to accumulate assets, but because the desired credit is not made available at a time of income decline. Even regional banking data can be interpreted differently. The Canadian banking data, for example, show an excess of assets (loans) over liabilities (deposits) in the lower-income regions, consistent with the orthodox notion that an integrated financial system serves to diminish regional payment problems. An alternative explanation is that deposits are generated by new loans (rather than vice versa) and the shortfall of deposits simply reflects net outflows on the trade account, or net purchases of assets outside the region. In short, if we had complete data, no issues would be settled; the arguments would only just begin. But at least there would be a concrete basis for argument.

CONCLUSION

The central argument of this paper has been that there is much to be learned from considering regional economic relationships in terms of the balance of payments. In particular, such a framework highlights the role of capital transactions and their interdependence with trade, output and employment. The focus on financial transactions at the international level has been dominated by global monetarism. Translated into the regional context, this type of approach has simply reinforced the popular perception that regions do not have balance of payment problems. But here we have explored an alternative approach which has highlighted the forces for divergence between regions, rather than convergence. This approach has demonstrated the importance of the scope for capital transactions to contribute to divergence, and the interdependence between these transactions and trade and direct investment, which is normally the sole focus of regional theory in this area.

The data problems are serious, although gradually they are lessening in the sense that more regional accounts are gradually being compiled. There will always be shortcomings to the data, and there will always be scope for different interpretations of the data. But a growing awareness of the importance of the issues at the theoretical level and an expanding data base should reinforce each other to provide a fruitful area of economic enquiry. Indeed, with the blurring of distinctions between national boundaries, the issues which arise in translating international concepts for application to regions will become increasingly relevant to the updating of international theory for application to changing institutional structures.

10. Money and Regional Development

This chapter was published as an article in Studies in Political Economy *23(2), pp. 73-94, 1987. It benefited from the helpful comments of Ian Parker.*

INTRODUCTION

It is a fact that economic development does not proceed evenly among the regions of Western economies. Yet, uneven regional development within developed capitalist economies has aroused little interest among orthodox economists of both the mainstream and Marxist schools of thought. It has been economists in the political economy tradition who have provided most insights, and it is in line with this tradition that we will address here the specific question of the role of money in uneven regional development.

Within the political economy tradition there are two views on money which are conventionally juxtaposed: Keynesian monetary theory, with its emphasis on liquidity preference, on the one hand, and the neo-Marxian theory, with money as the vehicle for realising surplus value and bankers as a sub-class struggling for a share of that surplus, on the other. Conventionally, the former is interpreted as a theory of short-run disequilibrium and the latter as a theory of longrun, historical development. It would appear therefore that only the neo-Marxian theory could contribute to an explanation of persistent uneven regional development. But the Post Keynesian interpretation of Keynesian monetary theory demonstrates its relevance to the longrun as a series of shortruns; as such it can be combined with features of the neo-Marxian long-run theory to provide a fuller analysis of money and economic development. The purpose of this paper is to demonstrate, using this combined theoretical approach, that money and financial institutions play an active part in promoting uneven regional development in capitalist countries.

The argument to be presented here is thus a particular, or partial, one, set within a much more general context. The development of economies, internationally as well as intranationally, is uneven. The forces behind this process of uneven development are many and complex, both real and financial; of the financial forces, money and the banks which create it are only a part. The focus here on money and regional development, therefore, should not be taken as a denial of the significance of more general forces between regional economies, or of the complexity of financial markets, or of the international dimension. The context of the argument will be spelled out in these terms where it is most relevant. But the overriding purpose here is to attempt to deal with one part of the economic process which has been relatively neglected in the literature: the relationship between money and regional development. The significance of the regional as opposed to international dimension is the national cohesion of banking systems particularly where there is nationwide branch banking as in Canada (although the degree of international cohesion in banking is progressively increasing).

The next section provides a brief review of the literature on regional development in general, and the role of money and financial institutions in particular. This puts into context the exposition which follows of the theoretical approach developed in the third section. The remaining discussion focuses on the case of regional development in Canada. This provides a particularly useful case-study, for a variety of reasons. First, Canada's pattern of regional development has been recently established, roughly coincident with the development of its financial system, and is relatively well-defined. Second, the role of financial institutions in the emergence of this pattern has always been a contentious political issue, sparking off an academic, as well as political, literature. Third, the high profile of the issue has encouraged the publication of a wide range of regional financial data which, for all their imperfections, allow some quantitative assessment of competing theories.

THE STATE OF THE ART ON MONEY AND REGIONAL DEVELOPMENT

The general tenor of theories of regional development is taken from the schools of thought to which their expositors subscribe. Thus, the orthodox mainstream theory is set in a general equilibrium framework. Full general equilibrium requires factor price equalisation and full employment of factors. Thus, in equilibrium, incomes may only differ between regions as a result of differing factor endowments (for example a higher skill level in the labour force) and no unemployment can persist. Mainstream theories thus focus on the adjustment mechanisms by which regional equilibrium, once disturbed, is restored.[1] The implication that there is little to be said about persistent differences in regional incomes and unemployment rates has not prevented the identification of this approach, by many, with regional economics. This is perhaps only less at odds with the issue of uneven development than the equivalent theoretical approach to international economics, which likewise examines the conditions for factor price equalisation. (Indeed the mainstream regional and international theories were originally developed in parallel by Ohlin, 1933.)

Orthodox Marxian theory has also made little direct contribution to explanations of uneven regional development, although Marx did discuss particular regional questions and posited an antagonism between country and city. But spatial divisions cut across class divisions. So there has been some resistance among orthodox Marxists to probing regional questions for fear of fostering divisions within the working class. However, a variety of theories has been developed in an attempt to provide a Marxian view of regional development; examples are applications of Lenin's theory of imperialism to regions, and Mandel's theory of the regional disposition of the reserve army of the unemployed. But Edel *et al.* (1978) punctuate an excellent review of the radical regional literature with the observation that none of these theories provides a satisfactorily class-based analysis.

Nevertheless, as long as one is prepared to countenance theories not explicitly grounded in class analysis, there is a wide range of useful theories in the middle ground between orthodox mainstream and orthodox Marxian analysis. Of these, the two we will concentrate on here are the theory of cumulative causation, originated by Myrdal (1964) and adopted by Keynesians (notably Kaldor, 1970b, and Dixon and Thirlwall, 1975), and dependency theory most widely associated with Frank (1967) and developed by neo-Marxians (notably Amin, 1974, and Wallerstein, 1974).[2] Both bodies of theory explain uneven regional development as an inherent feature of capitalist economies; the slow growth of some regions is a consequence of the faster growth of others.

Cumulative causation theory stresses the competitive advantages enjoyed by those regions already most developed; growth itself allows dynamic economies of scale to be reaped in a variety of contexts, leading to faster productivity growth, which makes it even harder for other regions to compete. These negative, 'backwash' effects are nevertheless offset by positive, 'spread' effects: the adoption of new technology by backward regions, an expanding market for their products in the faster-growing regions, and so on. (Myrdal in fact argued that spread effects tend to dominate backwash effects among regions, in developed economies.) Dependency theory emphasises the way in which development in the peripheral regions is governed by the imperatives of growth in the central regions. The former are dependent on the latter for markets for their products and for the finance and technology for production; the focus is thus on trade and investment as the vehicles of dependency.

Among the sectors of central regions which enjoy dynamic economies of scale, according to cumulative causation theory, is the financial sector. The fact that financial institutions tend to have head offices in the central regions implies a remoteness from sources of investment finance for businesses in peripheral regions; these businesses experience difficulties in borrowing in the same way as, in general, small businesses experience more difficulties than large businesses (because of the smaller size of loans relative to fixed processing costs, lack of information, etc.).

But not much has been made of the financial aspects of cumulative causation theory. Indeed Keynesians like Kaldor who have developed the theory in the regional context are noted for their view that the supply of money is endogenous at the national and regional levels; banks are prepared to supply credit indefinitely at a set interest rate, and acquire the reserves required to back the increase in deposits after the fact. In other words, all potential borrowers face the same borrowing conditions; all the emphasis is put on their expectations as to the return on their investment (relative to the going interest rate) since these determine investment plans. Money plays no active role in investment decisions, and thus in promoting uneven development.

Mainstream theorists go further, arguing that national financial markets if anything make regional development *more* even. Financial flows between regions are in fact a key variable in adjustment to equilibrium. Disequilibrium may be the result of an inequality of savings and investment in each region. If exports from one region are low relative to imports, there will be insufficient saving to finance investment; but the resulting excess demand for funds will be met by an inflow of funds from the other regions with high exports and thus excess saving, according to Scitovsky (1957). Further, if investment is earning a low return in one region relative to others, an outflow of capital will raise the average return on remaining projects in that region and lower it in others, promoting equality.[3] But in addition to ease of interregional capital mobility there is what Ingram (1959) calls the stock of 'generalised claims', that is financial instruments such as government bonds which are traded at a wider than regional level. Any temporary fluctuation in export earnings or in purchases of regional securities need not have the multiple effect on regional bank lending which would be suggested by bank multiplier theory. Faced with a reduction in deposits, banks can maintain their reserves by selling generalised claims rather than by calling in advances.

Ingram was writing in the context of a unit banking system. Where there is widespread bank branching, as in Canada, Ingram's argument is generally regarded as being strengthened where bank branches can settle payments across regions through Head Office book entries.[4] Branches experiencing a fall in deposits as a result of regional outflows of funds need not automatically curtail lending if the Head Office provides a book entry credit to match the outflow.

The problem with Ingram's argument is that regional differences in export performance and ability to attract capital are not generally temporary.[5] Unless it is the result of successful growth in import substitution, low regional net export growth is normally associated with poor investment prospects regardless of how much saving is available and would thus be more likely to encourage continued outflows of funds rather than inflows. By the time this process could raise the return on the remaining capital to that of capital in other regions, the level of economic activity could be critically depressed.

Nevertheless, dependency theory envisages continued capital inflows to peripheral regions, not as a result of equilibrating market forces, but as a vehicle for exploitation. Development of peripheral regions occurs as a result of investment from the central regions designed to generate a surplus; it is the form that this investment takes which ensures continued dependency and underdevelopment. While Lenin had emphasised portfolio investment governed by financial institutions, dependency theorists focus on direct investment by multinational corporations. The monetary aspect of the process is thus de-emphasised. Money's importance in neo-Marxian (and orthodox Marxian) theory stems from its role as the vehicle for exploitation. Money, even in Lenin's theory, is only important in the sense that it gives the bankers who lend it a share of the surplus; this is the primary significant distinction drawn between financial and physical capital.

Power over the provision of finance is important enough if there is some way in which investment finance is less readily available to borrowers in the peripheral regions or if its availability is biased towards particular types of industry (such as megaprojects) or firms (such as meso-economic corporations, in Holland's, 1976, terminology), leading to a separation between locus of investment and locus of control. The particular form of financial intermediation between savers and investors must influence the regional economic structure of an economy. This in itself is a large subject, a major focus of the dependency theory literature as it applies to regions as well as nations. Without wishing to belittle the importance of the full range of financial institutions for the pattern of regional development, the focus here will be rather on the purely monetary aspects of finance. Any financial institution whose liabilities are used as money plays a unique role in the economic system, not least because of its capacity to initiate monetary expansion through credit expansion. Such institutions in turn, because of this degree of independence, can bring about a financial crisis with widespread repercussions for the economy.

There is a growing awareness in Marxian circles about the possibility that production crisis may be initiated by financial crisis; just as unfulfilled expectations within product markets may initiate a production crisis, so may unfulfilled expectations within product markets.[6] The type of subjective element of value which is generated by non-deterministic expectations formation about the returns on real or financial assets is inherent in Post Keynesian monetary theory. Indeed, much of the renewed interest in Marxian monetary theory has developed along lines very similar to Post Keynesian theory.[7] Post Keynesian theory develops Keynes' theory of liquidity preference, demonstrating how economic upswings are associated with low liquidity preference, strong investment demand, and easy money, while the reverse is true of downswings, all governed by non-deterministic expectations. Expectations in turn are governed by group convention, thus having a closer affinity to class analysis than the atomistic subjectivity of neo-classical or neo-Austrian analysis.[8]

It would seem reasonable to translate this theory into a spatial context, where regions at different levels of development are connected by national financial institutions. This interpretation of Keynes is resisted strongly by Keynesians who identify with the Ricardian tradition for the same reason that it is dismissed by orthodox Marxists: subjective value theory smacks of neo-classicism and a focus on exchange rather than production. This is not the place to pursue that debate; the theoretical exposition in the next section will have to speak for itself. Suffice it to say that Joan Robinson's work demonstrates how successfully short-run Keynesian analysis can be translated into long-run analysis, where the long run is a series of short runs.[9]

A THEORY OF MONEY AND REGIONAL DEVELOPMENT: A PARADOX OF LIQUIDITY

For the sake of simplicity, let us consider the case of two regions, Centre and Periphery. Centre has long-established dominance in industry and commerce, housing the country's financial centre. In line with cumulative causation theory, this dominance is self-perpetuating since any pre-existing productivity differential makes it hard for establishments in Periphery to compete. Such a productivity differential in turn can be the outcome of a wide range of factors, extending from physical economies of scale to political power and influence. Since Centre has started with some initial advantage, it is here that the earliest accumulation of wealth occurs, creating a dependence of Periphery production on Centre finance. In the early stages of banking development,[10] when loans are the result more of intermediation than credit creation, the locus of control will coincide with the locus of wealth. The ensuing divorce between production and control in peripheral regions encourages the type of specialisation in production which promotes high returns on investment rather than development.

Where there is a nationwide branch banking system, regional borrowers can tap a national pool of credit. But, even in the narrow terms of relative project appraisal, the combination of favourable factors assisting existing Centre enterprise is such that, in the absence of any other distinguishing feature, the same new project in Centre as in Periphery would have a higher expected return, net of risk. The conventional subjective element in the assessment of new capital projects, where information is necessarily incomplete, is of crucial importance, not only for investment planning, but also in attracting the necessary finance. If the conventional valuation, other things being equal, is always in favour of projects located in the Centre, then more investment will be planned there and the necessary finance will be more readily available. A higher rate of investment in turn increases the rate of growth of effective demand and thus of incomes, justifying the confidence displayed in the region, and exacerbating the unevenness of development.

Of course, the nature of the Centre-Periphery juxtaposition is that other things are not equal, as a result of the different patterns of specialisation resulting from the initial pattern of wealth, and control. The economic structure of each region is quite different, with activity in Periphery geared towards exporting to Centre. Peripheral activity is usually in primary products, or manufacturing at low levels of processing. These products tend to be sold in flexprice markets, in contrast to the fixprice markets for Centre products which are at a higher level of processing, or in the service sector.[11] Earnings in Periphery as a result are sensitive to the conjuncture in Centre, and highly variable. That variability in itself is a significant discouragement to credit availability.[12] Employment in Periphery is vulnerable, too, in relation to the extent of branch plant penetration by Centre corporations. When activity in Centre goes through a downturn, not only is demand for Periphery products reduced, but Periphery's branch plants of firms producing in both regions are the ones more vulnerable to closure. There are positive, spread effects from Centre in the form of export demand, and the extension of technology, expertise and services to Periphery through branch plant operations. But the form of these spread effects is such as to promote Periphery's dependence on Centre.

The greater instability of Peripheral economies, relative to Centre economies, is well documented; national business cycles are composed of cycles of higher than average amplitude in Peripheries and lower than average in Centres.[13] Given the greater volatility of actual returns in Peripheral economies, the danger of overvaluation of expected returns during upswings and undervaluation during downswings is correspondingly greater for Periphery investments than for Centre investments. (Expectations formation is more stable, and more likely to be accurate in a more stable environment.) Thus, while large capital inflows may be attracted to finance projects in Periphery during boom periods, the capital flight will be all the greater once it becomes apparent that investors' expectations have been overoptimistic. Periphery is thus more prone to production crisis than is Centre. The industrial concentration which occurs during slumps to restore the rate of profit to previous levels proceeds on the closure of marginal plants, or the takeover of marginal firms; these are more likely to be the small indigenous concerns in Periphery than the branches of Centre corporations, further adding to Periphery's dependence.

But we are concerned here more with financial crisis, of which availability of credit (or its absence) is only one aspect. We need to consider investment more from the monetary side, as a vehicle for monetary accumulation. Since the goal of accumulation is served by speculative capital gains as much as by profits on production, investment decisions need to be placed in the broader context of trading in all assets new and old, real and financial. Further, we need to analyse the behaviour of all groups of actors in financial markets - business borrowers and lenders, financial institutions, and household borrowers and lenders.

Keynes' theory of liquidity preference is based on the principle that attempts are made to hold more liquid assets the greater the risk of capital loss, and to hold less liquid assets the greater the prospect of capital gain. These attempts drive down asset prices and raise interest rates in the case of expectations of a slump in asset prices, further fuelling pessimism. In the case of expectations of a boom, the rise in asset prices and fall in interest rates are equally self-fulfilling. Note that the onset of pessimism or optimism over asset prices may well, but still need not, have a connection with 'real' production conditions; a financial crisis *can* occur independently. But rising interest rates inhibit the financing of productive investment just as much as they inhibit purchases of existing assets (and vice versa for falling interest rates). A financial crisis can thus spark off a production crisis. (The rate of profit refers to the total return received by financial and industrial capitalists. The particular distribution of that profit between the two sub-classes need not *necessarily* affect investment and production decisions. But the closer the interest rate gets to the expected rate of profit on production, the more untenable it becomes to argue that bankers' behaviour does not affect investment and output, even if expressed in terms of class struggle between bankers and owners of physical capital.[14])

Keynes (*C.W. VII*, Chapter 12) drew a distinction between entrepreneurs, engaged in long-run investment decisions concerning physical assets and speculators, engaged in short-run investment decisions concerning financial assets (rather than financial and industrial capitalists). It was activity in speculative markets which determined the availability and cost of finance for productive activity, and thus posed a potential constraint on entrepreneurial investment. Keynes' archetypal speculator was the large dealer in bonds or stocks. But purchases and sales of financial assets are the activity also of firms and households. A bank manager assessing the return on an advance to finance a business project, relative to placing funds in the wholesale market, that is with other financial institutions, can be likened to workers deciding whether to buy a house or to acquire financial assets. Both are influenced by similar considerations: the viability of a business project is of the same order as the worker's job security and thus ability to meet mortgage payments, while speculative fever in financial markets holds promise of high returns for bank and individual investor alike.

In terms of the Centre-Periphery configuration, a pattern can be expected in the liquidity preference of all types of residents of each region and indeed in the regional distribution of liquid and illiquid assets. Liquidity preference will tend to be higher in Periphery for the following reasons:

1) Liquidity preference tends to be greater for lower-income firms, financial institutions and households than for more prosperous ones, because of their greater risk of needing credit for current (rather than capital) expenses. This increased risk in turn ensures that the availability of credit is limited and/or expensive because of the associated default risk, reinforcing the preference to hold assets in readily-realisable form (with low risk of capital loss).
2) This outcome is reinforced (as noted above) by regional differences in income variability, with higher liquidity preference the greater the variability of income. Even if average income is high, if there is a high risk of periodic, severe slumps, default risk can be high on medium - and long-term loans.

At the same time, it is Centre assets which provide liquidity more than Periphery assets for the following reasons:

1) The presence of the financial centre in Centre allows more direct access to markets, the largest volume of trading, and the greatest range of financial instruments.

2) Even if Periphery assets are traded in the financial centre, remoteness, poor information on borrowers and relatively low volume of trading in these assets will contribute to weaker markets than for Centre assets.

Thus the higher liquidity preference of Periphery residents will be met by attempts to hold Centre assets, thereby further driving down the price of Periphery assets relative to that of Centre assets, and increasing the incidence of capital loss on them. The result is added reason for financial institutions to make credit more readily available to concerns in Centre than in Periphery.

This configuration of liquidity preference holds a particular implication for banks: banks specific to Peripheral regions will prefer to hold excess reserves and restrict local loans, compared to the behaviour of nationwide banks whose liquidity structure will be nationally rather than regionally determined. On the one hand, Periphery banks will be at a competitive disadvantage, further encouraging banking concentration. On the other hand, while Periphery branches of national banks are not hampered directly by higher liquidity requirements, the problem of availability of credit to Periphery may remain, albeit internalised within the banks' own accounts. The same factors accounting for the relatively high Periphery liquidity preference (the real economic structure and the remoteness of control over Periphery industry and its bank branches) may also adversely affect willingness to lend in Periphery even within nationwide banks.[15]

Expressed in terms of the capital flows between the two regions the following pattern emerges. Capital inflows to Periphery for direct investment will be attracted by growth in primary industry responding to increased demand for primary products from Centre, but these flows will be reversed sharply as soon as that growth slows down. At all times, firms, financial institutions and households in Periphery will prefer to hold Centre assets for their liquidity relative to Periphery assets; Centre residents have less need for liquidity, but can satisfy such need as they have with Centre assets.

There is a 'prisoner's dilemma' problem in that, in-so-far as Periphery residents hold Periphery assets, attempts in Periphery to go liquid, during a slump phase particularly, cause Periphery asset prices to fall. (This phenomenon also causes an identification problem if attempts are made to interpret actual portfolio data.) The ensuing increased difficulty of acquiring credit forces asset sales on those requiring liquidity to meet current expenditure, involving them in capital loss. The outcome is that attempts to increase the stock of liquid assets only succeed in reducing it; this is a paradox of liquidity on a par with Keynes' paradox of saving.

The reverse holds for Centre residents. Having less need for liquidity, attempts are made to acquire less liquid assets with a view to making capital gains. The result is increased asset prices, capital gains and readily available credit; attempts to reduce liquidity succeed in increasing it. If Periphery residents do hold Centre assets as a potential source of liquidity, the actual process of liquidation should not unduly depress Centre asset prices, since Periphery wealth is, by definition of the notion of Peripheral economies, a small proportion of the national total. In any case the purpose of liquidation would generally be to meet payments to Centre, which in turn create additional demand for Centre assets, supporting their price.

This financial behaviour affects the pattern of regional development by exacerbating tendencies towards uneven development. It is not just a matter of Peripheral investors experiencing greater difficulty in acquiring credit, although that may be serious enough in itself. It is the behaviour of all Periphery sectors which tends to weaken the value of existing Periphery assets, and at the same time strengthen that of Centre assets. Not only does this promote disparities in the valuation of wealth in the two regions, but it influences unfavourably the willingness of Periphery producers to invest in new capital goods at the same time as reducing their credit-worthiness. Of course, capital inflows from Centre during expansions in Periphery finance developments which might otherwise not occur. But the volatility of that credit availability further adds to Periphery's dependence. In addition, the pull exerted by Centre's financial markets is such that Peripheral funds which might have been available to finance indigenous domestic investment are diverted out of the region. Centre direct investment in Periphery adds further to Periphery's dependence; depressed Periphery physical asset prices may be a particular inducement to such outside direct investment.

Interregional financial flows are constrained to balance; the regional equivalent of accommodating movements in foreign exchange reserves is movements in bank reserves.[16] Where banks are regionally distinct, a contraction in a region's banks' reserves will lead to regional credit contraction unless reserves can be borrowed (a balancing capital inflow). Credit contraction means liquidity contraction and thus an exacerbation of the region's difficulties. But if banks branch nationwide, there need be no *automatic* repercussions on regional credit. Indeed the maintenance of regional credit levels assists the maintenance of regional deposit levels.

This disparity between regionally-specific banks and national banks is reinforced by the fact that small banks tend to have a lower redeposit ratio and so cannot rely on deposits generated by new advances staying with the bank. This becomes less of a constraint on credit creation the more sophisticated the financial system of which the small bank is a part. If the bank holds a large stock of widely-traded assets, like government bonds, then any withdrawal of deposits can be offset by a sale of these assets. Further, if there is a well-developed wholesale market, the bank can borrow the funds from other financial institutions to back the new advances. But this type of facility is at its most developed within a branch bank network, where branches 'borrow from' and 'lend to' head office, that is other branches.

Further, we must consider again the implications of actual and expected asset price movements in Centre and Periphery, resulting from perceptions of their relative real economic conditions on the part of potential providers of loans. If loans in Periphery consistently lead to deposit outflows (in search of greater liquidity elsewhere), there is a limit to the interbank, or interbranch, borrowing which is feasible; eventually the credit-worthiness of the bank or branch is called into question. Bank branches are conventionally administered as profit centres, so that, in practice, their asset and liability structures are assessed together, as a whole. Except in unusual circumstances, persistently low redeposit ratios due to payments outside a Peripheral region, will be interpreted as reinforcing any pessimism about expected returns. Further, the greater the risk of capital loss on Periphery assets, the greater the incentive for Periphery banks to purchase Centre assets instead; this applies to all types of asset, not just loans. Thus it is not just a question of the credit-worthiness of Periphery borrowers which determines how much credit is extended in Periphery. The portfolio behaviour of all sectors may impose constraints on local banks' capacity and willingness to extend credit. In the event of financial crisis in Periphery, capital outflows may be so great as to lead to closure of financial institutions in Periphery, or Periphery branches of national institutions, further removing the locus of financial power.

THE CANADIAN CASE

The influence of financial markets on regional development has always been a political issue in Canada. As a result there is a body of political and academic thought devoted to the subject, policy measures have been introduced (mainly by the Quebec and Prairie provincial governments) in response, and regional data have been produced by most financial institutions as a contribution to the debate. All these features are also present with respect to the United States. But Canada provides a particularly interesting case because there is a highly concentrated financial sector, with nationwide branching. (In fact, the unit banking system in the States, which currently supports over 14,000 banks, has been supported by regional interests explicitly as a vehicle for promoting some regional balance.)

Canada's major period of development (from the early eighteenth century) coincided with the emergence of the British banking system; this was to be of great significance for the Canadian financial system which developed from the early nineteenth century, not only because of its dependence in the formative years on British capital, but also because of the subsequent exercise of British government jurisdiction over the Canadian financial system as it developed its national character. Canadian banking legislation, largely imposed by the British government, reflected the concerns of the British banking system of the early nineteenth century (notably the 1844 and 1845 legislation in Britain, which severely constrained banks' freedom to create credit, and the scope for the formation of new banks). It can be argued that this type of legislation was totally unsuited to a country such as Canada, still at an early stage of economic development. Indeed it can be argued that it was these undue restrictions imposed on the Canadian banking system which highlighted its impact on regional development. The Peripheral regions were vocal in their objections to the difficulties they experienced in gaining access to credit from the large banks, or in receiving permission to set up local, private banks.[17]

The central region of Ontario and Quebec, with its agricultural prosperity and strong population growth, established itself as the Centre, both in terms of direct control over economic activity in other regions, but also in terms of financial control. Although banking emerged in both the Atlantic region and Ontario and Quebec in the early 1820s, the Atlantic region soon took on, in banking, the characteristics of a Periphery to Ontario and Quebec's Centre. Even though one of the major banks, the Bank of Nova Scotia, still has it titular head office in Halifax, its management office has been in Toronto since the turn of the century. (It is symptomatic of the high degree of public consciousness of the regional dimension of banking that the Bank of Nova Scotia has attempted to maintain the appearance of its regional identity.) This regional configuration could well have been different if Canada had adopted a US-style unit banking system. Naylor (1978, Chapter 3) argues that it was the concentration of Canadian banking around the financial centres of Toronto and Montreal which led to the decline of the Atlantic region relative to the Eastern seaboard of the US. Indeed Acheson (1977) and Brym and Sacouman (1979, Introduction) argue that it was financial and corporate concentration which accounted for the shift westward in economic power, not any failure of productivity; with the centralisation of financial capital, the financial resources were not available within the

Maritimes to resist corporate takeovers and subsequent marginalisation of branch plant activity in the Maritimes.

Toronto and Montreal were also well-established as financial centres by the time the West was opened up, making it very difficult for Western banks to compete. The West benefited at the expense of the Atlantic region, by the banks channelling funds into such projects as the railroads, which were crucial to the Prairie economy, based as it was on trade in natural resources. At the same time, the Prairies took on the dependent character of a natural resource-based economy whose development is governed by trade and investment patterns established elsewhere. The Prairie economy is typically unstable, with marked boom and bust cycles. Being resource rich, much wealth has been generated; indeed the oil boom of the 1970s seemed to generate a shift westward of economic power, supporting the establishment of new Western banks. But subsequent events have reversed the fortunes of the West in time-honoured fashion. Two of the new Western banks, which were an innovative feature of the oil boom, had collapsed by the end of 1985.

Consciousness of the role of the financial system in the Prairie economy was raised most notably during the Depression, when foreclosures on farm mortgages and refusals of short-term debt were commonplace, exacerbating a situation of considerable hardship.[18] It is interesting to note that the Dominion Government's refusal to enforce a more expansive approach on the part of the banks was based on the fear that it would weaken the confidence of foreign investors in Canadian financial rectitude; Canada as a whole exhibits features of a dependent relationship on business and financial concerns elsewhere.[19] The product of the experience of the Depression was the emergence of populist movements on the left and the right, both of which identified the financial system as carrying much of the responsibility for the plight of peripheral regions.

On the left, the Cooperative Commonwealth Federation included in their manifesto the 'socialisation of finance' as a necessary adjunct to economic planning. The League for Social Reconstruction whose research expanded on features of the Manifesto (and some of whose members were educated in Cambridge during Keynes' time), argued that providing financial support to depressed regions, rather than pursuing speculative gains, went against the profit-making motivation of bankers; public ownership was therefore required to effect the desired change in financial behaviour. On the right, the Social Credit League identified finance as the sole cause of regional depression (and indeed all economic problems), along the lines of underconsumption theory. The League's inspiration came from Major Douglas and Silvio Gesell, a combination of whose proposals was adopted by the Social Credit Government of Alberta in the late 1930s. (The

Supreme Court, however, overturned all the financial reform legislation.)

The re-emergence of this issue in the 1970s[20] coincided with the temporary shift westward in economic power during the oil boom. As a result, the banks agreed to publish regional data in an effort to demonstrate their contribution to balanced regional growth. In general, the data show banks' assets exceeding liabilities in the Atlantic and Prairie regions, and liabilities exceeding assets in the Centre. The banks claim that this demonstrates a redistribution of Centre savings to finance investment in the other regions.[21] But the data are also consistent with an interpretation along the lines of the theory outlined here, which starts with credit creation rather than saving. The shortfall of liabilities in the lower-income regions thus reflects capital outflows following credit creation: in payment of profits to extra-regional owners, in payment for capital goods produced elsewhere, and in purchase of financial assets in the Central region. The relatively strong growth of liabilities in the Central region is the obverse of this process.

Comparing assets and liabilities by region is thus not fruitful, since it is consistent both with the traditional view that banks promote even regional development, and with the alternative view presented here. According to our theory, it is the strength of credit creation in each region in the first place which is of greatest importance. But then we are again faced with an identification problem, whereby the evidence supports both views. Credit growth in lower-income regions is relatively low; but is this because returns on investment are low (according to the traditional view) or is income growth low because credit growth is low (according to our view)?

But the banks' comparison of regional assets and liabilities, by their own calculations, have gone largely unchallenged and have indeed been employed by economists (such as Benson, 1978). It is necessary, therefore, to note the shortcomings of these data for *any* argument. A nationwide bank is centralised in various respects which makes a regional attribution of much of their assets and liabilities meaningless, most notably net worth, investments and large loans, none of which refers to any regional decision-making. Thus, for example, assets and liabilities may grow rapidly in a peripheral region during a boom period without any change in the locus of control over investment. Indeed, the scope for misinterpretation is enhanced by the possibility that industrial head offices may have their deposits booked in Centre branches but their loans booked in Periphery branches; the regional allocation of loans gives no indication of the regional allocation of control.

A final approach would be to compare portfolios in the different regions. The evidence is on balance in favour of the hypothesis that Periphery sectors attempt to hold more liquid portfolios than Centre sectors. (See Dow, 1990.) But even then the evidence is not strong, and we would not expect it to be. It was shown in the previous section that attempts to achieve greater liquidity tend to be self-defeating. In other words, the paradox of liquidity means that observed portfolios are unlikely to reflect preferred portfolios. In any case, the regional aggregative data are so problematic that it is difficult to maintain any strong assertion on the basis of them. Although there is a relatively good regional data base, then, the Canadian case cannot yield definitive conclusions by orthodox testing criteria.

CONCLUSION

The conventional view is that Canada's national financial system serves to promote regional equality by redirecting funds from high-income to low-income provinces. But the data on which this view relies cannot be conclusive. First, the fact that the statistical evidence is consistent both with the mainstream interpretation and our alternative interpretation should encourage further investigation of the alternative. There is no *prima facie* case at all for allowing the mainstream interpretation to rule the roost. Second, the well-known problems with regional data should not deter discussion of the underlying issues. International data are subject to equal, if not greater, problems; they are used nevertheless with great assurance in elaborate econometric models. This suggests that less weight should be given to international empirical work, but also that the regional question should not be dismissed so readily. However, the circular argument is often put forward in those countries without good regional financial data, that data need not be collected since there is no regional dimension to finance, and that there can be no discussion of regional finance since there are no data.

But in any case, the data are unlikely to distinguish successfully between the mainstream and alternative theories since what we are concerned with is a process of causation: are regional financial flows the result of regional disparities, or do they contribute to these disparities? Is the regional pattern of credit creation, in particular, the outcome of disparities, or part of the problem? A broader form of investigation is required than a regional comparison of (necessarily) *ex post* aggregative data. The argument must be fleshed out with detailed case studies of the behaviour of particular financial institutions, of particular investment projects and their finance in order to form some view of causative processes. This type of evidence for Canada does indeed support the theory presented here.[22]

Economic history evidence explains what has contributed to the emergence in the past of regional disparities. In the early days of a financial system, its primary purpose is in redirecting existing savings to finance investment, so that the argument may be couched in those clearly identifiable terms. As a financial system develops, however, the question of liquidity preference and the independent capacity of the banking system to create, as well as reallocate, credit increase in importance. An understanding of the current role of financial institutions in regional development thus requires that more attention be paid to the financial behaviour of all sectors in the economy, and how that behaviour, with financial institutions' own liquidity preference, influences the valuation of regional assets, the availability of credit and the willingness to invest in different types of region. Contemporary case studies along these lines will be a major task in themselves. The purpose here has been the limited one of assessing the existing analysis of the role of money in regional development, and suggesting a direction for future research.

NOTES

1. A precursor of dependency theory which also highlights the regional significance of liquidity is found in the Canadian literature; see Neill, 1972, pp. 57-61.
2. See Holland (1976, Chapter 1) for a review.
3. This argument is developed by Mundell (1976).
4. See Goodhart (1975, Chapter 14), for the theoretical argument, and Benson (1978) for the argument in terms of B.C. in relation to Canada-wide banks.
5. See Pfister (1960) and Whitman (1967).
6. This is reflected, for example, in Harvey (1982, Chapter 10).
7. See de Brunhoff (1976) for an exposition of Marxian monetary theory; Davidson (1978) and Dow and Earl (1982) for expositions of Post Keynesian monetary theory; and Dow (1985) for a comparison between the two.
8. See Keynes (*CW XIV*, pp. 109-23), for his clearest exposition on expectations. The origins of his thinking on expectations can be found in Keynes, (*CW VIII*).
9. See, for example, Robinson (1956).
10. See Chick (1986).
11. See Kaldor (1970b) and Hicks (1974).
12. Where risk is objectively determined, it is a conventional result in the orthodox literature that relatively high risk discourages funding, following Tobin (1958). This result is reinforced if high objective variability of returns is combined with remoteness between information and control.
13. A general and a particular discussion of this phenomenon as it occurs in Canada can be found in Economic Council of Canada (1968, Chapter 7) and Blain, Patterson and Rae (1974), respectively.
14. See Panico (1980).
15. This conclusion is borne out by comparisons between the portfolios of banks in the United States, in states with limited branching and in states with extensive branching.

(See Dow, 1981).
16. See Chapter 9 of this volume.
17. See, for example, Shortt (1896; 1964).
18. See, for example, McIvor (1958, p.148).
19. See Government of Canada (1940), Book I, p. 152.
20. See Premiers of Manitoba, Alberta, Saskatchewan and British Columbia (1973).
21. See Canadian Bankers' Association (1974).
22. See, for example, Sears (1972).

11. Money and the Pattern of International Development

This chapter has benefited from helpful comments and suggestions from Philip Arestis, Victoria Chick and Rogerio Studart.

INTRODUCTION

In looking forward to the next hundred years of economics in the special centenary issue of the *Economic Journal*, several leading economists identified the persistence of real economic disparities between countries as the major problem to which economics should be addressed. The size of the gap in terms of per capita income between developing and developed countries has been well documented, and much attention paid to the possible explanations arising from real factors: relative competitiveness, resource endowment, and so on. Here we will focus on the role which has been played by money and banking in the perpetuation or even promotion of economic disparities. Money and banking will not be treated as ultimately separable from the real economic processes at work in international economic relations. Rather they will be regarded as integral to these relations.

This chapter therefore continues the theme developed in earlier chapters with respect to real economic disparities between regional economies, and picks up where Chapter 5 left off, with the suggestion that capital flows might depress weaker national economies just as they depress any economy in a downturn phase of the business cycle. The mutuality of real and monetary forces can be explored by combining Post Keynesian monetary theory with an amalgam of dependency theory and cumulative causation theory. Dependency theory and cumulative causation theory have traditionally been applied both to the regional and the international contexts. But Post Keynesian monetary theory in general has not been applied spatially (Davidson, 1982, being a significant exception to the rule).

We will consider here, therefore, the consequences of combining dependency theory and cumulative causation theory with the theories of liquidity preference and endogenous money in an international context. In the process, the broad usage of the liquidity preference concept which has characterised earlier chapters will be clarified. Can different economies be characterised as having different liquidity preference? Does the greater power of the banks to create international credit than credit within any one national banking system strengthen the argument that all demand for credit at going interest rates can be accommodated? How does the proposed framework explain the debt crisis and the capital flight which has exacerbated it? On balance do developing countries benefit from access to international financial markets?

In this chapter we will address these questions in turn. In preparation for this discussion, the next section will discuss briefly the relevant distinctions between the regional and international contexts. The following section will briefly review the finance and development literature. The questions which naturally arise as to the optimal design of the international financial system will be dealt with in Chapter 12.

DISTINGUISHING THE INTERNATIONAL CONTEXT FROM THE REGIONAL CONTEXT

The first clear difference relevant to the present discussion is that international disparities are much more severe than regional disparities. Per capita GNP in the richest country in 1988, for example, was 275 times that of the poorest (see World Bank, 1990, pp. 178-9). Regional differences in per capita GNP in developed countries are of a totally different order: the richest Canadian region has a per capita GNP only around twice the level of the poorest regional for example (see Dow, 1990, p. 102). This difference must be due in part to the fact that physical factor endowments and their productivity are likely to be more similar among spatially proximate regions than among spatially remote nations. But much more important are the differences in institutions which govern production on the basis of these factors. Myrdal (1964) argues that spread effects tend to dominate backwash effects among regions only in developed countries; the weakness of spread effects for developing countries accounts for higher regional disparities there, and also the persistence of international disparities.

Kaldor (1970b) highlights the significance for regions of national governments. Even if there is no active regional policy, there is an automatic regional counterpart of the fiscal stabiliser; regions facing higher unemployment and lower-income growth than others receive a fiscal transfer in the form of benefits with a lower relative tax outflow. This automatic stabiliser is absent in the international context. Official development assistance only constituted 2.4% of the GNP of low-income countries in 1988 for example (see World Bank, 1990, p. 216). This compares with a public sector transfer of around 10% of GNP to the Atlantic provinces of Canada in 1980 (see Economic Council of Canada, 1982).

A further spread effect associated with the existence of a national government relates to education and training. It is generally the case that national governments aim to maintain at least a standard national minimum level of education and training, regardless of regional revenue base. Labour productivity is thus likely to be more uniform regionally than internationally; this not only facilitates labour mobility, but it also facilitates mobility of capital in the form of direct investment. To the international differences in education and skill levels must be added the cultural and linguistic impediments to labour mobility and direct investment. The resulting segmentation of the international labour market on the other hand means that wage bargaining is also segmented, allowing international wage differentials to persist. (This is not surprising given that the strict conditions for the Stolper-Samuelson factor price equalisation theorem clearly are not met.)

Technology transfer, too, is more effective regionally than internationally. It is more effective in two senses: first the transferred technology is more likely to be suited to another region in the same country than a different country with markedly different factor endowments, access to spare parts etc. Second, multi-regional companies are more common than multinational companies, other things being equal. Technology can thus be transferred readily within companies regionally. It is more difficult to transfer technology across companies internationally. This in itself provides multinational companies with a competitive edge, influencing the evolution of industrial structure in developing countries. In turn, this exacerbates the dualism of developing countries, between the monetised and non-monetised sectors, to which we will return in a later section.

A key spread effect in cumulative causation theory is the export demand generated by growth in the Centre. Dependency theory focuses on the fact that the downside of this spread effect is an overspecialisation in exports, often in the primary sector. The outcome is that export receipts are highly elastic with respect to the Centre's income; there has been a tendency too for the terms of trade to deteriorate for primary sector exports, (see World Bank, 1990, p. 165). It is not clear that there should be any regional-international difference in this phenomenon, only in the possibilities for averting its consequences.

The factor most commonly presumed to neutralise balance of payments problems for regions is capital mobility. Reference is made to automatic credit through national branch banking systems, or to the scope for portfolio adjustments within an integrated national financial system. At the international level, there is some financial integration. But whether this is sufficient to dampen economic disparities is the question at issue here. When considering the supply of credit, attention must be paid to the differing access of different parties within developing countries, the information problems faced by banks and the barrier posed by separate currencies. It has been concluded in earlier chapters that capital mobility may exacerbate disparities regionally. We will consider here how far this conclusion translates into the international context.

THE FINANCE AND DEVELOPMENT LITERATURE

The possibility that the banking system might have a role in international disparities is not a new one. Triffin's (1964) analysis of the gold standard of the late nineteenth century suggested that even then the international financial system was not neutral. Because London was then the dominant financial centre, exporters to Britain acquired their trade credit in London. This allowed Britain to correct a balance of trade deficit by raising interest rates. The resulting decline in export demand combined with the more immediate problem of meeting higher interest payments forced developing-country exporters to reduce export prices in order to generate revenue. Aside from the temporarily depressing effect of higher interest rates on the British economy, the payments imbalance was thus cured by an improvement in Britain's terms of trade. Kindleberger's (1974) study of financial centres suggests that this concentration of financial control (in a few locations) and the consequent imbalance of power in financial markets, far from being an aberration, has been a common feature of financial history.

But much of the finance and development literature has focused on the beneficial effects on developing countries of having access to credit from international sources. This literature relies on a loanable funds monetary theory, which equates the provision of credit with saving and capital flows with real transfers. The financial problem facing developing countries is identified as an inadequacy of saving relative to investment demand. Capital inflows constitute one solution to that problem. The implication is that the greater the degree of capital mobility the less likely it is that a shortage of saving will inhibit economic development. The other solution is seen to lie in financial liberalisation within developing countries in order to generate more saving internally. (See McKinnon, 1973 and Shaw, 1973;

see Van Vijnbergen, 1983, Beckerman, 1988, Burkett and Dutt, 1991 and Studart, 1991 for detailed critiques.) This theoretical approach underlies the structural adjustment programmes which the IMF has required of many debtor countries. Its sister organisation, the World Bank, similarly employs a loanable funds approach: 'The financial factor can play an important role by increasing the efficiency of the transformation of savings into investment' (World Bank, 1991, p. 122).

But this approach evades a number of important issues. First, as demonstrated by Triffin (1964), the provision of trade credit is as important as (and indeed prior to) the provision of capital to finance investment. Second, loanable funds theory cannot apply in a non-stationary state; the provision of bank finance outside such a state must take account of liquidity preference. Liquidity preference theory stresses the role of money markets as being distinct from capital markets; in particular it stresses the potential significance of a preference for holding liquid assets as an alternative to capital goods. Liquidity preference can then be seen to govern borrowing and lending behaviour as well as the willingness to purchase capital goods. (See the fourth section, below.) It follows then that saving is the consequence of income generated by such purchases of capital goods as can be financed, given the relative preference for more liquid assets on the part both of borrowers and lenders. Given the paradox of thrift, prior saving may be more an impediment to investment demand than a facilitator of it.

Most developing countries lack adequate internal capital markets and are driven therefore to international banks not only for initial financing but also for long-term finance. It is not a shortage of saving which is the problem, but rather the lack of a mechanism to turn saving into appropriate funding instruments. Further the resort to foreign borrowing does not necessarily reflect a demand for a transfer of real resources, since the investment should generate the saving to repay the debt. But repayment is made more difficult by virtue of the fact that it must be in the form of foreign exchange. (See Studart, forthcoming, for an exposition of these points.)

The most important factor not explicitly addressed by the traditional literature is the endogenity of credit creation within modern banking systems. (Lewis, 1954, raised this point, albeit within a traditional bank multiplier framework, but the point was not subsequently developed.) There is no longer any need for prior saving to finance investment when banks can create credit to finance investment which generates the saving to fund the credit. Chick's (1986) theory of the evolution of banking systems demonstrates how credit creation gradually ceases to be constrained by a given stock of reserves and then moves beyond the direct influence of the central bank. The issue of endogenous credit is picked up in the fifth section, below. But the pattern is complicated when considering financial relations between banking systems at different stages of evolution (see Chick and Dow, 1988). Then questions arise as to asymmetry in financial relationships and the consequences for the structure of international banking. In particular, the scope for creating credit is greater the higher the stage of development of the banking system. If the capacity to create credit for example in developing countries is constrained for this reason, borrowers can circumvent the historical process by gaining access to international banks. But, particularly since it is the projects perceived by international banks to be the safest which will gain finance in this way, the local banking system may be inhibited in its process of development, creating a vicious circle of limitations on domestic credit creating capacity. This issue is picked up again in the seventh section.

The structural adjustment policy of financial liberalisation is intended to strengthen the domestic financial system. McKinnon (1973) addresses his financial liberalisation argument to the particular issue of the characteristic dualism of developing countries. By exposing the rural sector to banking with high returns on deposits, domestic saving will be encouraged. (High returns will also encourage saving in the export enclave to be retained in the domestic banking system.) But McKinnon underestimates the significance of the dualism between the export enclave and the rural sector. First, much of production in the rural sector may be non-commercial so that any surplus may not be monetised. Improved access to banking in itself may not be sufficient to break down a dualism which is as much cultural as economic (see Ghosh, 1986a, 1986b and St. Hill, 1991). While it is presumed that banks would offer a preferable alternative to money-lenders, this may not in fact be the case. What appear to be exorbitant interest charges may be a realistic reflection of the lack of effective collateral. When faced with the type of credit demand which is the business of money-lenders, banks might simply refuse credit outright on the grounds that the risk is either excessive or cannot be assessed. The money-lenders have the advantage of extensive local knowledge which allows some measure to be attached to lenders' risk. (See Drake, 1980, Chapter 6.) In other words, it may be that freedom of capital movement within developing countries, and the general increased incidence of monetisation and banking habits which would bring it about, may exacerbate disparities between the export enclave and the rural sector.

There is finally a large body of literature on finance and development which has focused on the nature of the international financial system, and particularly on the debt crisis; see for example Helleiner, 1990 and Loxley, 1986. This literature provides detailed analysis of the conditions facing developing countries, and much of this analysis forms a backdrop to the argument to be developed below. Where the argument developed here differs is in using money and banking theory as a grounding for analysis; as a result some general principles will be put forward which can be applied to the diversity of developing-country experience.

On the basis of this brief critique of the finance and development literature we turn now to address in detail the questions posed in the Introduction with respect to the roles of liquidity preference and endogenous money, the causes of the debt crisis and capital flight, and the international structure of banking and its implications.

LIQUIDITY PREFERENCE

Keynes' theory of liquidity preference has generally been understood as a theory of the demand for money. This demand arises from transactions requirements, anticipated transactions (the finance motive), precautionary purposes and speculative purposes. Successive discussions in earlier chapters in this volume have applied the theory of liquidity preference more generally to all choices with respect to borrowing and lending. Keynes (*C.W. VII*, p. 166) introduced the concept as referring to the preferred constitution of a portfolio of assets; liquidity preference in turn arose from uncertainty (Keynes, *C.W. VII*, p. 167). In the previous chapter, Keynes had discussed long-term investment and its finance also in the context of uncertainty. It seems natural therefore to combine the two discussions into one of decision-making under uncertainty. Liquidity preference can then be extended to apply both to the volume and to the composition of assets. Increased liquidity preference then implies a reduced willingness to buy capital goods, and a reduced willingness on the part of the banks to create credit, as well as the more conventional preference on the part of individuals to hold their assets in more liquid form. (This argument is set out in more detail in Dow and Dow, 1988.)

The first implication is that the demand for money be distinguished from liquidity preference, since the demand for money may rise due to the finance motive which in turn is associated with a preference for borrowing and purchasing capital goods (low liquidity preference). (See Wray, 1990 and 1992.) Second, the focus has tended to be put on speculative demand for money (or liquidity) as the major source of instability. Speculative demand rises if there is an expectation of capital loss from holding alternative assets. While the choice is conventionally posed as being between money and bonds, it can be posed similarly between money and capital goods or, for banks, between investments and advances. (The comparison then involves a comparison between relative risks of capital loss.) Particularly relevant to the case of developing countries is the element of liquidity preference in the choice of financing mechanisms for investment. The least illiquid option is full long-term funding at an early stage, minimising the degree of short-term finance. But developing country borrowers are often constrained to use the most illiquid form of finance: short - and medium-term bank loans at variable interest.

It has also become conventional within the Post Keynesian literature to suggest that speculative demand increases with uncertainty as to the return on alternative assets, that is with an inability to quantify risk of capital loss. Recent developments in the theory of uncertainty allow some refinement of this idea. First, Keynes' notion of weight has been employed to develop the idea of uncertainty as a relative concept (see Dow, forthcoming, a). Then liquidity preference would be higher if the degree of uncertainty is higher. (With an absolute notion of uncertainty, liquidity preference would be higher only with a higher incidence of uncertainty.) Second, it has been suggested (by Runde, 1992) that it is the precautionary demand for money which varies with uncertainty, not the speculative demand. In other words, if there is a confident expectation of capital loss (and thus default) on a project to be financed by a bank, the bank will prefer to hold more liquid investments as a manifestation of speculative demand. On the other hand, if the bank is uncertain as to how to assess risk of default, the bank may prefer to hold investments as a manifestation of precautionary demand for liquidity, rather than create credit. Speculative demand for liquidity may be volatile; decisions have to be taken as if on the basis of certainty, and are thus vulnerable to new information and changes in confidence. But precautionary demand may be quite stable if conditions of uncertainty persist.

Different types of economy can then be characterised as having different degrees of liquidity preference as a result of different expectations as to capital loss on alternative assets and as a result of different degrees of uncertainty about the expected returns on alternative assets. Further, banks' lending behaviour in aggregate or with respect to different types of borrower can be analysed in terms of the expected risk of default and uncertainty about that risk assessment. If expectations about returns on assets are perpetually subject to high uncertainty (because of limited information), then liquidity preference can be expected to be consistently high, and the provision of bank credit consistently low.

In general an economy with good growth prospects will be characterised by low liquidity preference with respect to speculative demand. Investment demand will be strong and the demand for borrowed capital high. The opposite would be true for an economy with poor growth prospects. But overall liquidity preference would depend also on the degree of uncertainty attached to the expectations of growth prospects, that is on precautionary demand. An economy with high investment demand might also express a high precautionary demand for liquidity if the optimistic expectations are uncertain. This uncertainty might arise from a lack of relevant knowledge about the source of growth: if it is to come from expanding a new sector or market for example. But it could also arise from uncertainty about constraints which might impede the investment. Thus for example if the future availability of finance is uncertain, or if the wealth base is small so that dependence on external finance is high should unforeseen circumstances require increased borrowing, then the precautionary demand for liquidity will be high.

As was suggested in Chapter 10 with respect to peripheral regional economies, liquidity preference may also be high because of a greater risk of a need for working capital combined with high-income variability, which in turn increase default risk and thus reduce the availability of credit. This argument is reinforced for developing countries by the inadequacy of local financing mechanisms. But in turn the exposure of banks to high default risk makes more difficult the evolution of the domestic banking system. Banks evolve by means of a virtuous circle of increased confidence which in turn allows banks to reduce the apparent liquidity of their portfolios. But just as banks in developing countries are less likely to extend credit than money-lenders with good local knowledge, so international banks are less likely to accept the perceived risk than domestic banks with better local knowledge.

In summary, the highest liquidity preference would be expressed by those countries with poor growth prospects, low wealth and uncertain future need for and availability of credit. The lowest-income developing countries would fit this category. The lowest liquidity preference would be expressed by countries with good growth prospects, high wealth and assured access to credit whenever required. The higher-growth developed countries which are well-integrated with the international financial system would fit this category.

Finally, how would national liquidity preference be expressed? The most liquid assets for developing countries are foreign assets, for example short-term deposits in the Euro-currency market. The most illiquid of liabilities is foreign borrowing, which must be serviced with scarce foreign exchange, or else rescheduled on condition that structural adjustment programmes are adopted. High liquidity preference would thus be expressed in a high ratio of foreign deposits to foreign borrowing. It is indeed the case that, in periods when it is likely that low-income developing countries have been most able to satisfy liquidity preference, there is evidence of high liquidity preference. (See Dow, forthcoming, c and Dow and Ghosh, forthcoming.) These studies considered the ratio of international assets to liabilities as an indicator of liquidity preference.

The use of this ratio must take account not only of constraints on acquisition of liquidity, but also of constraints on availability of foreign credit. Indeed the issue is complicated by the proposition that liquidity preference increases if there is an expectation of credit constraints. We cannot proceed further without addressing directly the issue of credit availability.

THE ENDOGENEITY OF CREDIT SUPPLY

There is a growing acceptance in the monetary literature that the private sector has a significant amount of control over the volume of new credit, that is credit creation is largely endogenous to the private sector. In its extreme form, as expressed by Kaldor (1970a, 1982) and Moore (1979b, 1988), this endogeneity is perfect in the sense that all demand for credit is satisfied at the interest rate established by the central bank. This is the 'horizontalist' position, referring to the money supply function. If this accurately represented the international provision of credit, then there would be no difference in the availability of credit for different types of economy, and that availability would be assured. Liquidity preference would then differ only on account of differences in expected returns on domestic investment, that is with respect to speculative demand. There would be no difference due to precautionary demand.

But there is good reason to question the horizontalist position, as expressed above. Even if banks undertake to supply credit at a particular interest rate, there is always the proviso that the default risk be acceptable. Indeed banks supply credit within an interest rate structure, whereby a rate is chosen to reflect expected risk (once the risk is accepted). This requires that risk be quantified. Since the build-up of the debt crisis, banks have engaged in sovereign risk assessment, using a range of indicators (see Sargen, 1977). But ultimately sovereign risk does not satisfy the criteria for quantification, that there be limited independent variety. For example, the usefulness of a debt/exports ratio depends on exports remaining stable during the term of the debt. But developing-country export receipts are notoriously volatile, depending on external demand conditions. Indeed, in general, sovereign risk assessment cannot take account of unanticipated global developments (such as the aftermath of oil price rises). The past is then not necessarily a good guide for the future, in attempting to quantify risk. Even if full information on the past were available then, sovereign risk is inevitably a matter of uncertainty. For low-income developing economies this uncertainty is compounded by poor information. Even if credit were perfectly endogenous in the horizontalist sense, therefore, economies for which default risk is assessed as high or uncertain will inevitably encounter constraints on credit availability.

This argument has already found expression in the literature on credit rationing with respect to small firms (see Fazzari *et al.*, 1988). Small firms tend to be assessed as high default risks because of their small asset base and their relatively volatile earnings; but in any case relevant information is costly to acquire relative to the value of the loans sought. The portfolio behaviour of small firms thus tends to conform to that suggested in the previous section for low-income developing countries: Fazzari *et al.* show that their reliance on retained earnings is much greater than for larger firms, consistent with the hypothesis of high liquidity preference for precautionary purposes. (A similar result emerged for Scottish firms relative to the rest of the UK in Dow, 1992.)

The control of the banking system over credit creation at the international level is considerable. The essence of the Euro-currency market is that it is subject to much less regulation than other money markets. But the discussion above suggests that the banks nevertheless use their discretion in providing credit, employing risk assessment procedures. Credit then will be rationed for economies which are perceived as high risks. The perception of high risk then is likely to become entrenched because the consequence of credit rationing for low-income countries is that the growth process is inhibited. Indeed such countries may not even seek credit because of their high liquidity preference.

In addition to controlling the distribution of credit, banks control the volume of credit. This brings us back to the liquidity preference of the banks themselves. Banks have speculative preference for liquidity if uncertainty increases as to the risk attached to advances. If banks exercise liquidity preference, they create less credit. Thinking of the demand for credit as constituting a queue, ordered in terms of perceived risk, then borrowers with higher perceived risk, other things being equal, will find it difficult to borrow.

There is considerable debate over the presence or otherwise or credit rationing at the microlevel. There is growing evidence that rationing is present at this level due to information limitations. But the situation of developing countries in international financial markets provides ample macro-evidence. As we shall discuss in the next section, the debt crisis can be explained partly as the result of variations in the degree of rationing. But more generally developing countries can be seen as experiencing more endemic financing difficulties (see Studart, 1991).

THE DEBT CRISIS AND CAPITAL FLIGHT

The debt crisis provides a case study of particular interest which can serve to illuminate the theory outlined above. The conventional analysis of the debt crisis explains the massive increase in developing-country borrowing in the 1970s in terms of the factors causing an increase in developing-country demand (primarily the rises in oil prices) and the factors causing an increase in supply (the contraction in developed-country demand as developed countries absorbed the contractionary effects of the oil price rises). Demand was further enhanced by the fall in export receipts as developed countries contracted and by the rise in world interest rates. The situation reached crisis point when Mexico's default in 1982 suggested that continuing to roll over developing-country debt was exposing banks to undue risk.

Let us first examine the proposition about increased demand for credit. Although all non-OPEC developing countries experienced balance of payments difficulties following the rise in oil prices, the low-income developing countries did not borrow to the same extent as the middle-income countries. Indeed, in 1979 when the supply of credit to developing countries was still fairly elastic, the low-income developing countries were more likely to be net creditors of international banks than net debtors. Whether this low level of borrowing was the result of a preference for maintaining liquidity for precautionary purposes (in the expectation of credit rationing) or of actual credit rationing is not clear. Given the interdependence between liquidity preference and credit availability outlined in the previous two sections, the distinction is not of fundamental importance. It is interesting however that the difference in pattern of liquidity preference between middle-income and low-income developing countries was discrete rather than continuous; no further information is gained by relating liquidity to per capita income by country rather than simply the two categories, 'middle' and 'low' income (see Dow and Ghosh, forthcoming). This is consistent with the hypothesis that information gathering on low-income borrowers was too costly for banks, so that they were either rationed *en masse*, or else expected to be rationed *en masse*.

Second, we question the implication of the conventional view that there was a fixed stock of credit which banks could allocate according to the pattern of demand. The argument that banks simply reallocated credit from developed-country borrowers to developing-country borrowers implies a loanable funds view of international finance. If it is the banking system itself which decides how much credit to create, then there was in effect a conscious decision to extend credit to developing countries.

Indeed the 1970s saw the emergence of liability management, whereby banks struggled over market share. The expansion of developing-country lending was spearheaded by Citicorp; the others simply copied this market leader on the basis (it would appear with hindsight) of very little information about the credit-worthiness of the borrowers. Indeed there was an acceptance which was historically extraordinarily myopic of Citibank's Walter Wriston's maxim that governments do not default. The push factor was no doubt the weakening in credit demand in developed countries; the banks sought an alternative market into which to expand. But if expectations about debt default had been more pessimistic, there would simply have been a general credit contraction.

Minsky's (1982) financial instability hypothesis is particularly apposite. If banks perceive their lenders' risk to be stable, an increased demand for credit will be met by an increased supply. Borrowers may see their situation as one of hedge finance, whereby current earnings are sufficient to service the debt. But if interest rates rise because of restrictive monetary policies in developed countries, borrowers may be pushed into speculative finance, whereby the debt can only be serviced if further debt is undertaken. If then the banks reassess their lenders' risk (as they did in 1982), then borrowers may be pushed into Ponzi finance such that only postponement of debt-servicing followed by some miraculous growth in export receipts will allow debt eventually to be serviced.

What then ultimately caused the debt crisis? Was it an ill-informed and thus faulty risk-assessment by the banks? Was it the unwillingness of the borrowing countries to undertake the structural adjustment necessary to bring about a long-lasting improvement in their balance of payments position? If either of these explanations holds, the implication is that the debt crisis could not recur. The banks now use a range of ratios to measure country risk, and many debtor countries are now in the throes of structural adjustment programmes imposed by the IMF.

But to argue that the debt crisis could not recur is to argue that the business cycle could not recur. Yet the business cycle plays itself out again and again. In the expansion phase banks have low liquidity preference because of low perceived lenders' risk; they expand credit accordingly further fuelling the expansion. But then the cycle peaks and there is a fundamental reassessment of risks. Loans which in the expansion phase were assessed as low risk may now have to be written off as bad debts. Banks' liquidity preference increases and credit contracts, exacerbating the fall in asset prices which started off the contractionary phase. In just the same way there is no reason why the banks might not yet again engage in massive lending to developing countries if the risks appeared to have abated. And again there might follow an upward reassessment of risk which induced a contraction of credit.

Capital flight has been raised as a contributory factor in the deepening of the debt crisis (see for example Lessard and Williamson, 1987). Using one technique for isolating capital flight from 'normal outflows', the Bank of England (1989) estimates that the accumulated level of capital flight was over 30% of outstanding debt during the period 1981-87. Capital flight is generally perceived as flight induced by undue domestic restrictions on financial markets (for example, interest rate ceilings). But again the issue has been raised as something peculiar to developing countries at a particular juncture when it is in fact a general phenomenon. Capital flight from developing countries has been encouraged by political uncertainties, including those arising from structural adjustment programmes. But capital flows from developed countries into the Euro-currency market can also be said to fit into the capital flight category, since the nature of the market is that it is less regulated than domestic markets, and thus offers higher returns.

Nevertheless there may be particular characteristics of developing countries which induce capital outflows. It has already been suggested that low-income countries in particular are likely to have a high liquidity preference which would be satisfied by deposits with foreign banks. Further expectations of relative decline in domestic asset prices and/or of greater difficulty in acquiring foreign credit in the event of balance of payments problems would increase liquidity preference and thus capital outflows. (If the balance of payments problems materialise then it may become difficult to satisfy liquidity preference.) Then capital flight indeed worsens a debt crisis; it is the natural expression of the interdependence between liquidity preference and endogenous credit creation.

BANKING STRUCTURE AND ECONOMIC DEVELOPMENT

The argument developed above is based on the presumption that the financial centre is remote from low-income developing countries; this accounts for the relatively poor information base for risk assessment and for the need to buy external assets in order to satisfy liquidity preference. The combination of these two factors serves to reinforce the development difficulties faced by low-income countries: poor credit availability requiring greater liquidity preference which is satisfied by capital outflows, when the development effort in general requires capital inflows.

Yet access to sophisticated international financial markets can be seen as a spread effect from growth in the Centre. Indeed financial integration which improves access to external financial markets is one of the goals of the EC; it is envisaged (see Commission for the European Communities, 1990) that all members would benefit from this access. It is certainly the case that without such access, oil-importing developing countries would not have been able to borrow in the 1970s, they would have been forced to adjust immediately, and there would have been no debt crisis. But such an argument is unhelpful: the dependence of developing countries on oil imports was a product of a more general economic dependence, of which financial relations are an integral part.

International financial relations have advantages and disadvantages for developing countries, both arising from the increased opportunities for borrowing and lending. But low-income countries are often net creditors of international financial markets, although the opportunity cost to them of this position must be extremely high. Their net creditor position is the expression of preferences, but preferences which are the product of economic and financial dependency. These preferences also are constrained by inadequate internal sources of financing, as well as possible constraints on availability of external finance. The satisfaction of these preferences for low borrowing relative to liquid assets means a retardation of the development process and thus a perpetuation of the constraints which generated the preferences in the first place. Since the counterfactual of isolation from international financial markets involves a complete change in structure, it is impossible to conduct a conventional cost-benefit analysis, which requires a common structure for the cases under consideration. It can simply be concluded, as for regional economies, that peripheral national economies experience significant backwash effects from international financial markets.

In considering the implications of this conclusion, account must be taken of the differences in banking structure as between regions and nations. The regional literature suggests an element of dualism between local banks and the local businesses which depend on them on the one hand and multi-regional banks and the multi-regional businesses which use them. (See Moore and Hill, 1982, Harrigan and McGregor, 1987 and Chapter 7 of this volume.) The general import of this literature is that small local businesses pay an interest premium on credit, as local monopoly rent, to local banks. This conclusion is not without challenge (see Hutchison and McKillop, 1990, on Northern Ireland). But in any case there may well be differences in credit availability; if small firms suffer from poor information held by national banks and high-perceived risk, then they may find better availability from local banks which have a better information base. (There is evidence that banks in American states with tighter branching regulations allocate a relatively high proportion of their assets to advances rather than investments; see Dow, 1981.) There is some dispute with respect to the EC as to whether increased financial integration would allow small local banks to survive in the face of competition from large national and multinational banks (see Commission for the European Communities, 1990, Goodhart, 1987 and Branson, 1990). If not, then availability of credit to small local business is likely to deteriorate.

Developing countries start off with a much more severe dualism in banking. In the export enclave multinational firms use multinational banks. National banks operating in the export enclave benefit from technology transfer, and can achieve some degree of integration with international money markets through the foreign banks operating locally. On the other hand, the rural sector is generally largely unbanked, many transactions are not monetised, and credit is supplied by money-lenders. Again there is a premium charged on this credit, compared with charges levied by urban banks. But the counterpart is availability on the basis of the local knowledge of the money-lender; it is not clear that urban banks would consider that credit to small local farmers with low collateral would constitute an acceptable risk.

The structure of banking in developing countries can thus be characterised as follows, in terms of Chick's (1986) stages of banking framework. The rural sector is in the first stage, where private sector bank liabilities are not accepted as money, so that the volume of credit is constrained by the supply of savings - here the loanable funds theory does apply, and investment is accordingly heavily constrained. The indigenous urban sector banks will be at a later stage of banking development. Since central banking with a lender-of-last-resort is now general, the banks will be at least in stage four. Then banks can create credit in response to demand, with the assurance that the central bank will provide reserves as required. Investment is no longer constrained by saving. The major constraint rather will be foreign exchange, given that many inputs may be imported and there will be a need for trade credit. The foreign banks in the urban sector will be at the latest stage in banking development. The current stage may be characterised as stage seven; having gone through the stage of liability management where banks compete for market share by enticing funding for credit creation (stage five), they have now reduced the risks created by all this credit by securitisation (stage six) and have moved to the point where the traditional distinction between banks and other firms has broken down. (See Gardner, 1988.) Now many firms have internalised banking services. Indeed this has been true for some time of multinational corporations, which have been particularly conscious on the one hand of exchange risk and on the other of the tax advantages of internalising accounting.

The implication of having a banking system with banks at different stages of evolution is that competitive forces favour banks at later stages of evolution. German universal banks could be at a competitive disadvantage with respect to banks which have developed the practice of securitisation. In developing countries, indigenous banks will find it hard to sell their services to firms which have already internalised banking services. They will also find it hard to compete with foreign banks which have expanded their portfolios, but have hived off the risks by securitising them. The degree of competition can be controlled, but is being made more difficult by IMF structural adjustment programmes which require financial liberalisation. The more international banks dominate developing-country banking, the more the focus of the sector will be on international markets, and the less on the domestic market. The international market has a tremendous capacity to create credit, but the information problems alluded to earlier will reinforce the credit availability problems of small local business; credit rather will be directed more to multinational corporations on which information is good and collateral in general high. Further, the greater the integration with international banking, the greater the ease with which liquidity preference may be satisfied by capital outflows. In the meantime there is no evidence to suggest that the multinational banks will see any advantage in expanding into the rural sector, which will thus continue to be credit constrained.

CONCLUSION

As with the regional context, the conclusion has been reached that financial behaviour can serve to increase economic disparities. It has been suggested that peripheral economies (the low-income developing countries) have a high liquidity preference not only because of the vulnerability of real economic conditions, but also because this is compounded by uncertainty about the availability of long-term finance in general (regardless of domestic saving) and of external credit in terms of balance of payments difficulty in particular. The availability of credit in turn is the outcome of banks' decisions as to liquidity preference in general and their assessment of country risk (and the degree of uncertainty attached to that assessment) in particular.

The debt crisis can thus be understood as the outcome of a massive increase in developing-country credit, followed by a massive reversal in banks' liquidity preference in general and in the assessment of risk associated with developing-country debt in particular. The capital flight which compounded the debt crisis was the expression of liquidity preference by residents of debtor countries which coincided with the reduction in credit availability. These patterns can be seen to conform to Minsky's account of the business cycle. They can similarly be understood as a natural phenomenon within financial markets. There is no reason therefore to conclude that the debt crisis could not happen again.

The situation for developing countries was shown to be more serious than for peripheral regions within one country because of the greater disparities in stage of banking development as between the rural sector, indigenous banks in the urban sector, and foreign banks. The increased competition that will follow from the liberalisation programmes currently being undertaken by many developing countries at the instigation of the IMF will increase the market power of the foreign banks. The outcome is likely to be increased credit constraints for small local concerns, combined with increased facilitation of capital flight.

There are two policy approaches which might be taken in response to this analysis. One is to examine the possibilities for using regulation to influence the structure of banking within developing countries. This avenue will be explored by St. Hill (forthcoming). The other approach is to examine the institutional arrangements within which international banking operates; the problems identified for developing countries stem from systemic forces, but these may be amenable to modification by means of regulation. This will be the subject matter of the next chapter.

12. The International Financial System: Institutional Arrangements

This chapter has benefited from helpful comments from Philip Arestis, Victoria Chick and John Smithin.

INTRODUCTION

The analysis developed in Chapter 11 suggests that there are systemic forces within modern banking systems which aggravate real economic disparities between developed and developing countries. These distributional concerns raise questions about the scope for policy to ameliorate the situation. These questions are pressing in several contexts, notably the debt crisis and the design of the European Monetary Union. They arise also in contexts where the issue is not widely recognised: design of the new monetary systems in Eastern Europe, and with respect to regional policy within national economies, for example.

It is the purpose of this chapter to consider policy with respect to institutional arrangements within financial systems at the most general level, and then to consider the implications for two particular contexts: the International Monetary Fund (IMF) and European Monetary Union (EMU). We start with a general account of institutional arrangements within the international financial system and the systemic forces operating within financial systems (including the distributional issue as one of many implications of these forces). As a backdrop for the discussion of policy, the next section attempts to analyse the current institutional arrangements in terms of the roles of convention and regulation in order to address the question of policy at a general (and fundamental) level. There is now a well-articulated body of thought which argues that most problems with financial systems arise from state interference. A justification for policy of some sort is therefore required before further consideration of policy detail. Some of the ideas put forward for institutional arrangements within the international financial system are explored in the fourth section, with an emphasis on Keynes' ideas. The discussion then focuses on the design of European Monetary Union.

THE INTERNATIONAL FINANCIAL SYSTEM

The international financial system consists of a wide range of private sector banks, some of which operate in more than one country, central banks which issue national currencies and international organisations, notably the IMF which issues its own currency (SDR, for intergovernmental transactions) and the Bank for International Settlements (BIS) which negotiates agreements on regulation of international banking. There are plans for a European central bank which will issue Ecu, a currency which was originally created by the European Commission for intergovernmental transactions but which is also now used in private sector transactions. While the IMF was originally designed to administer a system of fixed exchange rates between national currencies, the value of most currencies is now market determined. However some countries choose to peg their exchange rate to a dominant currency (notably the dollar), and the countries participating in the European Monetary System (EMS) have elected to peg their currencies against each other.

Triffin (1991) points out the significant and increasing degree to which foreign exchange deposits now dominate international money (relative to anational assets like gold and IMF instruments). The value of international money is therefore increasingly determined in foreign exchange markets which have become increasingly unstable. Exchange controls at one time prevented banks from operating across currencies themselves; the central bank intermediated. But now a massive volume of international transactions by-passes central banks altogether. The most notable development has been the growth of borrowing and lending in third currencies within the Euro-currency market. The attraction of the market is that it is subject to less restrictions than banking in the home currency. Being a large wholesale market, it enjoys economies of scale. But in addition it avoids the costs associated with reserve requirements and other regulatory restrictions. (See Dufey and Giddy, 1978.)

Before this growth of anational banking, as we might call it, the growth in world credit was determined by the growth in credit in terms of domestic currencies extended by domestic banks and that extended by foreign banks and channelled through the central bank, supplemented by IMF credit and SDR creation. Even then the growth in domestic and foreign credit was not under the full control of the central banks: the more advanced the banking system, the greater the capacity of banks to determine themselves the supply of credit. (See Chick, 1986 and 1989.) But with the growth of the Euro-currency market, the scope for credit determination within the private sector increased markedly. Indeed since one of the restrictions which banks avoid by operating in the

Euro-currency market is full disclosure of information, the size of the market cannot even be measured (see Strange, 1986).

Since the banks themselves have broken down national boundaries between banking systems, facilitated by the increasing absence of exchange controls, the systemic forces can be analysed to some extent as for national banking systems. The Minsky (1982) analysis can then be applied. At the microlevel, credit is extended if perceived borrower's risk justifies the demand and if perceived lender's risk justifies the supply. Investment can then be financed in advance of saving, and income and employment accordingly generated. At the macrolevel, there is a systematic pattern behind risk assessment on both sides. As the world economy expands, liquidity preference and perceived risk fall and credit creation increases; the reverse is true of downturns. At the global level, banks decide how much credit to create according to assessment of macro-risk (and thus their liquidity preference); the distribution of that credit is determined by country-risk assessment. Strange (1986) argues that banks' response to the debt crisis was to attempt to increase the liquidity of their portfolios, particularly by reducing the term of lending, which in turn reduces the supply of liquidity to the borrowing countries.

As discussed in the previous chapter, the import of the uncertainty surrounding risk assessment is potentially more serious in an international than a national context. The differences in stage of banking development are greater internationally than nationally, so that the market dominance by banks at the latest stage of development means that credit creation decisions with respect to countries which are remote from the financial centre suffer from poor information. As securitisation becomes more widespread, it is the market's information, rather than that of particular lending banks, which assumes importance (see Chick, 1989 and Gardner, 1988). This reinforces the tendency for credit in developing countries to be directed to multinational companies on which information is relatively good, with consequences for the industrial structure and economic dependency of the countries involved.

But international borrowing and lending is of particular significance because of the barrier posed by separate currencies. A region can settle payments using a common currency, but a nation cannot. International credit constraints play a double role in meeting capital requirements and in meeting foreign exchange requirements. Thus to the extent that some countries do not face a perfectly elastic supply of credit, their problems are compounded by a lack of foreign exchange. This kind of problem does not in general arise for countries like the US and UK which can borrow readily on international markets and whose currencies are vehicle currencies. While this would not be true of periodic crisis situations, this contrasts with the normality of the problem for low-income developing countries. Nevertheless a sanguine confidence in the capacity of capital markets to finance payments imbalances has led to what is termed the 'new view' of balance of payments problems (see Corden, 1977, 1990). This 'new view' is an international version of the horizontalist argument, that all demand for credit at the going interest rate may be met.

The other consequence of separate currencies is the opportunity offered for speculation. Thus availability of credit within a national banking system can be influenced significantly by speculative capital flows. Within a nation, capital flows towards assets whose price is expected to rise, but there is a significant range of assets (money assets) whose capital value is invariant. Internationally all assets, including domestic money, vary in value with the exchange rate. So the currency which serves the role not only of international money but also possibly that of domestic money is that whose value is most stable. One problem which has emerged during the period of floating exchange rates is that the US dollar, which is the dominant international currency, has been the most unstable (see for example Crockett, 1989). For other countries whose currency is unstable that instability itself may induce capital outflows, or at least the expectation of unstable capital flows, diminishing the capacity to create credit domestically. But exchange rate expectations, like risk assessment, depend on information. There is still no satisfactory theory of exchange rate determination; exchange rate expectations are heavily conditioned by uncertainty, which contributes to exchange rate instability.

The international financial system in general can be characterised as unstable (see for example Weiner, 1989). This instability was most evident at the time of the 1987 stock market crisis which spread worldwide at astonishing speed regardless of differences in national economic conditions. Just as domestic banking systems have increasingly taken on a life of their own (relative to central bank control), so international banking increasingly has taken on a life of its own. Just as banks domestically have been creating and marketing credit and liabilities in a struggle over market share and attempting to reduce the riskiness of their portfolios and evade monetary controls by securitisation, while facing increasing competition in financial services from non-banks (see Chick, 1989), so the same trends can be identified in international banking. Indeed international banking has provided a vehicle for banks to pursue these trends: the greater international spread of stages of banking development has created particular competitive opportunities, and the Euro-currency market has provided an opportunity to evade domestic controls. The upshot has been an inflationary bias due to upward pressure on interest rates and thus on nominal returns required to service debt, and an increasing detachment of credit creation from real economic conditions (the driving force instead being increasingly the internal competitive conditions within the banking sector). As a result, there is no reason why the global total of credit and its distribution should be stable and they have indeed proved to be unstable. The consequence has been that there has been an enhanced access to credit for some countries, but not for others, and that the instability in capital markets and foreign exchange markets has created new constraints for countries facing both capital and foreign exchange requirements.

THE ROLE OF THE STATE IN THE INTERNATIONAL FINANCIAL SYSTEM

In considering the implications of this account for policy action, we need to start by considering carefully the present role of the state. In particular the question must be addressed as to how far the present instability is in fact due to state intervention, without which the international financial system would work more smoothly. In other words, should the policy response be deregulation rather than increased (or modified) regulation?

The modern free banking (MFB) school (see Hayek, 1976; 1978; 1990, White, 1989, Dowd, 1989 and Glasner, 1989) takes the deregulation argument much further than the policy of financial liberalisation advocated by the IMF. They argue that the current problems with the international financial system arise from state control of banking and from state issuance of currency. Because the state acts as lender-of-last-resort, and possibly administers a deposit-insurance scheme, there is a moral hazard problem: unduly risky lending (to developing countries for example) and fraudulent behaviour are tolerated or not investigated by the market because there is an assumption that the central bank will protect depositors. Further, because states enter into fixed exchange rate arrangements which are subject to revision, opportunities are offered for destabilising speculation. (Speculation in free markets is generally assumed to be stabilising.)

The argument is put forward therefore that money should not be issued by the state at all, but rather by private sector banks. Competition would determine which moneys were used (worldwide) and at the same time ensure the prudent behaviour of the issuing banks. Banks would be free to operate worldwide, borrowing and lending according to market requirements. Rather than being concerned at the increasing endogenity of credit creation, the MFB school welcomes it and seeks to increase it. But they insist that there be a monetary standard in the form of a precious metal or commodity bundle to underpin the pyramid of credit. Individual banks would have to guarantee convertibility of their liabilities into this reserve asset in order to discipline their credit creation. (It is envisaged that this requirement would be the natural outcome of competition.)

The New Monetary Economics/Legal Restrictions Theory (NME/LRT) view (see for example Black, 1970, Fama, 1980, Yeager, 1985 and Wallace, 1988) goes further in that they deny the need for a monetary standard. This stems from the view that money-assets (and therefore banks) are not distinctive. Rather there is a continuum of financial assets issued by a range of financial and non-financial institutions which attract a market according to the conventions of market processes. Money is whatever is accepted in exchange. As a corollary, there need be no 'system' underpinning the value of money. They welcome the encroachment of non-banks into banking and wish to encourage it by removing regulatory distinctions between banks and non-banks.

The MFB and NME/LRT views share a vision (often implicit) of the suppression of nation-states. This is part of a wider view termed 'globalism' (see Arndt, 1992), one of whose tenets is that the national balance of payments is no longer meaningful in the light of multinational companies and financial institutions. Nor is it viewed as a basis for policy in practice, given the capacity for multinational institutions to evade national fiscal and monetary policy. But as Arndt points out, there are clear indications of the resistance of national governments to giving up sovereignty over fiscal and monetary policy and the issuing of a national currency, even in the particular instance of the European Community where there is a political momentum towards economic unification. It seems more realistic therefore to continue to think in terms of national currencies and national policies. But the questions posed by the MFB and NME/LRT theories still have relevance: is there something distinctive about money (at the international level) and if so should there be a monetary standard? Further, should banks be the subject of particular regulation in international transactions, should international money consist of something other than foreign exchange deposits with banks, and if so should the alternative be defined in terms of a monetary standard?

The state currently exerts an influence on the international monetary system almost exclusively through the actions of individual national governments, particularly those which issue international currencies. The IMF's role has been gradually restricted to high conditionality lending to countries heavily indebted to international banks (see Dell, 1989). That the IMF should have found this role for itself is extremely interesting in relation to the MFB and NME/LRT arguments. The banks have voluntarily expressed the need for a supranational body to resolve the difficulties created by market forces. Private sector banks now rely on IMF conditionality to introduce structural adjustment policies which, it is hoped, will reduce the default risk attached to further bank credit. Not only does the IMF have a superior information base, but it has procedures for introducing conditionality and also the capacity to bring together the creditor banks to take a collective view of the borrower's economy. Without the IMF it is very unlikely that bank lending to developing countries would have been forthcoming and that the debt crisis could have been held in abeyance. Whether the structural adjustment policies actually reduce default risk is a highly debatable question; but it is symptomatic of the way in which risk is assessed that the view propagated by the IMF should have become the conventional view.

Conventional views as a substitute for hard information under conditions of uncertainty are of universal and fundamental importance to the functioning of financial markets. Banks can attract capital if the market has confidence in the banks' assets, on the basis of available information. Investment projects do not proceed if the information available does not attract creditors, no matter how persuaded the investor is of the worth of the project. Balance of payments problems arise when private sector capital flows do not accommodate any payments imbalance, because of perceptions of default risk or expectations of currency devaluation. Yet these flows must respond to expectations about return and risk which must of necessity be formed under conditions of uncertainty. Thus for example the EMS is currently (August 1992) under threat because of the imbalance between the strength of the Deutschmark and the weakness of other European currencies. Germany is undergoing a period of upheaval in the aftermath of unification; yet this does not seem to dampen the conventional enthusiasm for the strength of the Deutschmark, which is self-fulfilling. Other periods may be recalled when conventional wisdoms persisted in the face of actual developments and then underwent dramatic revisions: the delay until Mexico's default in 1982 in perceiving the extent and nature of the debt crisis, the delay then until 1987 when banks started to reflect the debt crisis by making debt provision in their balance sheets, and the ambivalence to the size of the US budgetary deficit until October 1987, when a sudden realisation of the situation led to the stock market crash.

The state can play a crucial role with respect to information. First it has the power and resources to collect information often from confidential sources on a consistent basis. This has clearly been an important service provided to the banks by the IMF. But more important, the state can take a macro-view of information, convey this view to markets and act on it (with stabilisation policy for example) if it would not be in the market's interest to do so. During a boom phase, for example, assets may be overvalued, but movement traders will reinforce this overvaluation by pursuing short-term profit. The market itself has no vehicle or incentive for moderating this behaviour and its consequences.

There is in fact a continuum between information and convention and regulation. In the absence in general of hard information about future asset values, decisions must rely on conventional views (which are built on such facts as are perceived). It is a short step from a conventional view that it is wise to hold a certain proportion of assets liquid to its enshrinement in regulation. The prospect of free banking as being dualistically opposed to the current regulated system is thus a chimera. (See Gowland, 1990.)

In considering possibilities for regulation of international banking, therefore, it must be emphasised first that a totally deregulated market is hard to envisage and second that markets function with a continuum of regulation and convention, such that if regulation is withdrawn the role of conventions increases accordingly. First whether the issuers of money are distinct or not, they must be registered according to company law. Not only does this entail at least some minimal company legislation, but it establishes a country of jurisdiction. Second, vehicles of exchange inevitably involve a degree of trust (see Hicks, 1979) and a whole range of conventional attitudes and behaviour. Where banking systems have developed largely unregulated, notably in Scotland, there has been a tendency to self-regulate (see Dow and Smithin, 1992). At the international level, if there were free banking, one or more banks would eventually dominate the market, their liabilities would be used as international money and they would police the system like a world central bank. If national currencies persisted one or more would dominate in the same way. But this is currently the case and is the source of problems to which an additional solution needs to be found. But in any case, rather than taking the circuitous, and highly risky, route of freeing money and seeing what conventions the market comes up with, it seems legitimate instead to consider in the context of the present system what regulations and/or conventions would be desirable, with the state taking a lead in introducing them (see Dow and Smithin, 1991).

PROBLEMS AND PLANS FOR REFORM

The putting forward of plans to reform the international monetary system goes back at least to the breaking up of the gold standard system as a result of the first world war. The Bretton Woods system established in 1944 was the first to involve a supranational institution; the plans to reform that system have changed with the perceived problems with the system. In the 1960s there was concern that the supply of world money was not growing in line with world trade; as a result the SDR was introduced as a central bank reserve asset, and there were infrequent new issues as demand increased. But there have been no new issues since 1981, mirroring the 'new view' that private sector markets can adequately meet international liquidity requirements. Even within the IMF's programmes for extending credit, its unconditional lending has contracted relative to highly conditional lending, indicating further that the IMF no longer sees itself as supplying international liquidity except in emergency situations (see Dell, 1989).

A further problem which was overtaken by events was the rigidity of the par value system which in practise overly inhibited rate changes (although these could be authorised in cases of 'fundamental disequilibrium'). But now, with floating rates, the concern is more with exchange instability and the consequences of conflicting domestic policies 'protected' by floating rates. The current system of floating exchange rates emerged from the suspension of dollar convertibility into gold in 1971. It was hoped that floating rates would eliminate persistent payments imbalances, allow capital markets to direct funds from capital-rich countries to capital-poor countries and insulate domestic policy-making from external influences. None of these outcomes has materialised (see Davidson, 1991). Indeed conflicting domestic problems have created what many see as the most pressing need: the need for policy coordination (see for example Crockett, 1989). This need is particularly pressing because of the high degree of integration of capital markets and because the bulk of central bank reserves is in the form of foreign exchange, that is they are the liabilities of national governments. The need for policy control is in fact a need independent of exchange rate regime (see for example Bryant, 1980).

One solution frequently put forward to reduce exchange instability is that there be 'target zones' (see Crockett, 1989) or what Davidson (1982) calls Unionized Monetary Systems (UMS) within which exchange rates would be fixed, but between which they would be floating. Indeed this solution seems to be evolving naturally in the form of a dollar zone, or with some institutional help in the form of the European Monetary System. Exchange rates then can be fixed for international transactions within these areas. McKinnon's (1988) proposal is rather to fix exchange rates between the dollar, Ecu and yen at their purchasing power parities in the expectation that speculation will then be stabilising. A second approach is to attempt to reduce the source of exchange instability, which is generally recognised to be speculative capital movements. In their initial plans prepared for Bretton Woods, both Keynes and White supported the use of exchange controls to discourage short-term capital movements between currencies (see de Cecco, 1979, for one interpretation of the motivation behind their views on speculation). This proposal was subsequently dropped from the plans. It had been assumed then that all international transactions would be routed through central banks, which would have allowed some mechanism for distinguishing and preventing short-term capital movements. But the general dismantling of exchange controls and the rise of international banking outside national jurisdictions opened the floodgates to speculative capital movements. Nevertheless, proposals continue to be put forward to try to inhibit speculation: through taxation of short-term capital movements (Tobin, 1978) or through a dual-exchange rate system (see Soloman, 1989).

One cause for concern with exchange instability is the predominance of reserves in the form of foreign exchange. The Bretton Woods system was set up as a gold-exchange standard system, with all currencies valued in terms of gold or the US dollar, and the US guaranteeing convertibility of the dollar into gold. This system came under strain as US gold reserves became an ever-smaller proportion of international dollar holdings. Further the growing demand for dollars as reserves required a growing deficit on the US current account. While the first issue was resolved by the US suspending dollar convertibility, the second remains and is endemic to an exchange standard. Further, the solution to the fixed gold stocks problem meant that the international monetary system no longer has a monetary standard aside from national currencies.

Machlup and Triffin have long been critics of the exchange element of the gold-exchange standard, and then of the exchange standard, because of the potential conflict between internal US policies and the requirements of the international monetary system (see Triffin, 1991). Indeed Keynes (*C.W. XXV*) had originally proposed that instead of a gold-exchange standard there be an international currency, bancor, created by an International Clearing Union (ICU) which would in effect be a world central bank. The ICU would thus control the supply of international reserves, independent of national economic conditions. Although exchange rates would be expressed in terms of gold, the supply of bancor would respond to need, not to gold holdings. Need was conceived as including the financing of buffer-stock facilities to stabilise commodity prices. Further, all payments imbalances would be settled through accounts with the ICU. Keynes was particularly concerned at the asymmetry of adjustment to payments imbalance; the need to adjust is always more pressing for countries in deficit than for those in surplus. So the former are forced to employ deflationary policies, which automatically correct the surpluses for surplus countries. Keynes advocated a system of penalties for countries with excessive credit balances with the ICU to ensure a more balanced and more expansionary process of adjustment. All that survived of this proposal was the scarce currency clause in the IMF Articles of Agreement, a clause that has never been invoked. Nevertheless, the asymmetry in the pressure for adjustment persists: the solution to the debt crisis has been identified as adjustment by developing countries, not creditor countries, and the Maastricht agreement involves an institutionalisation of a deflationary bias (see the next section below).

Davidson (1991) and Guttman (1988) have adapted Keynes' proposals for application to modern circumstances. The relevance of Keynes' ideas for the debt crisis is that they involve a recognition that balance of payments deficits are as much the product of domestic policies in surplus countries as those of deficit countries; correction of the general imbalance thus requires adjustment on all sides, including notably expansion among surplus countries. Triffin and Machlup have gone further than Keynes' proposal for financing buffer stocks in proposing that the control over credit creation be applied to its distribution (to developing countries, to finance natural resource conservation projects for example) as well as its total (see Triffin, 1991). Kaldor (1983b) has developed further Keynes' proposal for commodity-price stabilisation by means of an international buffer-stock system.

While Keynes had envisaged a gold valuation of bancor, Davidson and Guttman relinquish the idea of a commodity-based monetary standard. But for some the absence of such a standard is at the root of the current problems with the international financial system. Some argue strongly in favour of a gold or commodity standard (see Hart, 1989, White, 1989 and Dowd, 1989); Glasner (1989) argues in favour of a wage index standard. McKinnon (1988) argues for a fixed exchange rate system based on purchasing power parity (implicitly a commodity bundle standard), while growth in world money would be determined by agreement between the US, Japan and the EC (a 'gold standard without gold' as he calls it).

Alongside many of these proposals goes the view that a gold or commodity standard will ensure control over the world money supply. But the issue of the determination of world money growth is quite separate from that of a monetary standard. Implicit in much of the literature is a monetarist view of credit creation, whereby international reserves form the core of national banking systems, with base money and larger monetary aggregates stable multiples of this core. If we reject this characterisation in favour of an endogenous credit creation theory of money supply, then the question of an international reserve asset takes on a different complexion (see Keynes, *C.W. XXV*, p. 140 and Guttman, 1989).

If international credit is supplied according to the prerogatives of the international banking system largely independently of national central banks, then controlling the supply of international reserves will not control the supply of credit. Keynes presumably assumed that banks would continue to operate only in domestic currencies when he proposed that bancor only be held by central banks. Guttman proposes rather that the international reserve asset be used for private sector transactions, and indeed be mandatory for international transactions, but prohibited in domestic transactions. This would have the significant consequence of eliminating the *raison d'ètre* of the Euro-currency market. (Interestingly, much of the Euro-currency market is doomed anyway as a consequence of plans for European Monetary Union.) In so far as a central monetary authority can influence private sector credit creation, the IMF or its substitute would then be able to influence the world supply of credit; but there would be no question of controlling it. What is required therefore is a vehicle for a world monetary authority to orchestrate credit creation at the macro-level (see Strange, 1986, Chapter 6 and Earl, 1990, Chapter 14 for specific proposals).

Then the valuation of the international reserve asset becomes an issue on a par with the valuation of national currencies. The successful functioning of a domestic banking system rests on confidence. If gold or commodity valuation engenders confidence then it should be advocated. But now confidence in domestic banking systems depends more on confidence in the authorities' willingness to act as a lender-of-last-resort, and in their proven capacity to supervise the banking system. The BIS has responded to the need for enhanced confidence in banks by fostering agreement on national jurisdiction regarding international banks (the Concordat of 1975); but subsequent cases of confusion over the jurisdiction of failed banks demonstrate that the problems are not yet fully resolved. The success of the international monetary system is thus not just a matter of establishing an international money which instils confidence but also of being seen successfully to supervise international banks. Any plan for reform should thus specify the supervisory functions of the IMF or its substitute (that is the functions of the BIS should be absorbed into the IMF). If world politics allow a world central bank of this sort to be established, then by the same token the need for a gold or commodity standard (other than for psychological reasons) becomes redundant (see Smithin, 1989).

A more recent agreement of the BIS has been agreement on capital adequacy ratios to be observed by banks in the Euro-currency market (see Hall, 1989, 1992). Now that reserves no longer act as a constraint on credit creation (given the lender-of-last-resort function of central banks), the ability to raise capital, it is hoped, will act as a substitute constraint. Certainly this should be so for individual banks. But referring again to the Minsky-style analysis of credit-creation set out above, it is at the macro-level of credit creation that the serious problems of excessive or inadequate credit creation arise. If international financial markets are bullish and anxious to expand credit rapidly, and if their optimism is shared by capital markets, then they will be able to raise the capital to back the credit creation. On the other hand, if banks are bearish and wishing to contract credit, that will tend to coincide with a reduced capacity to raise capital. In other words, capital adequacy ratios at the macrolevel simply add a further dimension through which the market can determine global credit creation; it is now the stock market which has the final say, rather than the banks themselves. While the capital adequacy rules go some way to ensuring prudent behaviour on the part of banks, further measures would therefore be required not only to deal with the ways in which banks try to evade these rules (see for example Gardner, 1988) but also to deal with the fact that it is the market which decides on the supply of capital to banks. Some procyclical adjustment to the ratios could prevent an overextension of credit in booms when market confidence is (unreasonably) high and an over-contraction of credit in slumps when confidence is (unreasonably) low (see St. Hill, 1991). This would not put the solvency of the banking system at risk if it were an integral part of stabilisation policy.

This proposal to make supervision an integral part of central banking counters the trend to divorce supervisory issues from other aspects of the international financial system, or indeed to argue that the debt crisis is not a product of the system itself (see Soloman, 1989). Rather, by recognising that the modern international financial system is based on bank credit, it is being proposed that that be the starting point both for analysis and for policy design.

EUROPEAN MONETARY UNION

Plans for reform of the international monetary system in general have not had much impact on the actual workings of the system. But plans for European Monetary Union (EMU) are well advanced and their realisation is becoming a real possibility. In this section we consider briefly how far these plans meet the concerns raised with respect to the global financial system: does Maastricht provide a blue-print for world monetary reform?

The final goal of EMU is to replace national currencies with Ecu issued by a European Central Bank; in the interim, the Ecu is to circulate alongside national currencies whose values fluctuate within narrow bands around a rate expressed in Ecu. The Ecu is currently valued in relation to a basket of EC currencies; with the eventual demise of these currencies, the Ecu will be valued by its exchange rate relative to other major currencies. The amount of Ecu created is to be determined by the European Central

Bank which will be given the primary goal of inflation control. In the meantime, national central banks are to be made independent of government and similarly charged with responsibility for controlling inflation. The theory implicit in this design is clearly monetarist; there is no suggestion that the authority to create a reserve asset and ultimately base money might not be sufficient to control inflation.

There are some elements in common with plans for international monetary reform. First there is the creation of an anational international reserve asset, which is designed to prevent conflict of interest between issuers of reserve currencies and domestic national goals. Then there is the notion that there must be an international body with responsibility for the international money supply. But the international reserve asset is for general use, eventually to become the universal currency of the EC; none of the global plans go so far. Further the Ecu is not to be tied to a standard of any kind, which would be of concern to many, but need not be if the European Central Bank attracts confidence in its capacity to maintain the value of the Ecu and the general stability of the banking system.

Bank supervision in fact scarcely gets a mention in the Maastricht proposals, being seen as an issue separable from the issue of monetary control. Attempts are being made through other channels within the EC to standardise the regulation of banks and other financial institutions (as part of the general level-playing-field policy to encourage increased competition in all sectors). Further, the influence of German institutional arrangements on plans for EMU can be seen in this separation of monetary control and supervision (and the separation of both from government). The EMU proposals therefore go counter to the suggestion in the previous section that, since the money creation process starts with private sector banks, not the core of international reserves held by the central bank, monetary policy should start with banks' credit creation, a matter which cannot reasonably be distinguished from bank supervision.

The interdependence between national macroeconomic policy and the international financial system has been fully recognised in the EC context, and policy coordination (with a view to controlling inflation) is a central feature of the EMU plans. The prospects of success in coordination are greatest among a group of countries, as in the EC, which have a political commitment to integrate economically. Dornbusch (1988), in commenting on McKinnon's purchasing power parity fixed exchange rate system, points to the dangers posed by the different priorities between the US and the EC with respect to inflation. But the independence of the European central banking system from government will require that governments coordinate policy with a common set of monetary conditions established by the central banking system. One area of negotiation is thus to be removed and governments' degrees of freedom will accordingly be limited. In the case of a world central bank, governments would have the right to participate democratically in the design of world monetary policy, allowing scope for negotiation between the central bank and governments. If, as has been suggested here, the world money supply cannot be controlled arbitrarily, and in any case does not deterministically cause the rate of inflation, then such a two-way negotiation of policy between the two levels of government seems highly desirable. The proposal that the European Central Bank and national central banks be independent of government makes sense only with a monetarist view that controlling the money supply is feasible, and that this on its own will control inflation.

As far as the global proposals are concerned, there is some wariness of the idea of a world central bank. It may be that the greater concern at the global level with a gold or commodity base for international money is because this is seen as an alternative, automatic form of money supply control. Those who advocate the establishment of a world central bank (Keynes, *C.W. XXV*, Davidson, 1991 and Guttman, 1988) do not envisage it as being independent of government; but then since they reject the relevance of a gold standard mechanism they see the central bank as performing a more complex range of functions than strict monetary control. These functions include ensuring a more equitable (and expansionary) distribution of the burden of balance of payments adjustment, and acting as a vehicle for redistribution in more direct forms.

As far as the first is concerned the reverse is the case for EMU. EC members which experience balance of payments difficulties are those which cannot induce adequate capital inflows to finance the deficit. If exchange realignment and an independent interest rate policy are both ruled out, either deficit countries must induce a fiscal deflation or surplus countries a fiscal reflation. But the provisions of Maastricht put limitations on the size of budgetary deficit and the size of the national debt apparently to serve the primary goal of price stability. If Maastricht is implemented, surplus countries will then not have the option to reflate, and deficit countries will be forced to bear the burden of adjustment. Those members which cannot meet these targets (or the targets with respect to price stability, interest rate stability and exchange stability) by 1996 will not be able to participate in EMU and therefore will not be able to contribute to policy design for Europe. Since policy will then be designed by successfully deflationary governments, there will be a deflationary bias to policy. Further, once in EMU, members which fail to meet the fiscal policy limitations will be subject to penalties. No such limitations are placed on budgetary surpluses. This will reinforce the deflationary bias in European fiscal policy.

In effect this means that the normal situation whereby there is more pressure on countries with balance of payments deficits to adjust would become institutionalised and automised by the provisions of Maastricht. There is already concern about the distributional implications of these provisions, and proposals are being considered for a substantial system of subsidy for members who would otherwise have to deflate to politically unacceptable degrees. This is enshrined in the 'cohesion' principle, that there should be balanced growth in the Community. Within nations this transfer occurs automatically through the fiscal system, with declining regions attracting higher benefits and raising lower taxes than other regions. Such an automatic stabiliser is to be prohibited in the EC by the limitations on budgetary deficits. The EC therefore requires an equivalent of regional policy which actively redistributes in order to ameliorate national differences. The import of the argument presented in Chapter 11 is that the distribution of credit availability plays a part in the process of perpetuating international income disparities. (See Dow, forthcoming, b, for the development of this argument with respect to the EC.) Countervailing redistribution policy should therefore be co-ordinated with other elements of monetary/macroeconomic policy. This has implications for consideration of the case for a European central bank.

Just as there is a strong case for a world central bank, so there is a strong case for a European central bank (at least in the absence of a world central bank). What is being suggested here is that the design enshrined in Maastricht can be faulted for presuming a capacity to control the money supply which an independent central bank could not hope to have, for separating monetary policy not only from other elements of macroeconomic policy but also from bank supervision, and for removing so many degrees of freedom from member governments that monetary policy will impose a deflationary bias on the Community which will jeopardise the cohesion principle,

Nevertheless a European central bank could be designed along lines similar to those suggested for a world central bank. The bank would be an integral part of macroeconomic policy-making and policy-making with respect to issues such as income distribution, recognising the interdependencies between these areas. Given that a primary goal of the bank would be to promote confidence in European banking, supervision would be an integral part of its function.

The proposal for an international money which would be mandatory for international transactions but not for domestic transactions does not necessarily carry forward to the European context. There are good arguments for introducing a European currency for all transactions, domestic and international: removal of the transactions costs and the uncertainty associated with separate currencies. Alternative redistributive measures could substitute for the freedom to change the value of the domestic currency. But on the other hand separate currencies give national governments some leverage, not least on information about capital flows: further the freedom to change currency value confers a very real advantage in times of severe balance of payments problems. If there were in addition a European currency as the standard, which was not tied to any one national economy, then the uncertainty attached to foreign exchange values would be moderated: national currencies would no longer act as vehicle currencies. In short the issue of maintaining separate currencies is not clear cut within the ideal institutional arrangements being proposed here. The important point of issue is the existence of a European currency to be used in all international transactions.

The European central bank which issued a European currency would have the means by which to enforce symmetrical adjustment if the bank were designed along the lines of Keynes' International Clearing Union, regardless of whether or not national currencies continued to be used in domestic transactions. European-wide private sector banks might choose to engage in capital flows in domestic currencies which could be disguised as domestic transactions; this would cloud the information contained in the European central bank's accounts in its own currency. But a balance of payments deficit resulting from a need to finance international transactions would still manifest itself in the normal way in the form of an excess demand for means of international payment and a surplus in the form of an excess supply. The European central bank would then be in a position to identify sources of imbalance and the required distribution of the burden of adjustment. It is ultimately information which is the key to implementing monetary policy of any type; in line with Keynes' proposals the type advocated here is one which promotes symmetrical adjustment, in order to counteract the deflationary bias of current institutional arrangements.

CONCLUSION

The major problems identified with the current international financial system are threefold. First the absence of an international money whose value is not determined by the internal policies of a national government, which causes exchange instability. Second the asymmetric pressures for balance of payments adjustment create a deflationary bias and exacerbate the maldistribution of income. Third the power of international banks to determine the volume, terms and distribution of world credit has in general created instability in international capital markets and the foreign exchange market. In addition it has created the vicious circle of the debt crisis, with debtors being required to deflate and banks to contract credit, which has further increased default risk and imposed an immense burden on the debtor countries.

It has been suggested here that these problems have arisen more from the increasing free play given to market forces in international finance than from the role of the state. Policy recommendations are therefore addressed to the question of how to provide a more stable environment for market forces on the one hand and how to channel market forces more constructively on the other. An international money for use in international but not domestic transactions as proposed by Guttman would provide a stable linch-pin for credit creation. At the same time it would allow better information on and scope for direction of international credit. A world central bank whose responsibility this money was would ensure its stability by acting like a national central bank: influencing (rather than controlling) the total supply of credit, acting as a lender-of-last-resort, orchestrating supervision of international banks and generally promoting confidence in the international financial system; this would obviate the need for a commodity standard as an inspirer of confidence. (The possibility that a commodity standard would facilitate control of monetary aggregates is denied.)

Equally important would be the scope for the world central bank to take the macro-view. It has been argued that the debt crisis was the outcome of a general risk assessment which was proved wrong, but which could not necessarily have been anticipated by private banks. Just as national governments can seek to stabilise the business cycle, so a world central bank could seek to modify excessive swings in credit supply. Procyclical capital adequacy ratios and the distribution to banks of better information on local borrowers in peripheral economies are proposed as two measures to promote more stable and balanced credit provision.

Finally, the central bank could take an explicit view on distributional issues. So for example it could have been decided that the rises in oil prices in the 1970s imposed an excessive real burden on developing countries which could not reasonably be dealt with by private sector credit, but rather required a distribution of funds through the central bank. The situation would be ameliorated further by a system of incentives and penalties which ensured a more balanced distribution of the burden of adjustment: the adjustment imposed then on surplus countries would in itself constitute a significant contribution to curing the debt crisis.

Plans are in train within the European Community for the setting up of an international central bank which would administer the Ecu, the European currency. While this would address the problems of currency instability and the need to coordinate monetary policy, the problems of financial instability due to lack of confidence in the banking system and asymmetry in balance of payments adjustment would remain; indeed additional problems would emerge from the separation of monetary policy from macroeconomic policy and from the institutionalisation of limits on the scope for fiscal reflation.

It has been suggested here that Europe would benefit from the type of international central bank proposed above for the global economy. This would involve an integration of monetary policy with macroeconomic policy (to promote macroeconomic stability), with bank supervision (to promote financial stability) and with redistribution policy through measures to promote a more symmetrical pattern of balance of payments adjustment and to ensure a stable distribution of credit. The European central bank could coordinate with regional policy-making to direct credit towards projects whose returns could be perceived at the macrolevel, even if not at the microlevel of individual banks.

References

Acheson, T.W. (1977), 'The Maritimes and Empire Canada', in Bercuson, D. (ed.), *Canada and the Burden of Unity*, Macmillan, Toronto.

Addison, J.T., Burton, J. K. and Torrance, T. S. (1980), 'On the Causes of Inflation', *The Manchester School*, vol. 48, June.

Addison, J. T., Burton, J. K. and Torrance, T. S. (1984), 'Causation, Social Science and Sir John Hicks', *Oxford Economic Papers*, NS vol. 36, March.

Amin, S. (1974), *Accumulation on a World Scale: A Critique of the Theory of Underdevelopment*, Harvester, Brighton.

Ando, A. and Modigliani, F. (1965), 'The Relative Stability of Monetary Velocity and the Investment Multiplier', *American Economic Review*, vol. 55.

Archibald, G.C. (1969), 'The Phillips Curve and the Distribution of Unemployment', *American Economic Review*, vol. 59, March.

Arestis, P. (1987), 'Post-Keynesian Theory of Money, Credit and Finance', *Thames Papers in Political Economy*, Spring.

Arndt, H.W. (1992), 'The Economics of Globalism', *Banca Nazionale del Lavoro Quarterly Review*, no. 180, March.

Bank of England (1989), 'Capital Flight', *Bank of England Quarterly Bulletin*, August.

Barro, R.J. (1984), 'Rational Expectations and Macroeconomics in 1984', *American Economic Review, Papers and Proceedings*, vol. 74, May.

Bausor, R. (1983), 'Conceptual Evolution in Economics: The Case of Rational Expectations', paper presented to the History of Economics Conference, Charlottesville, Virginia.

Beare, J.B. (1976), 'A Monetarist Model of Regional Business Cycles', *Journal of Regional Science*, vol. 16, February.

Beckerman, P. (1988), 'The Consequences of Upward Financial Repression', *International Review of Applied Economics*, vol. 2.

Beek, D.C. (1977), 'Commercial Bank Lending to the Developing Countries', *Federal Reserve Bank of New York Quarterly Review*, vol. 2, Summer.

Benson, J. (1978), *Provincial Government Banks*, Fraser Institute, Vancouver.

Black, F. (1970), 'Banking and Interest Rates in a World without Money', *Journal of Bank Research*, vol. 1.

Blain, L., Patterson, D. G. and Rae, J. D. (1974), 'The Regional Impact of Economic Fluctuations during the Inter-War Period: the Case of British Columbia', *Canadian Journal of Economics*, vol. 7, August.

Board of Governors of the Federal Reserve System (1976), *Banking and Monetary Statistics 1941-1970*, Board of Governors of the Federal Reserve System, Washington, DC.

Boland, L.A. (1982), *The Foundations of Economic Method*, George Allen & Unwin, London.

Bowsher, N.H., Daane, J. D. and Einzig, R. (1958), 'The Flows of Funds between Regions of the United States', *Journal of Finance*, vol. 13.

Branson, W.H. (1990), 'Financial Market Integration, Macroeconomic Policy and the EMS', in Brago de Macedo, J. and Bliss, C. (eds), *Unity with Diversity within the European Economy: the Community's Southern Frontier*, Cambridge University Press, Cambridge.

Bryant, R.C. (1980), *Money and Monetary Policy in Interdependent Nations*, Brookings Institution, Washington.

Brym, R.J. and Sacouman, R.J. (1979), *Underdevelopment and Social Movements in Atlantic Canada*, New Hogtown Press, Toronto.

Burkett, P. and Dutt, A.K. (1991), 'Interest Rate Policy, Effective Demand and Growth in LDCs', *International Review of Applied Economics*, vol. 5, May.

Canadian Bankers' Association (1974), 'Governments' Place in Bank Ownership: The Industry View', *CBA Bulletin*, vol. 17, special edition.

Carvalho, F. (1983-84), 'On the Concept of Time in Shacklean and Sraffian Economies', *Journal of Post Keynesian Economics*, vol. 6, Winter.

Chick, V. (1977), *The Theory of Monetary Policy*, second edition, Parkgate & Blackwell, Oxford.

Chick, V. (1983), *Macroeconomics after Keynes: A Reconsideration of the General Theory*, Philip Allen, Oxford.

Chick, V. (1986; 1992), 'The Evolution of the Banking System and the Theory of Saving, Investment and Interest', *Economies et Sociétés*, vol. 20, *Monnaie et Production*, no. 3. Reprinted in Arestis, P. and Dow, S. C. (eds), *On Money, Method and Keynes*, Macmillan, London.

Chick, V. (1989), 'The Evolution of the Banking System and the Theory of Monetary Policy', University College London Discussion Paper 89-03. Forthcoming in Frowen, S. F. (ed.), *Monetary Theory and Monetary Policy: New Tracks for the 1990s*, Macmillan, London.

Chick, V. and Dow, S. C. (1988), 'A Post-Keynesian Perspective on the Relation between Banking and Regional Development', in Arestis, P.

(ed.), *Post-Keynesian Monetary Economics*, Elgar, Aldershot.
Clower, R. W. (1969), 'The Keynesian Counter-revolution: A Theoretical Appraisal', in Monetary Theory: Selected Readings, Penguin, Harmondsworth.
Coddington, A. (1976), 'Keynesian Economics: The Search for First Principles', *Journal of Economic Literature*, vol. 14, December.
Commission for the European Communities (1990), 'One Market, One Money', *European Economy*, no. 44, October.
Cooley, T.F. and LeRoy, S.F. (1981), 'Identification and Estimation of Money Demand', *American Economic Review*, vol. 71, December.
Corden, W.M. (1977), *Inflation, Exchange Rates and the World Economy*, Clarendon, Oxford.
Corden, W.M. (1990), 'Does the Current Account Matter? The Old and the New View', mimeo, Washington, DC.
Courchene, T.J. (1981), 'A Market Perspective on Regional Disparities', *Canadian Public Policy*, vol. 7, Autumn.
Crockett, A. (1989), 'International Monetary Reform, Coordination and Indicators', in Hamouda, O., Rowley, R. and Wolf, B. (eds), *The Future of the International Monetary System*, Elgar, Aldershot.
Cross, R. (1982), 'The Duhem-Quine Thesis, Lakatos and the Appraisal of Theories in Macroeconomics', *Economic Journal*, vol. 92, June.
Davidson, P. (1978), *Money and the Real World*, second edition, Macmillan, London.
Davidson, P. (1982), *International Money and the Real World*, Macmillan, London.
Davidson, P. (1982-83), 'Rational Expectations: A Fallacious Foundation for Studying Crucial Decision-Making Processes', *Journal of Post Keynesian Economics*, vol. 5, Winter.
Davidson, P. (1991), 'What International Payments Scheme would Keynes have Suggested for the Twenty-first Century?', in Davidson, P. and Kregel J.A. (eds), *Economic Problems of the 1990s*, Elgar, Aldershot.
Davidson, P. and Weintraub, S. (1973), 'Money as Cause and Effect', *Economic Journal*, vol. 83, December.
de Brunhoff, S. (1976), *Marx on Money*, Urizen, New York.
de Cecco, M. (1979), 'Origins of the Post-War Payments System', *Cambridge Journal of Economics*, vol. 3, March.
Dell, S. (1989), 'The Future of the International Monetary System', in Hamouda, O., Rowley, R. and Wolf, B. (eds), *The Future of the International Monetary System*, Elgar, Aldershot.
Desai, M. (1981), *Testing Monetarism*, Frances Pinter, London.
Dixon, R.J. and Thirlwall, A.P. (1975), 'A Model of Regional Growth Rate Differences on Kaldorian Lines', Oxford Economic Papers, vol. 27, July.

Dornbusch, R. (1988), 'Doubts about the McKinnon Standard', *Journal of Economic Perspectives*, vol. 2, Winter.

Dow, A.C. and Dow, S.C. (1985), 'Animal Spirits and Rationality', in Lawson, T. and Pesaran, H. (eds), *Keynes' Economics: Methodological Issues*, Croom Helm, London.

Dow, A.C. and Dow, S.C. (1988), 'Endogenous Money Creation and Idle Balances', in Pheby, J. (ed.), *New Directions in Post-Keynesian Economics*, Elgar, Aldershot.

Dow, S.C. (1980), 'Methodological Morality in the Cambridge Controversies', *Journal of Post-Keynesian Economics*, vol. 2, Spring.

Dow, S.C. (1981), 'Money and Real Economic Disparities Between Nations and Between Regions', unpublished PhD Thesis, University of Glasgow.

Dow, S.C. (1983), Review of Short with Nicholas (1981), *Urban Studies*, vol. 20.

Dow, S.C. (1985), *Macroeconomic Thought: A Methodological Approach*, Basil Blackwell, Oxford.

Dow, S.C. (1990), *Financial Markets and Regional Economic Development: The Canadian Experience*, Gower, Aldershot.

Dow, S.C. (1991a), 'The Capital Account of the Scottish Balance of Payments: The Evidence', *Research Report 2*, Scottish Foundation for Economic Research, Glasgow.

Dow, S.C. (1991b), 'The Capital Account of the Scottish Balance of Payments: Theory and Policy Considerations', *Discussion Paper 2*, Scottish Foundation for Economic Research, Glasgow.

Dow, S.C. (1992), 'The Regional Financial Sector: A Scottish Case Study', *Regional Studies*, vol.26, no.7.

Dow, S.C. (forthcoming, a), 'Uncertainty', in Arestis, P. and Sawyer, M. (eds.), *Handbook of Radical Political Economy*, Elgar, Aldershot.

Dow, S.C. (forthcoming, b), 'European Monetary Integration and the Distribution of Credit Availability', in Corbridge, S., Martin, R. and Thrift, N. (eds), *Money, Power and Space*, Blackwell, Oxford.

Dow, S.C. (forthcoming, c), 'Liquidity Preference in International Finance: the Case of Developing Countries', in Wells, P. (ed.), *Post Keynesian Economic Theory*, Kluwer, Boston.

Dow, S.C. and Earl, P.E. (1982), *Money Matters: A Keynesian Approach to Monetary Economics*, Martin Robertson, Oxford.

Dow, S.C. and Ghosh, D. (forthcoming), 'International Banks and the Liquidity Preference of Developing Countries', University of Stirling mimeo.

Dow, S.C. and Smithin, J. (1991), 'Change in Financial Markets and the "First Principles" of Monetary Economics', *University of Stirling*

Discussion Papers in Economics, 91/23.
Dow, S.C. and Smithin, J. (1992), 'Free Banking in Scotland, 1695-1845', *Scottish Journal of Political Economy*, vol. 39, November.
Dowd, K. (1989), *The State and The Monetary System*, Philip Allan, Hemel Hempstead.
Drake, P.J. (1980), *Money, Finance and Development*, Martin Robertson, Oxford.
Dreese, R.G. (1974), 'Banks and Economic Development', *Southern Economic Journal*, April.
Dufey, G. and Giddy, I.H. (1978), *The International Money Market*, Prentice-Hall, Englewood Cliffs, N.J.
Earl, P.E. (1990), *Monetary Scenarios: A Modern Approach to Financial Systems*, Elgar, Aldershot.
Eaton, J. and Gersowitz, M. (1980), 'LDC Participation in International Financial Markets: Debt and Reserves', *Journal of Development Economics*, vol. 7, March.
Economic Council of Canada, (1968), *Fifth Annual Review: The Challenge of Growth and Change*, Queens Printer, Ottawa.
Economic Council of Canada (1982), *Financing Confederation: Today and Tomorrow*, Queen's Printer, Ottawa.
Edel, C. *et al.* (1978), 'Uneven Regional Development: An Introduction to this Issue', *Review of Radical Political Economy*, vol. 10, Fall.
Fama, E.F. (1980), 'Banking in the Theory of Finance', *Journal of Monetary Economics*, vol. 6.
Fazzari, S.M., Hubbard, G. and Peterson, B.C. (1988), 'Financing Constraints and Corporate Investment', *Brookings Papers on Economic Activity*, no. 1.
Feder, G. and Just, R.E. (1977), 'An Analysis of Credit Terms in the Eurodollar Market', *European Economic Review*, vol. 9, May.
Feyerabend, P.K. (1975), *Against Method: Outline of an Anarchistic Theory of Knowledge*, NLB, London.
Fishkind, H.H. (1977), 'The Regional Impact of Monetary Policy: An Economic Simulation Study of Indiana 1958-1973', *Journal of Regional Science*, vol. 17, February.
Foster, J. (1987), 'Understanding Movements in M3 from 1963-86', Department of Political Economy, University of Glasgow, mimeo.
Frank, A.G.(1967), 'The Development of Underdevelopment', *Monthly Review*, vol. 17, September.
Frenkel, J.A. and Johnson, H.G. (eds) (1976), *The Monetary Approach to the Balance of Payments*, University of Toronto Press, Toronto.
Friedman, M. (1953), 'The Methodology of Positive Economics', in *Essays in Positive Economics*, University of Chicago Press, Chicago.

Friedman, M. (1970a), 'A Theoretical Framework for Monetary Analysis', *Journal of Political Economy*, vol. 78, March/April.

Friedman, M. (1970b), 'Comment on Tobin', *Quarterly Journal of Economics*, vol. 84, May.

Friedman, M. (1971), 'The Euro-Dollar Market: Some First Principles', *Federal Reserve Bank of St Louis Review*, vol. 53, July.

Friedman, M. and Meiselman, D. (1963), 'The Relative Stability of Monetary Velocity and the Investment Multiplier in the United States', in Commission on Money and Credit, *Stabilization Policies*, Prentice-Hall, Englewood Cliffs, NJ.

Friedman, M. and Schwartz, A. J. (1963a), *A Monetary History of the United States, 1867-1960*, Princeton University Press, Princeton for NBER.

Friedman, M. and Schwartz A.J. (1963b), 'Money and Business Cycles', *Review of Economics and Statistics*, vol. 45, supplement.

Friedman, M. and Schwartz A.J. (1982), *Monetary Trends in the United States and the United Kingdom: Their Relation to Income Prices and Interest Rates, 1867-1975*, Chicago University Press, Chicago for NBER.

Gale, D. (1982), *Money: In Equilibrium*, Cambridge University Press, Cambridge.

Gale, D. (1983), *Money: In Disequilibrium*, Cambridge University Press, Cambridge.

Gardner, E.P.M. (1988), 'Innovations and New Structural Frontiers in Banking', in Arestis, P. (ed.), *Contemporary Issues in Money and Banking*, Macmillan, London.

Garvy, G. (1959), *Debits and Clearings Statistics and Their Use*, Board of Governors of the Federal Reserve System, Washington, DC.

Gaskin, M. (1960), 'Credit Policy and the Regional Problem', *The Banker's Magazine*, September.

Gaskin, M. (1965), *The Scottish Banks: A Modern Survey*, George Allen & Unwin, London.

Ghosh, D. (1986a), 'Savings Behaviour in the Non-monetized Sector and its Implications', *Savings and Development*, vol. 10, no. 2.

Ghosh, D. (1986b), 'Monetary Dualism in Developing Economies', *Economies et Sociétés*, vol. 30, *Monnaie et Politique Monetaire dans les Pays du Tiers Monde*.

Glasner, D. (1989), *Free Banking and Monetary Reform*, Cambridge University Press, Cambridge.

Godley, W. and Cripps, F. (1983), *Macroeconomics*, Fontana, Oxford.

Goodhart, C.A.E. (1975), *Money, Information and Uncertainty*, Macmillan, London.

Goodhart, C.A.E. (1987), 'Structural Change in the British Capital Markets', in Goodhart, C.A.E., Currie, D. and Llewllyn, D.T. (eds), *The Operation and Regulation of Financial Markets*, Macmillan, London.

Government of Canada (1940), *Report of the Royal Commission on Dominion-Provincial Relations*, Queen's Printer, Ottawa.

Gowland, D.H. (1990), *The Regulation of Financial Markets in the 1990s*, Elgar, Aldershot.

Guttman, R. (1988), 'Crisis and Reform of the International Monetary System, in Arestis, P. (ed.), *Post-Keynesian Monetary Economics*, Elgar, Aldershot.

Hahn, F.H. (1973), *On the Notion of Equilibrium in Economics*, Cambridge University Press, Cambridge.

Hahn, F.H. (1981), 'General Equilibrium Theory', in Bell, D. and Kristol, I. (eds), *The Crisis in Economic Theory*, Basic Books, New York.

Hahn, F.H. (1983), *Money and Inflation*, MIT Press, Cambridge, Mass.

Hall, M.J.B. (1989), 'The BIS Capital Adequacy "Rules", A Critique', *Banca Nazionale del Lavoro Quarterly Review*, no. 169, June.

Hall, M.J.B. (1992), 'Implementation of the BIS "Rules" on Capital Adequacy Assessment', *Banca Nazionale del Lavoro Quarterly Review*, no. 180, March.

Harrigan, F.J. and McGregor, P.G. (1987), 'Interregional Arbitrage and the Supply of Loanable Funds: A Model of Intermediate Financial Capital Mobility', *Journal of Regional Science*, vol. 27, August.

Hart, A.G. (1989), 'A Neglected Monetary Standard Alternative: Gold/Commodity Bimetalism', in Hamouda, O., Rowley, R. and Wolf, B. (eds), *The Future of the International Monetary System*, Elgar, Aldershot.

Hartland, P. (1949), 'Interregional Payments Compared with International Payments', *Quarterly Journal of Economics*, vol. 63.

Harvey, D. (1982), *The Limits to Capital*, University of Chicago Press, Chicago.

Hayek, F.A. (1976; 1978; 1990), *Denationalisation of Money - the Argument Refined*, IEA, London, successive editions.

Helleiner, G.K. (1990), *The New Global Economy and the Developing Economy*, Elgar, Aldershot.

Hendry, D.F. and Eriksson, N.R. (1983), 'Assertion Without Empirical Basis: An Econometric Appraisal of Friedman and Schwartz (1982)', Bank of England Panel of Academic Consultants, Paper No. 22, October.

Hicks, J.R. (1974), *The Crisis in Keynesian Economics*, Blackwell, Oxford.

Hicks, J.R. (1979), 'Review of Microfoundations', *Journal of Economic Literature*, vol. 17.

Holland, S. (1976), *Capital versus the Regions*, Macmillan, London.

Hutchison, R.W. and McKillop, D.G. (1990), 'Regional Financial Sector Models: An Application to the Northern Ireland Financial Sector', *Regional Studies*, vol. 24, no. 5.

Industry Department for Scotland (1984), 'Input - Output Study of the Scottish Economy in 1979', *Scottish Office News Release*, 499/84, 10 May

Ingram, J.C. (1959), 'State and Regional Payments Mechanisms', *Quarterly Journal of Economics*, vol. 73.

Johnson, H.G. (1971), 'The Keynesian Revolution and the Monetarist Counter-Revolution', *American Economic Review*, vol. 61, May.

Kahn, R.F. (1976), 'Inflation - A Keynesian View', *Scottish Journal of Political Economy*, vol. 23, February.

Kaldor, N. (1970a), 'The New Monetarism', *Lloyds Bank Review*, no. 110, July.

Kaldor, N. (1970b), 'The Case for Regional Policies', *Scottish Journal of Political Economy*, vol. 17, November.

Kaldor, N. (1981), *Origins of the New Monetarism*, University of Cardiff Press, Cardiff.

Kaldor, N. (1982), *The Scourge of Monetarism*, Oxford University Press, Oxford.

Kaldor, N. (1983a), 'Keynesian Economics After Fifty Years', in Worswick, D. and Trevithick, J. (eds) *Keynes in the Modern World*, Cambridge University Press, Cambridge.

Kaldor, N. (1983b), 'The Role of Commodity Prices in Economic Recovery', *Lloyds Bank Review*, July.

Katouzian, H. (1980), *Ideology and Method in Economics*, Macmillan, London.

Keller, R.R. and Carson, J. L. (1982), 'A Neglected Chapter in the *General Theory*', *Journal of Post Keynesian Economics*, vol. 4, Spring.

Kenen, P.B. (1969), 'The Theory of Optimal Currency Areas: An Eclectic View', in Swoboda, A. and Mundell, R. A. (eds), *Monetary Problems of the International Economy*, University of Chicago Press, Chicago.

Kenen, P.B. (1976), 'Capital Mobility and Financial Integration: A Survey', *Princeton Studies in International Finance*, no. 39.

Keynes, J.M. (1973a), *The General Theory of Employment, Interest and Money. Collected Writings Vol. VII*, Macmillan, London, for the Royal Economic Society.

Keynes, J.M. (1973b), *A Treatise on Probability. Collected Writings, Vol. VIII*, Macmillan, London, for the Royal Economic Society.

Keynes, J.M. (1973c), *The General Theory and After. Part I: Preparation, Collected Writings Vol. XIII*, Macmillan, London, for the Royal Economic Society.

Keynes, J.M. (1973d), *The General Theory and After. Part II: Defence and*

Development, Collected Writings, Vol. XIV, Macmillan, London, for the Royal Economic Society.
Keynes, J.M. (1979), *The General Theory and After. A Supplement, Collected Writings Vol. XXIX*, Macmillan, London, for the Royal Economic Society.
Keynes, J.M. (1980), *Activities 1940-1944: Shaping the Post-War World, The Clearing Union, Collected Writings Vol. XXV*, Macmillan, London, for the Royal Economic Society.
Keynes, J.M. (1982), 'How to Avoid a Slump', *Activities 1931-9. Collected Writings Vol. XXI*, Macmillan, London for the Royal Economic Society.
Khatkhate, D.R. (1980), 'False Issues in the Debate on Interest Rate Policies in Less Developed Countries', *Banca Nazionale del Lavoro Quarterly Review*, no. 105, June.
Kindleberger, C.P. (1974), 'The Formation of Financial Centres: A Study in Comparative Economic History', *Princeton Studies in International Finance*, no. 36.
Kregel, J. (1984-85), 'Constraints on the Expansion of Output and Employment: Real or Monetary?', *Journal of Post Keynesian Economics*, vol. 7, Winter.
Kuhn, T.S. (1970), *The Structure of Scientific Revolutions*, Chicago University Press, Chicago.
Kuhn, T.S. (1974), 'Second Thoughts on Paradigms', in Suppe, F. (ed.), *The Structure of Scientific Theories*, University of Illinois Press, Urbana.
Lakatos, I. (1978), *The Methodology of Scientific Research Programmes. Philosophical Papers*, in Worrall, J. and Currie, G. (eds), Cambridge University Press, Cambridge.
Lamfalussy, A. (1989), 'Globalization of Financial Markets: International Supervisory and Regulatory Issues', *Federal Reserve Bank of Kansas City Economic Review*, January.
Lavoie, M. (1984), 'Un modèle post-Keynesian d'économie monétaire fondé sur la théorie du circuit', *Economies et Sociétés*, vol. 18, *Monnaie et Production*, vol. 1.
Leijonhufvud, A. (1968), *On Keynesian Economics and the Economics of Keynes*, Oxford University Press, New York.
Lessard, D.R. and Williamson, J. (1987), *Capital Flight and Third World Debt*, Institution for International Economics, Washington.
Lewis, A.W. (1954), 'Economic Development with Unlimited Supplies of Labour', *Manchester School*, vol. 22, May.
Lipsey, R.G. (1960), 'The Relation between Unemployment and the Rate of Change of Wage Rates in the UK, 1862-1957: A Further Analysis',

Economica, vol. 27, February.
Lösch, A. (1954), *The Economics of Location*, Woglom, W. H. and Stolper, W. F. (trans.), Yale University Press, New Haven.
Loxley, J. (1986), *Debt and Disorder: External Financing for Development*, Westview, London.
Lucas, R.E., Jr. (1980), 'Methods and Problems in Business Cycle Theory', *Journal of Money, Credit and Banking*, vol. 12, November.
Macfie, A.L. (1955) 'The Scottish Tradition in Economic Thought', *Scottish Journal of Political Economy*, vol. 2, June.
Machlup, F. (1967), 'Theories of the Firm: Marginalist, Behavioural, Managerial', *American Economic Review*, vol. 57, March.
Mao Tse-Tung (1967), *Quotations from Chairman Mao Tse-Tung*, Foreign Language Press, Peking.
McCallum, J. and Vines, D. (1981), 'Cambridge and Chicago on the Balance of Payments', *Economic Journal*, vol. 91, June.
McCloskey, D.N. (1983), 'The Rhetoric of Economics', *Journal of Economic Literature*, vol. 21, June.
McIvor, R.C. (1958), *Canadian Monetary, Banking and Fiscal Development*, Macmillan, Toronto.
McKinnon, R.I. (1963), 'Optimal Currency Areas', *American Economic Review*, vol. 53.
McKinnon, R.I. (1973), *Money and Capital in Economic Development*, Brookings Institution, Washington.
McKinnon, R.I. (1988), 'Monetary and Exchange Rate Policies for International Financial Stability: A Proposal', *Journal of Economic Perspectives*, vol. 2, Winter.
Meltzer, A.H. (1981), 'On Keynes's General Theory', *Journal of Economic Literature*, vol. 19, March.
Miles, M.A. and Davidson, P. (1979), 'Monetary Policy, Regulation and International Adjustments', *Economies et Sociétés*, vol. 1.
Miller, R.J. (1978), *The Regional Impact of Monetary Policy in the United States*, Lexington Books, Lexington, Mass.
Minsky, H.P. (1976), *John Maynard Keynes*, Macmillan, London.
Minsky, H.P. (1982), *Inflation, Recession and Economic Policy*, Wheatsheaf, Brighton.
Moore, B.J. (1979a), 'Monetary Factors', in Eichner, A. S. (ed.), *A Guide to Post Keynesian Economics*, M. E. Sharpe, New York.
Moore, B.J. (1979b), 'The Endogenous Money Stock', *Journal of Post Keynesian Economics*, vol. 2, Fall.
Moore, B.J. (1983), 'Unpacking the Post Keynesian Black Box: Bank Lending and the Money Supply', *Journal of Post Keynesian Economics*, vol. 5, Summer.

Moore, B.J. (1984a), 'Wages, Bank Lending and the Endogeneity of Credit Money', in Jarsulic, M. (ed.), *Money and Macro Policy*, Kluwer-Nijhoff, Boston, MA.

Moore, B.J. (1984b), 'Contemporaneous Reserve Accounting: Can Reserves be Quantity-Constrained?', *Journal of Post Keynesian Economics*, vol. 7, Fall.

Moore, B.J. (1988), *Horizontalists and Verticalists*, Cambridge University Press, Cambridge.

Moore, C.L. and Hill, J.M. (1982), 'Interregional Arbitrage and the Supply of Loanable Funds', *Journal of Regional Science*, vol. 22, November.

Morgan, E.V. (1973), 'Regional Problems and Common Currencies', *Lloyds Bank Review*, no. 110, October.

Mott, T. (1985-86), 'Towards a Post-Keynesian Formulation of Liquidity Preference', *Journal of Post Keynesian Economics*, vol. 8, Winter.

Mundell, R.A. (1961), 'A Theory of Optimum Currency Areas', *American Economic Review*, vol. 51.

Mundell, R.A. (1976), 'The International Distribution of Money in a Growing Economy', in Frenkel, J. A. and Johnson, H. G. (eds), *The Monetary Approach to the Balance of Payments*, University of Toronto Press, Toronto.

Myrdal, G. (1964), *Economic Theory and Under-developed Regions*, Methuen, London.

Naylor, T. (1978), *The History of Canadian Business 1867-1914: The Banks and Finance Capital*, Lorimer, Toronto.

Neill, R. (1972), *A New Theory of Value: The Canadian Economics of H. A. Innis*, University of Toronto, Toronto.

OECD (1980), *Development Cooperation: Efforts and Policies of the Members of the Development Assistance Committee*, OECD, Paris.

Ohlin, B. (1933), *Interregional and International Trade*, Harvard University Press, Camb., Mass.

Panico, C. (1980), 'Marx's Analysis of the Relationship between the Rate of Interest and the Rate of Profit', *Cambridge Journal of Economics*, vol. 4, December.

Pfister, R.L. (1960), 'State and Regional Payments Mechanism: A Comment', *Quarterly Journal of Economics*, vol. 74.

Popper, K.R. (1970), 'Normal Science and Its Dangers' in Lakatos, I. and Musgrave, A. (eds), *Criticism and the Growth of Knowledge*, Cambridge University Press, Cambridge.

Porter, R. D., Simpson, T. D. and Mauskopf, E. (1979), 'Financial Innovation and the Monetary Aggregates', *Brookings Papers on Economic Activity*, no. 1.

Premiers of Manitoba, Alberta, Saskatchewan and British Columbia

(1973), *Capital Financing and Regional Financial Institutions*, Calgary.

Radcliffe, Lord (1959), *The Committee on the Working of the Monetary System Report*, Cmnd 827, HMSO, London.

Richardson, H.W. (1978), *Regional Economics*, Urbana, University of Illinois Press.

Roberts, R.B. and Fishkind, H. (1979), 'The Role of Monetary Forces in Regional Economic Activity: An Econometric Simulation Analysis', *Journal of Regional Science*, vol. 19, February.

Robinson, J. (1952), 'The Rate of Interest', in *The Rate of Interest and Other Essays*, Macmillan, London.

Robinson, J. (1956) ,*The Accumulation of Capital*, Macmillan, London.

Robinson, J. (1964), *Economic Philosophy*, Penguin, Harmondsworth.

Robinson, J. (1965), *Collected Economic Papers*, vol. 3, Basil Blackwell, Oxford.

Robinson, J. (1978), 'History versus Equilibrium', in *Contributions to Modern Economics*, Basil Blackwell, Oxford.

Robinson, J. (1979), *Collected Economic Papers*, vol. 5, Basil Blackwell, Oxford.

Rotheim, R.J. (1981), 'Keynes' Monetary Theory of Value (1933)' *Journal of Post-Keynesian Economics*, vol. 3, Summer.

Runde, J. (1992), *Essays on Keynesian Uncertainty*, Cambridge University Ph.D. thesis.

Russell, B. (1946; 1961), *History of Western Philosophy and its connections with Political and Social Circumstances from the Earliest Times to the Present Day*, George Allen & Unwin, London.

Sardoni, C. (1987), *Marx and Keynes on Economic Recession*, Wheatsheaf, Brighton.

Sargen, N. (1976), 'Commercial Bank Lending to Developing Countries', *Federal Reserve Bank of San Francisco Economic Review*, Spring.

Sargen, N. (1977), 'Economic Indicators and Country Risk Appraisal', *Federal Reserve Bank of San Francisco Economic Review*, Fall.

Schofield, J.A. (1974), 'Regional Unemployment Rate Dispersion and the Aggregate Phillips Curve: Some Additional Research', *Bulletin of Economic Research*, vol. 26, May.

Scitovsky, T. (1957), 'The Theory of the Balance of Payments and the Problems of a Common European Currency', *Kyklos*, vol. 10.

Sears, J.T. (1972), *Institutional Financing of Small Business in Nova Scotia*, University of Toronto Press, Toronto.

Shackle, G.L.S. (1955), *Uncertainty and Economics*, Cambridge University Press, Cambridge.

Shackle, G.L.S. (1974), *Keynesian Kaleidics*, Edinburgh University Press, Edinburgh.

Shapiro, N. (1978), 'Keynes and Equilibrium Economics', *Australian Economic Papers*, vol. 17, December.

Shaw, E.S. (1973), *Financial Deepening in Economic Development*, Oxford University Press, New York.

Short, J. with Nicholas, D. J. (1981), *Money Flows in the UK Regions*, Gower, Farnborough.

Shortt, A. (1896; 1964), 'The Early History of Canadian Banking', *Journal of the Canadian Bankers' Association*, reprinted as 'Origin of the Canadian Banking System', in Neufeld, E. (ed.), *Money and Banking in Canada*, McClelland & Stewart, Toronto.

Smithin, J. (1989),' Comment on Hart (1989)', in Hamouda, O., Rowley, R. and Wolf, B. (eds), *The Future of the International Monetary System*, Elgar, Aldershot.

Soloman, R. (1989), 'International Monetary Reform: The future is not what it used to be!', in Hamouda, O., Rowley, R. and Wolf, B. (eds), *The Future of the International Monetary System*, Elgar, Aldershot.

St. Hill, R. (1991), 'A Post-Keynesian Analysis of Commercial Bank Regulation', Lincoln University mimeo.

St. Hill, R. (forthcoming), *Money, Banking and Economic Development*, Elgar, Aldershot.

Stohs, M. (1983), 'Uncertainty in Keynes's *General Theory*: A Rejoinder', *History of Political Economy*, vol. 15, Spring.

Strange, S. (1986), *Casino Capitalism*, Blackwell, Oxford.

Studart, R. (1991), 'Financial Repression and Economic Development: A Post Keynesian Response', University College London Discussion Paper in Economics, 91-19.

Studart, R. (forthcoming), 'Investment Finance, Saving, Funding and Financial systems in Economic Development: Theory and Lessons from Brazil', unpublished PhD Thesis, University College, London.

Termini, V. (1981), 'Logical, Mechanical and Historical Time in Economics', *Monte dei Paschi di Siena Economic Notes*, vol. 10.

Termini, V. (1984), 'A Note on Hick's "Contemporaneous Causality"', *Cambridge Journal of Economics*, vol. 8, March.

Thirlwall, A. P. (1980), 'Regional Problems are Balance of Payments Problems', *Regional Studies*, vol. 14, no. 5.

Tobin, J. (1958), 'Liquidity Preference as Behaviour Towards Risk', *Review of Economic Studies*, vol. 25, February.

Tobin, J. (1963), 'Commercial Banks as Creators of "Money"' in Carson, D. (ed.), *Banking and Monetary Studies*, Richard D. Irwin, Homewood, Ill.

Tobin, T. (1970), 'Money and Income: Post Hoc Ergo Propter Hoc?', *Quarterly Journal of Economics*, vol. 84, May.

Tobin, J. (1978), 'A Proposal for International Monetary Reform', *Eastern Economic Journal*, vol. 3.

Townshend, H. (1937), 'Liquidity Premium and the Theory of Value', *Economic Journal*, vol 47.

Triffin, R. (1964; 1969), 'The Myth and Realities of the So-Called Gold Standard', reprinted in Cooper, R.N. (ed.), *International Finance*, Penguin, Harmondsworth.

Triffin, R. (1991), 'The IMS (International Monetary System - or Scandal?) and the EMS (European Monetary System - or Success?)', *Banca Nazionale del Lavoro Quarterly Review*, no. 179.

Tsiang, S.C. (1978), 'The Diffusion of Reserves and the Money Supply Multiplier', *Economic Journal*, vol. 88, June.

UK Government (1978), *The European Monetary System*, Cmnd 7405, HMSO, London.

Van Vijnbergen, S. (1983), 'Interest Rate Management in LDCs', *Journal of Monetary Economics*, vol. 12.

Wallace, N. (1988), 'A Suggestion for Oversimplifying the Theory of Money', *Economic Journal* (supplement), vol. 98.

Wallerstein, I. (1974), *The Modern World System*, Academic Press, New York.

Weiner, S.E. (1989), 'Financial Market Volatility: Summary of the Bank's 1988 Symposium', *Federal Reserve Bank of Kansas City Economic Review*, January.

Weintraub, E.R. (1979), *Microfoundations*, Cambridge University Press, Cambridge.

Weintraub, S. (1978), *Capitalism's Inflation and Unemployment Crisis: Beyond Monetarism and Keynesianism*, Addison-Wesley, Reading, Mass.

Wells, P. (1983), 'A Post-Keynesian View of Liquidity Preference and the Demand for Money', *Journal of Post Keynesian Economics*, vol. 5, Summer.

White, L.H. (1989), Competition and Currency: Essays on Free Banking and Money, New York University Press, New York.

Whitman, M. von N. (1967), 'International and Interregional Payments Adjustment: A Synthetic View', *Princeton Studies in International Finance*, no. 19.

Wilson, T. (1968), 'The Regional Multiplier - A Critique', *Oxford Economic Papers*, November.

Wimsatt, K.C. (1981), 'Robustness, Reliability and Overdetermination', in Brewer, M. B. and Collins, B. E. (eds), *Scientific Inquiry and the Social Sciences*, Jossey Bass, San Francisco.

World Bank (1990), *World Development Report 1990*, Oxford University

Press for the World Bank, Oxford.
World Bank (1991), *World Development Report 1991*, Oxford University Press for the World Bank, Oxford.
Wray, L.R. (1990), *Money and Credit in Capitalist Economies: the Endogenous Money Approach*, Elgar, Aldershot.
Wray, L.R. (1992), 'Alternative Theories of the Rate of Interest', *Cambridge Journal of Economics*, vol. 16, March.
Yeager, L.B. (1985), 'Deregulation and Monetary Reform', *American Economic Review Papers and Proceedings*, vol. 75, May.

Author Index

Subject Index

Printed and bound by CPI Group (UK) Ltd, Croydon, CR0 4YY

23/04/2025

14660984-0002